THE SIX DAYS OF CREATION

THE SIX DAYS
of CREATION

Thomas Mary Sennott

THE RAVENGATE PRESS
Cambridge

FOR

MARY

CONCEIVED

WITHOUT

SIN

CONTENTS

ILLUSTRATIONS

"In his extremely personal rendering of the biblical story, for motives of composition and economy of space Michaelangelo sometines changes, or rather inverts, the chronological order of the episodes of Genesis. In fact the Holy Scriptures place the separation of the earth from the waters together with the creation of the plants on the third Day, and narrate that the Sun, Moon and Stars were created on the fourth. Whereas here the latter stage precedes the former and also takes in the creation of the plants, symbolized in the tuft of green leaves that appears in the bottom left hand corner of the fresco...

In the...paintings...Michaelangelo tries to express symbolically two difficult attributes of Divinity, eternity and infinity...The difficult metaphysical idea of eternity is conceived by the imagination as an everlasting moment, and therefore eternally youthful, and as an endless flow of time. A visual equivalent of this twin conception is present in the figure of God as a being with a young, vigourous body and the head of an old man..."

D. Redig de Campos, *Cappella Sistina*

Cover and photography by Bro. Bartholomew, o.s.b.

PLATES

Plates by the author.

INTRODUCTION

We have just completed the 1950th anniversary of our Redemption which was declared a Holy Year by Pope John Paul ii. Very few Catholics seem to realize that the theory of the evolution of man, even so-called "theistic evolution," at least in its current scientific form, is implicitly a denial of the doctrine of the Redemption. As Wallace Johnson has so convincingly pointed out: "No Adam and Eve [a basic teaching of the theory, as we shall see], no original sin; no original sin, no Redemption." Also no original sin, no Immaculate Conception, which is why I have dedicated this little work to Our Lady under that beautiful title.

Evolution is much more than a scientific theory; it has social, philosophical and religious implications as well. Pope St. Pius x, in his encyclical *Pascendi Gregis*, says that religious evolutionism, the false notion that the dogmas of the faith evolve, is the basis of the still wide-spread heresy of Modernism. It is because liberal Catholic Scripture scholars feel they have to accept the theory of the evolution of man, that they reject the historicity of the biblical story of Adam and Eve, and consequently are compelled to throw doubt on the defined doctrine of original sin.

I am writing primarily for a Catholic audience, and my main purpose is offer some kind of a rebuttal to the continuous barrage of secular humanism with its central dogma of evolutionism, especially as set forth in popular television series like *The Ascent of Man* by Jacob Bronowski, and *Cosmos* by Carl Sagan.

Secondarily, I would like to try to clear up some Catholic misconceptions regarding the largely Protestant creationist movement. Pope Pius xii in his encyclical *Humani Generis* said that Catholics cannot accept the theory of the evolution of man as a proven scientific fact, but should weigh carefully the pros and cons. So in principle, at least, Pope Pius would support the ongoing legal battle of the creationists to obtain equal time with the evolutionists in the public schools, a struggle which I believe merits the support of every Catholic.

To explore these and other questions, I have imagined a dialogue in a college setting between four fictional speakers: a secular humanist, a liberal Catholic, a conservative Catholic (my own position, though I dislike the label), and a Protestant creationist. I have tried, I hope successfully, to present each position as fairly as possible, despite my own personal bias.

Easter, 1984
St. Benedict Priory,
Still River, Massachusetts.

ACKNOWLEDGEMENTS

I would like to thank all my kind friends who read the manuscript of *The Six Days of Creation* for their suggestions and encouragement, especially: Fr. Giles Dimock, o.p., Dom Rembert Sorg, o.s.b., Fr. Richard Gilsdorf, Fr. Thomas Carleton, Fr. Francis Steinmetz, o.s.b., Fr. James P. O'Reilly, m.s., and Dr. Anthony Ostric.

I would also like to thank the following authors who generously gave me permission to quote from their books and articles: to Fr. Bruce Vawter, c.m., for excerpts from *A Path Through Genesis* published by Sheed and Ward of New York in 1956; to Fr. Owen Garrigan and Francis Nead (who wrote the Preface) for excerpts from *Man's Intervention in Nature* published by Hawthorne Books of New York in 1967; to Fr. Robert Faricy, s.j., for excerpts from *Teilhard de Chardin's Theology of the Christian in the World* published by Sheed and Ward of New York in 1967; to Jack Catran for excerpts from *Gee Whiz Scientists Searching for Life* which appeared in the *Los Angeles Times* on March 13, 1983; and to George Alexander for excerpts from *How Life on Earth Began* which appeared in the *Los Angeles Times* and was reprinted in *Reader's Digest* in November of 1982.

I am also grateful to the following publishers for the use of copyrighted material, especially Creation-Life Publishers of San Diego, California for excerpts from *Scientific Creationism* by Dr. Henry Morris, copyright © Creation-Life Publishers, 1974, and *Ebla Tablets: Secrets of a Forgotten City* by Clifford Wilson, copyright © Master Books, Creation-Life Publishers, 1979; to Random House Inc. and Alfred Knopf Inc. of New York for excerpts from *Broca's Brain* by Carl Sagan, copyright © Random House, 1967, *Chance and Necessity*, by Jacques Monod translated by Austryn Wainhouse, copyright © Vintage Books, Random House, 1972, and *Nim* by Herbert Terrace, copyright © Alfred Knopf, 1979; to Viking Penguin Inc. of New York for excerpts from *Violent Universe* by Nigel Calder, copyright © by Nigel Calder, 1969, and *Einstein's Universe* by Nigel Calder, copyright © by Nigel Calder, 1979, and for *Entropy* by Jeremy Rifkin, copyright © by the Foundation on Economic Trends, 1980; to the

xiv THE SIX DAYS OF CREATION

Homiletic and Pastoral Review of New York for excerpts from *Cosmos: A Trap or a Home?* by Fr. Owen Bennett, O.F.M., CONV.; to Prow Books, Franciscan Marytown Press, Libertyville, Illinois, for excerpts from *Immaculate Conception and the Holy Spirit* by Fr. F.H.M. Manteau-Bonamy, O.P. copyright © Franciscan Marytown Press, 1977; to Keep the Faith Inc. of Montvale, New Jersey for excerpts from a taped lecture, *Evolution: The Hoax That's Destroying Christendom* by J.W.G. Johnson; to America Press Inc. of New York for excerpts from *Are There Others Out Yonder?* by Fr. L.C. McHugh, S.J., copyright © America Press 1966; to the *National Catholic Register* of Los Angeles for excerpts from the *Nazi-Abortion Link* by Michael Schwartz, copyright © the *National Catholic Register*, 1978; to the Paulist Press of Ramsey, New Jersey for excerpts from *Biblical Reflections on Crises Facing the Church* by Fr. Raymond Brown, S.S., copyright © the Missionary Society of St. Paul the Apostle in the State of New York, 1975; to Fr. Stanley Jaki, O.S.B. and the University of Chicago Press for excerpts from *The Road of Science and the Ways to God* by Fr. Stanley Jaki, O.S.B., copyright © University of Chicago Press, 1978; to *Discover* Magazine of Time Inc., New York for excerpts from *The Universe according to Guth* by Dennis Overbye, copyright © *Discover* Magazine, 1983; to CNS College Publishing of New York for excerpts from *Exploration of the Universe* by George Abell, copyright © Holt, Rinehart and Winston, 1964; to Anchor Books, Doubleday and Co. of New York for excerpts from *Where the Wasteland Ends* by Theodore Roszak, copyright © Theodore Roszak, 1978; to Little, Brown and Co. of Boston for excerpts from *The Ascent of Man* by Jacob Bronowski, copyright © Jacob Bronowski, 1972; to Avon Books, Walker and Co. of New York for excerpts from *The Universe* by Isaac Asimov, copyright © Isaac Asimov, 1966, and the *Ultimate Experiment* by Nicholas Wade, copyright © Nicholas Wade, 1977; to the Sterling Lord Agency Inc. for the Estate of Arthur Koestler of New York for excerpts from *The Sleepwalkers* by Arthur Koestler, copyright © Arthur Koestler, 1959, published by MacMillan of New York, and *The Ghost in the Machine* by Arthur Koestler copyright © Arthur Koestler, 1968, also published by MacMillan.

THE FIRST DAY

The Origin of Matter and Energy

Separation of the Light from the Darkness

"As in Michaelangelo's last work of sculpture, the unfinished *Rondanini Pieta*, the spirit here transforms, 'eats into' the body, clothing it in an almost immaterial veil of light - just enough to make it visible to men's eyes. Never has the ineffable been expressed in art with so much force."

D. Redig de Campos, *Cappella Sistina*

THE FIRST MEETING
A) The Existence of God
B) The Origin of Religion

THE SPEAKERS

Dr. Edward Smalley	*Dean of the Divinity School at Cabot University, the moderator,*
Dr. Arthur Schonfield	*Professor of Mathematics at Cabot University, a secular humanist,*
Fr. Robert A. Staatz	*Professor of Theology at Cheverus College, a liberal Catholic,*
Mrs. Maria Stepan	*Professor of History at Cheverus College, a conservative Catholic,*
Rev. De Verne Swezey	*Protestant Chaplain at Cabot University, a creationist.*

Scene: A lecture hall at Cabot University, a prestigious secular university. The capacity audience is made up of faculty and students from Cabot and from nearby Cheverus, a large Catholic college.

Dean Smalley

Good evening, and welcome to Cabot University. For those of you who don't know me, my name is Edward Smalley and I am the Dean of the Divinity School here at Cabot University. Originally Dr. Schonfield and Rev. Swezey had intended these meetings to be a series of debates entitled *Evolution or Creation?* with Dr. Schonfield presenting the evolutionist and Rev. Swezey the creationist positions. The topic aroused intense interest, and it was suggested that the debate be enlarged to include Catholic participation. Accordingly, Fr. Staatz, who as you from Cheverus know, is very outspoken in his liberal views, and Mrs. Stepan, who is considered very conservative, were invited to participate, and both agreed enthusiastically. I was invited to moderate the discussions and I also accepted enthusiastically, since it is the first time ever, at least to my knowledge, that these four divergent viewpoints have been brought together.

We held a few preliminary meetings to work out the details, and it was decided to use the term "dialogue" rather than debate, and to enlarge the subject matter to include what Carl Sagan calls the "ultimate questions" - the existence of God, the origin of religion, the origin of the universe, the origin of life, the origin of man, the existence of the soul, and so on. Rev. Swezey suggested, and we all concurred, that the dialogue be given a biblical format and entitled *The Six Days of Creation.* We decided to hold at least one meeting on each of the "days" of creation, and to alternate each week between Cabot and Cheverus. We also agreed for the sake of simplicity and clarity to keep the same order of speaking throughout; namely: I will introduce the topic for each session; Dr. Schonfield will present the secular humanist position; Fr. Staatz the liberal or progressive Catholic position; Mrs. Stepan the conservative Catholic position; Rev. Swezey the fundamentalist or creationist position; and finally I will conclude the meeting with a brief summary.

The first day of Genesis deals with the origin of "light," or as we have chosen to phrase it, *The Origin of Matter and Energy.* But we decided to use this first meeting mainly to get acquainted with our four speakers and with our somewhat unusual format. The two topics we have chosen for tonight's discussion are the existence of God and the origin of religion, topics which are basic to our dialogue and will permeate all succeeding meetings.

It was suggested that I begin each meeting with a reading of the Scriptural account of the day under discussion. Fr. Staatz urged that for the sake of unity, we all use the same version of the Bible and suggested the Revised Standard Version, which has a Catholic edition. This Protestant version of the Bible is a revision of the famous King James Version, and in the so-called "Catholic edition," the seven books considered apocryphal by Protestants, but deuterocanonical by Catholics, have been added, otherwise the text is substantially the same in both Protestant and Catholic editions. Mrs. Stepan, our conservative Catholic, agreed to this version for the sake of unity, but expressed a reservation I should mention. She said that any translation or revision of the Bible necessarily involves a certain interpretation, and any interpretation, which did not reflect the constant teaching of the Church, she considered unacceptable. However, she found nothing objectionable in the RSV's account of the six days, so without further ado, let me read the Scriptural account of the first day of creation:

> In the beginning God created the heavens and the earth. The earth was without form and void, and darkness was upon the face of the deep; and the Spirit of God was moving over the face of the waters.
> And God said, "Let there be light," and there was light. And God saw that the light was good; and God separated the light from the darkness. God called the light Day, and the darkness he called Night. And there was evening and there was morning one day (Gen 1:1-5).

Dr. Arthur Schonfield

I should say at the outset that, although I am of Jewish origin, I consider myself an agnostic in matters of religion. So accordingly, I will be presenting the humanist or, as my religious friends prefer to call it, the secular humanist position, during the course of these meetings. One of the best-known spokesmen for humanism is the astronomer, Carl Sagan, the host of the very popular television series, *Cosmos*, which I am sure many of you watched. The opening line told it all. "The cosmos is all that is or ever was or ever will be." However, I prefer to begin with another of Sagan's best-selling books entitled *Broca's Brain* - but before I go on, let me explain this intriguing title.

The book begins with Sagan strolling through the *Musée de l'*

Homme in Paris, where he wanders into a room containing a collection of human brains in glass jars. This collection, we learn, was begun by Paul Broca, the founder of the science of neurology, the study of the human brain. Sagan takes down one of the glass jars from the shelf; it is marked *P. Broca* - Broca had evidently left his own brain to the collection. Then holding Broca's brain in his hands, like Hamlet holding Yorick's skull ("Alas, poor Yorick"), Sagan begins a soliloquy on the meaning of life and death. He wonders if somehow Broca might still be *in* there, preserved some way in the configuration of the neurons. He asks, "where do we go when we die?" So Sagan is using this clever literary device to ask the ultimate questions about the meaning of life and death. But first he has to establish his authority, which is the authority of science, to give those answers. He does this mainly by a long rebuttal of Immanuel Velikovsky whose pseudo-scientific theories were very popular in the sixties and early seventies. Then in the last section of the book entitled *The Ultimate Questions*, we finally get down to business. Sagan says that two of the ultimate questions are the existence of God, and the origin of religion.

Sagan, who has a wonderful sense of humor, unfortunately somewhat of a rarity among us scientists, begins with this witty comment about theologians in general, and Thomas Aquinas in particular:

> Many statements about God are confidently made by theologians that today at least sound specious. Thomas Aquinas claimed to prove that God cannot make another God, or commit suicide, or make a man without a soul, or even make a triangle whose interior angles do not equal 180 degrees. But Bolyai and Lobachevsky were able to accomplish this last feat (on a curved surface) in the nineteenth century, and they were not even approximately gods. It is a curious concept this, of an omnipotent God, with a long list of things he is forbidden to do by the fiat of theologians. [1]

Sagan then goes on to reject Aquinas' so-called "proofs" from reason for the existence of God, because, he says, they are based on the supposed absurdity of an infinite regression of causes. This notion was derived from Aristotelian physics which, of course, has little or no relevance today. Sagan then gives an example of a legitimate infinite regression, the Oscillating Universe, which we will take up on the second day of creation when we discuss the origin of the universe:

> It is often considered that at least the origin of the universe requires a God - indeed, an Aristotelian idea. This is a point worth looking at in a little more detail. First of all, it is perfectly possible that the universe is infinitely old and therefore requires no Creator. This is consistent with existing knowledge, which permits an oscillating universe in which events since the Big Bang are merely the latest incarnation in an infinite series of creations and destructions of the universe. But secondly, let us consider the idea of a universe created somehow from nothing by God. The question naturally arises - and many ten-year olds spontaneously think of it before being discouraged by their elders - Where does God come from? If we answer that God is infinitely old or present simultaneously in all epochs, we have solved nothing, except perhaps verbally. We have merely postponed by one step coming to grips with the problem. A universe that is infinitely old and a God that is infinitely old, are I think, equally deep mysteries. It is not readily apparent why any one should be considered more reliably established than the other. Spinoza might have said that the two possibilities are not really different ideas at all. [2]

Let me go on now to our second topic, another of Carl Sagan's "ultimate questions," the origin of religion. Sagan begins with a fascinating, true story about one William Wolcott who had apparently died during an operation. Wolcott later said that he seemed to see himself looking back on his wasted body and ascending toward a great light, in the midst of which he could dimly make out a great god-like figure. When a heart machine was rushed to the operating room, Wolcott recovered and later claimed to have caught a glimpse of heaven.

Such incidents are quite common and have happened to all

kinds of people, believers and non-believers alike. Ernest Hemingway claimed to have had such an experience during World War I. They are now called "perithanatic" or "near-death" experiences, and most probably have occurred throughout the course of human history. Such stories of people returning from the dead and claiming to have "caught a glimpse of heaven," could well be the source of belief in a life after death. But if these perithanatic experiences have indeed occurred throughout human history, they must be founded on a common human experience. Many scientists now believe that this common experience is our own birth.

This speculation is based mainly on the experiments of the Czech psychiatrist, Stanislav Grof. Dr. Grof discovered that by using LSD, he could induce many of his patients to re-experience, not just remember, their own births. Dr. Grof found that these "perinatal" or "around-birth" experiences, could be broken down into at least three stages. Stage 1 is the peaceful existence of the fetus in the womb, the so-called "oceanic experience," where the child is, as it were, at one with the universe. Freud considered this "oceanic experience" the ultimate source of all religious belief. In Stage 2 the birth pains of the mother begin, and the peaceful universe of the womb is transformed into one of suffering and pain. Stage 3 is the actual birth, when the child emerges from the dark universe of the womb into a world of light and is lifted up by a strange god-like figure, the doctor or the nurse.

These ideas may cast some light on the origin and nature of religion. Most Western religions long for a life after death; Eastern religions for a relief from an extended cycle of deaths and rebirths. But both promise a heaven or satori, an idyllic reunion of the individual and the universe, a return to Stage 1...Might not the Western fascination with punishment and redemption be a poignant attempt to make sense out of perinatal Stage 2? Is it not better to be punished for something - no matter how implausible, such as original sin - than for nothing? And Stage 3 looks very much like a common experience, shared by all human beings, implanted into our earliest memories and occasionally retrieved in such religious epiphanies as the near-death experience. It is tempting to try to understand other puzzling religious motifs in these terms.

In utero we know virtually nothing. In Stage 2 the fetus gains experience of what might well in later life be called evil - and then is forced to leave the uterus. This is entrancingly close to eating the fruit of the knowledge of good and evil and then experiencing the "expulsion" from Eden. In Michaelangelo's famous painting on the ceiling of the Sistine Chapel, is the finger of God an obsterical finger? Why is baptism, especially total-immersion baptism, widely considered a symbolic rebirth? Is holy water a metaphor for amniotic fluid? Is not the entire concept of baptism and the "born again" experience an explicit acknowledgement of the connection between birth and mystical religiosity? [3]

Sagan concludes by asking, why are so many people of religious conviction afraid to submit that conviction to a reasonable examination? He suggests that this fear is based largely on the fear of death, a fear which both believers and non-believers share in common. Religion is seen as offering the one hope that death may not be final, that somehow we might survive, while science is seen as depriving us of that one last hope. But such an irrational fear should not cause us to reject a reasonable discussion of such a common human problem. Here is Sagan's final statement on the greatest of the "ultimate questions," the existence of God:

...An atheist is someone who is certain that God does not exist. Someone who has compelling evidence against the existence of God. I know of no such compelling evidence. Because God can be relegated to remote times and places and to ultimate causes, we should have to know a great deal more about the universe that we do now to be sure that no such God exists. To be certain of the existence of God and to be certain of the nonexistence of God seem to me to be the confident extremes in a subject so riddled with doubt and uncertainty as to inspire very little confidence indeed. A wide range of intermediate positions seems admissable, and considering the enormous emotional energies with which the subject is invested, a questing, courageous, and open mind seems to be the essential tool for narrowing the range of our collective ignorance on the existence of God. [4]

This is of course, what we are trying to do here.

Fr. Robert A. Staatz

I am afraid that Dr. Schonfield might feel a little intimidated to-night since we have him outnumbered three to one - three believers to one non-believer. So to put him at his ease, I would like to read a few paragraphs from an intervention or speech delivered during the Second Vatican Council by Archbishop Marty of Rheims. It has the amusing title *Atheism Is People*. Archbishop Marty begins with a quote from the well-loved Pope John xxiii:

> "One must never confuse error and the person who errs...The person who errs is always and above all a human being, and he retains in every case his dignity as a human person; and must always be regarded and treated in accord-ance with that lofty dignity." [Archbishop Marty continues:]

> The atheist in the world today - I am speaking of the conscious atheist who reflects on his position - appears as a humanist who wishes to save man and his transcendency but within the boundaries of this terrestrial universe. Whether he is a positivist, or a Marxist, or imbued with existentialism, or devoted to psychoanalysis, the atheist is not a man who denies God systematically. What he refuses is faith in God insofar as such faith seems to him an illusion which diminish-es man. What he puts forward positively is what he would like to think of as a message of salvation, an ethic and a spir-ituality which are more successful at delivering man from the servitudes which oppress him than with the older ethic drawn from a religious inspiration. In a country like France, Chris-tians and atheists are in daily contact; Marxism is simply one component in a broadly diffused atheism. But dialogue on the essential questions between Christians and atheists only rarely begins. Those who have attempted it, whether priests

or laymen, know how difficult such a dialogue is, and how great the demands it makes on both sides. [5]

At our preliminary meetings all the speakers agreed to use easily available and popular books in order to encourage student participation in our dialogue. So I was very pleased to hear Dr. Schonfield using the popular Carl Sagan to present the humanist position. In the so-called liberal or progressive Catholic position a very popular writer is the Vincentian, Bruce Vawter, the author of *A Path Through Genesis*, which is considered a classic in its field. This book first appeared back in 1956, but is still extremely relevant today. Fr. Vawter was very much ahead of his time, and is still in the forefront of the progressive movement in the Church. He is currently teaching at De Paul University in Chicago, and his name appeared recently at the head of a list of over two hundred priests and nuns from the Chicago area, protesting statements made by Pope John Paul ii, during his recent visit to this country. Let me read a few excerpts from this excellent statement:

> We wish to state our regret at the narrow vision of the Church proposed by Pope John Paul ii during his recent pastoral visit. The Catholic Church in America is one of rich diversity, of pluralism in not only ethnic heritage, but also in critical opinion. There had developed in our Church a spirit of tolerance for public discussion of reasoned dissent on many issues, such as priestly celibacy, birth control, homosexuality, divorce and the ordination of women. We do not regard this diversity as a threat to truth, but rather the authentic means by which to discover a fuller truth. We find the vision of a monolithic Church incompatible with the best of our experience and also with the inspiring vision of human rights and dignity of persons enunciated by the Pope in his speeches to non-Catholics. But we think that a Church which is not willing to apply the message of human rights first of all to itself is not a credible bearer of it to the rest of humanity. We admire Pope John Paul's ability to communicate pastoral concern, but we regret the closed model of hierarchical authority that he also communicated. This closed model be-

trays the ideal of religious liberty, not only for the American experience, but also for the rich diversity of the Catholic tradition. We ask that Pope John Paul will be open to dialogue with critical Catholic thought on these important issues. [6]

In January of 1982 while contesting a state law in Arkansas requiring equal time in the public schools for the teaching of creationism, the American Civil Liberties Union, representing, among others, the Catholic Bishop of Little Rock, called Bruce Vawter to the stand as an expert witness on the book of Genesis. His testimony was influential in defeating the fundamentalist cause.

I was very interested to hear Carl Sagan's presentation of some of the latest scientific speculations on the origin of religion. But rather than comment on them directly, I would like to turn to an older theory concerning the origin and evolution of religion. It is called the *Religionsgeschichte*, which means in German, the history or evolution of religions, and it began around the middle of the nineteenth century. One of the many variations of this theory maintains that men first worshipped the forces of nature, animism; and that this evolved into the worship of many gods, polytheism; then out of this multitude of gods, the various nations chose one national god, henotheism; finally there evolved monotheism, the idea of one supreme God, the Creator of the universe.

In 1876 Julius Wellhausen, a liberal Protestant, proposed a theory on the origin of the Pentateuch, the first five books of the Bible, based on the ideas of the *Religionsgeschichte*. It had been thought that Moses who was supposed to have lived around 1500 B.C., was the author of the Pentateuch, but by careful literary analysis, Wellhaused discovered that the Pentateuch was actually a composite of four different documents. Then by means of the *Religionsgeschichte* Wellhausen determined the state of religious development in each of these documents, and was thus able to assign them approximate dates, all long after the time of Moses. Wellhausen called this theory the Documentary Theory, or J E D P for short. The oldest document which he called J because of its author's preference for the name of God, Yahweh or Javeh in German, was written around 900 B.C., the time of Solomon. The next document which he called E, because of its author's preference for the name of God, Elohim, was written around 800 B.C., the time of the schism of Jerobam. Then around 600 B.C., the time of king Josiah, came D, the Deuteronomist document; and about 500 B.C., during the Babylonian Captivity, P, the Priestly document appeared. Finally after the Captivity, in approximately 400 B.C., a redactor or editor put the Pentateuch into the form we have today.

These four authors, according to Wellhausen, reflect the evolution of religion as proposed by the *Religionsgeschichte*. In J and E we find henotheism, one national god, and in D and P we discover monotheism, one God, the Creator of the world. Now, whatever we might think of the *Religionsgeschichte*, the great majority of Catholic biblical scholars today accept its literary analysis, the four sources. However, the only one of these sources we will be directly concerned with in our study of the Hexameron, the six days of creation, is P, the Priestly Author, who wrote his account of the creation of the world during the Babylonian Captivity. This will be crucial to our understanding of the Hexameron.

Studies like the Documentary Theory of Wellhausen are now called "source criticism." Another method of studying the Bible called by the Germans *Formsgeschichte*, form criticism, or the study of literary forms, will also be important for our discussion.

In 1876, the same year that Wellhausen published his study of the Pentateuch, George Smith, an English epigrapher, published his translation of a Babylonian creation myth which began *Enuma elish*, "When on high." This story written in cuneiform script on seven clay tablets, had recently been discovered in the ruins of Assurbanipal's library at Niniveh. Wellhausen had claimed that the Priestly Author had written to encourage a six day work week and a sabbath day's rest. But in 1895 Herman Gunkel, another liberal Protestant, a former pupil of Wellhausen, added that the Priestly Author had purified the *Enuma elish* of its gross polytheism. So the literary form of the Hexameron, according to Gunkel, was the myth, which means of course, that instead of looking for historical truth in our story, we should be looking for religious truth. Here is Bruce Vawter's comment in *A Path Through Genesis:*

The author of Genesis was undoubtedly acquainted with the creation myths of the polytheistic religions of Egypt and Babylon; there are enough indications in Genesis to suggest that the author was consciously opposing his account to the Babylonian story. According to the myth, matter had already existed at the beginning of time in the person of the first gods, from whom were fashioned the earth and the heavens, and who gave birth to other gods. The world became the battleground of rival deities, and out of their struggle, as a kind of by-product, living creatures were formed, and finally man to be the slave of the gods. [7]

The Hexameron, then, is primarily a poem or hymn to the one true God, the Creator of heaven and earth, and secondarily a polemic against the *Enuma elish* myth. If this interpretation is properly understood, it can immediately be seen that it would be impossible to make a concord or harmony between the scientific account of the origin of the universe and the Hexameron. Bruce Vawter gives an example of one such well-meaning attempt by Raymond Murray in his *Man's Unknown Ancestors:*

"Most educated Catholics take the word *yom* (day) of the first chapter of Genesis to mean a certain undefined period of time, an interpretation which incidentally fits very well with the evidence of historical geology concerning the sequence of different forms of plant and animal life and the length of time, perhaps millions of years, often estimated to be necessary for this development to have taken place..." [Bruce Vawter continues:]

This sally into bad science and bad interpretation surely does not represent the belief of most educated Catholics...On what grounds is the author of Genesis presumed to have anticipated the discovery of the geological ages (which in any case are four, not six)? He would have needed divine revelation, which he did not have; and to what purpose would God reveal such an inconsequential thing?

The creation story of Genesis neither affirms not denies our scientific knowledge of the universe; it disregards it. The

author has used his story to teach that there is one transcendent God who is Creator of all things...Positive science knows
nothing of this, just as he knows nothing of positive science. [8]

If the concordist interpretation of the Hexameron is no longer
tenable, we would know *a fortiori* that the fundamentalist or
strictly literal interpretation is also obsolete. Two recent
discoveries have conspired to make these methods of Scriptural
exegesis out-dated: the theory of evolution as applied to both the
origin of the universe and the origin of man, and the discovery of
the ancient literatures of the Near East:

> ..."But now unexpected witnesses have emerged from the
> shadows where they were thought to have been buried forev-
> er." These witnesses were the fossil remains which proved the
> tremendous age of the world and the newly discovered litera-
> tures of ancient Egypt and Mesopotamia, far older than
> Moses. Israel was a newcomer among the nations of men,
> and its traditions could not be very old...Traditions can be
> preserved with astounding accuracy of detail even over cen-
> turies, as the Pentateuch makes clear, but who could imagine
> a tradition kept intact for hundreds of thousands, a half mil-
> lion or more years. For the life of man upon earth, we now
> know, is no less than this...Any interpretation of Scripture
> that contradicts a known fact of science we may be very sure
> is no true interpretation. This principle was established fif-
> teen hundred years ago by St. Augustine, who in his *De
> Genesi ad Litteram* ["On the Literal Meaning of Genesis"] at-
> tacked the problem of Genesis in the light of the knowledge
> of his age. We can do no better than imitate his spirit.
>   "Fundamentalism" or "literalism" has never had a home in
> the Catholic Church. It is regrettable, however, that some
> Catholics have felt that the fundamentalists are "on our side"
> in their reverence for the letter of God's word amid a world
> that has largely gone over to unbelief. Fundamentalism is not
> born of respect for the Bible. It is born of contempt for man's
> God-given intellect. It has failed the most elementary task of
> religion, which is the rational service of God. [9]

In conclusion let me repeat a line from Archbishop Marty concerning our dialogue which will be critical for us during the coming weeks. "Those who have attempted it, whether priests or laymen, know how difficult such a dialogue is, and how great the demands it makes on both sides."

Mrs. Maria Stepan

I would like to say at the beginning that while I agree with the excerpt which Fr. Staatz read from Archbishop Marty's intervention during Vatican II, *Atheism Is People*, I thought it incomplete. Let me read a fuller treatment of just what the term "dialogue" should mean to Catholics, because I think that it is very important that we lay all our cards on the table at the very beginning, lest there be any misunderstanding on the part of our non-Catholic friends. This is from Pope Paul VI's wonderful encyclical *Ecclesiam Suam*, which appeared in 1964:

Before speaking, it is necessary to listen, not only to a man's voice, but to his heart. A man must first be understood, and where he merits it, agreed with. In the very act of trying to make ourselves pastors, fathers, and teachers of men, we must make ourselves their brothers. The spirit of dialogue is friendship and, even more, service. All this we must remember and strive to put into practice according to the example and commandment Christ left us.

But the danger remains. The Apostle's art is a risky one. The desire to come together as brothers must not lead us to a watering-down or substracting from the truth. Our dialogue must not weaken our attachment to our faith. In our apostolate we cannot make vague compromises about principles of faith and action on which our profession of Christianity is based.

An immoderate desire to make peace and sink differences at all costs is, fundamentally, a kind of skepticism about the power and content of the Word of God which we desire to preach. [10]

Let me go on now to Carl Sagan who, if you remember, began his treatment of the existence of God with a humorous jibe at St. Thomas Aquinas. St. Thomas, he claimed, said that God could not make a triangle whose interior angles were less than 180 degrees, and that this feat had been accomplished by Bolyai and Lobachevsky, hardly gods, in the nineteenth century by drawing a triangle on a curved surface. Now Sagan does not tell us where he got this alleged statement of St. Thomas, but as far as I can make out, he is referring to the *Summa Contra Gentiles*, which St. Thomas wrote at the request of his friend St. Raymond of Pennafort to assist him in his efforts in converting the Moslems and Jews. Let us see just what St. Thomas actually said:

> God cannot make one and the same thing to be and not to be. He cannot make a thing lacking in any of its essential constituents, while a thing itself remains: for instance, a man without a soul. Since the principles of some sciences, as logic, geometry, and arithmetic, rest on formal, or abstract constituents on which the essence of a thing depends, it follows that God cannot effect anything contrary to these principles, as that genus should not be predicable of species, or that *lines drawn from the center of a circle to the circumference should not be equal.* [11]

There is no mention of God being unable to make a triangle whose interior angles are less than 180 degrees. The example that St. Thomas does actually give is that God cannot make a circle in which the lines drawn from the center to the circumference would not be equal. The standard definition of a circle is: *a closed plane curve, all points of which are equidistant from a point within called the center* - the same definition as St. Thomas'. If the radii of a circle were of unequal lengths, it would not be a circle. God cannot make something that is both a circle and not a circle at the same time, or a thing cannot be and not be at the same time. This is known as the principle of contradiction, and is one of the basic principles which makes rational thought, including science, possible.

The standard definition of a triangle, on the other hand, is: *a polygon having three sides*. A figure would not be a triangle if it had four sides. So again God cannot make something that is both a triangle and not a triangle at the same time, or as Paracelsus so colorfully put it, "God can make an ass with three tails, but not a triangle with four sides."

The statement that the sum of the interior angles of a triangle equals 180 degrees is not part of the definition of a triangle, but rather what is called a "postulate" derived from that definition. So Sagan has not only substituted a triangle for a circle in St. Thomas but also a postulate for a definition!

After this somewhat questionable start, Sagan went on to St. Thomas' famous five proofs from reason for the existence of God. He said that they were based mainly on the supposed absurdity of an infinite regression of causes, a notion derived from Aristotelian physics which, he said, is irrelevant today. Again let us turn to St. Thomas and see just what he actually said. In his *Summa Theologica* St. Thomas asks *Whether God Exists?* and then proposes some of the still current objections to the existence of God, even more convincingly, it seems to me, than many of our contemporary humanists, and then proceeds to refute them.

> *On the contrary:* It is said in the Person of God: *I am Who am* (Exod 3:4).
> *I answer that* the existence of God can be proved in five ways. The first and more manifest way is the argument from motion...Whatever is put in motion is put in motion by another. If that by which it is put in motion be itself in motion, then this also must needs be put in motion by another, and that by another again. But this cannot go to infinity, because then there would be no first mover, and consequently no other mover; seeing that subsequent movers move only inasmuch as they are put in motion by the first movers; as the staff moves only because it is put in motion by the hand. Therefore it is necessary to arrive at a first mover, put in motion by no other; and this everyone understands to be God. [12]

St. Thomas is not just arguing from Aristotelian physics, but from common sense as well. He thinks of motion primarily in terms of change, and as we look around us we see that everything in the world is in a constant state of change. Nothing is permanent, unchangeable, or immovable. Indeed, Sheldon Glashow in his "Grand Unified Theory" claims that even the most stable of all the subatomic particles, the protons, the very core of matter, are in the process of breaking down. Thus we are led logically to the consideration of a changeless, permanent, unmoved Being, the First or Prime Mover, the source of all motion.

Let me go on now to our second topic for tonight, the origin of religion. Fr. Staatz discussed the so-called *Religionsgeschichte*, the history of the origin and evolution of religions, which maintains that religion is of natural rather than supernatural origin. One of its many variations maintains that men first worshipped the forces of nature, animism; then personalized those various forces, polytheism; then they chose one particular god for their own national god, henotheism; and finally they worshipped the one and only God, monotheism. Fr. Staatz said that the Documentary Theory of Wellhausen was based on the *Religionsgeschichte*, and the evolution of religion was reflected in the four documents J E D P which make up the Pentateuch. Let me read a few comments on this theory by Msgr. John Steinmueller from his excellent, *A Companion to Scripture Studies:*

> The basic thesis of the critics, that in the science of religion monotheism is the ultimate result and culmination of progressive evolution among peoples, cannot be sustained. The learned anthropologist, Rev. W. Schmidt, s.v.d., has proved conclusively that the outstanding mark of the religion of primitive peoples is its fundamental monotheism (i.e., their belief in one Supreme Being). Professor Langdon has defended the thesis that the early Sumerians were originally monotheists, and Lagrange did the same for the early Semites. The internationally known biblical scholar, Professor Johann Goetsberger of Munich is thus correct when he writes: "The prevailing Pentateuchal theories in particular instances are still unconsciously derived or consciously influenced by preconceived notions of religious and historic ev-

olution, which by no means can be regarded as permanent scientific conclusions." [13]

Thus the so-called "scientific" *Religionsgeschichte* seems to me to be a better model for the *de*volution rather than the *e*volution of religion. Religion is of supernatural origin, that is, revealed by God. So religion began as monotheism, but unfortunately among some people devolved into henotheism, polytheism, and animism.

Fr. Vawter also said that there can never be a conflict between a proven scientific fact and a proper interpretation of Scripture. I would add - there can never be a conflict between a proven scientific fact, and a proper interpretation of Scripture as proposed by the Church. The Church has always been opposed to the principle of *sola Scriptura*, "Scripture alone," or private interpretation of the Bible. The Church has been appointed by God to be the official interpreter of the Bible and she does this through Tradition, the teachings of the Fathers and Doctors, and through what is called the Magisterium.

A good example of the Magisterium is the work of the Pontifical Biblical Commission. This Commission was founded by Pope Leo XIII in 1902 to combat the errors of liberal Protestantism which were then seeping into the Church, where they became known as Modernism. The Biblical Commission is a group of Cardinals assisted by consultors, expert biblical scholars, which hands down decisions on biblical problems after they have been approved by the Holy Father. These decisions even after they have been approved by the Pope, are not infallible, so theoretically they could be in error and later revoked, but not if they are simply a reflection of the constant Tradition of the Church.

In 1906 the Biblical Commission condemned the Documentary Theory of Wellhausen. Then in 1907 Pope St. Pius x in a *Motu proprio*, that is, on his own motion, raised the authority of these decisions to the same level enjoyed by the decisions of the Holy Office in matters of doctrine. He said that they should be considered "binding in conscience" on all Catholics. This is, of course, true of all the teachings of the Magisterium, since a Catholic is always expected to "think with the mind of the Church."

Fr. Vawter seems to be quite a bit behind the times despite his "progressive" label, apparently a common characteristic of American biblical scholarship, and not only with regard to the Documentary Theory. Certainly no Catholic would consider the Jerusalem Bible a conservative document, yet even its editors, the Dominican Fathers of the *École Biblique* in Jerusalem, have abandoned the theory. Here is Msgr. Steinmueller quoting from the Dominican Fathers and from W.E. Albright, the famous Protestant biblical archaelogist:

> The *Jerusalem Bible*, while admitting final written forms, denies the validity of the system for its textual origin. "The Documentary Theory in its classical form is...in the melting pot. Continued effort to give it further precision has served only to show that the task is impossible...The attempts to satisfy these data by a theory of assembled 'documents' scissored, reshuffled, and recombined by some mechanical process of literary compilation must be abandoned." [And here is W.E. Albright in *Christianity Today:*]
>
> "It is quite impossible to cut the Pentateuch into a patchwork of J E P with any hope of increasing knowledge...That the Pentateuchal law is substantially Mosaic in origin and that patriarchal and Mosaic historical traditions are astonishingly early and dependable seems, in my opinion, certain." [14]

In 1909 the Biblical Commission condemned the Mythical Theory of Herman Gunkel, which claimed that the Hexameron was merely a purified version of the *Enuma elish* myth. Let me read a few excerpts from the encyclical *Humani Generis* of Pope Pius XII, in which he discusses the question of history versus myth in the book of Genesis:

> The first eleven chapters of Genesis, although they do not properly conform to the rules of historical composition used by the great Greek and Latin historians or by the historians of our time do nevertheless pertain to history in a true sense to be further studied and determined by exegetes;...the same chapters contain in simple and metaphorical language adapted to the mentality of a people of low culture, the prin-

cipal truths fundamental for our eternal salvation and a popular description of the origin of the human race and the chosen people. For the rest, if the ancient hagiographers have taken anything from popular narratives (and this may be conceded), we must not forget that they did so with the help of divine inspiration which preserved them from error in selecting and appraising those documents.

In any case, whatever of popular narratives have found a place in the Sacred Scriptures, must in no way be considered on a par with myths or other such things; these are more the product of an exuberant imagination than of that striving for truth and simplicity which is so apparent in the Sacred books. [15]

Finally let me conclude by repeating Pope Paul vi's warning on the dangers of dialogue: "An immoderate desire to make peace and sink differences at all costs is, fundamentally, a kind of skepticism about the power and content of the Word of God which we desire to preach."

Rev. De Verne Swezey

Dean Smalley mentioned in his introduction that these meetings were originally intended to be a debate between myself and Dr. Schonfield entitled *Evolution or Creation?* When it was suggested that the debate be enlarged to include Catholic participation, I was at first somewhat reluctant, but later realized that it would be a good opportunity to present the real aims of the creationist movement to an audience which included Catholics. I think that the unfortunate opposition of some Catholic bishops to State laws granting equal time for the teaching of creationism in the public schools, which by the way is something that the majority of Americans want, is the result of a misunderstanding concerning the real goals of the creationist movement.

One of the founders of the creationist movement is Dr. Henry Morris, a professional geologist and the Director of the Institute for Creation Research in San Diego, California. Dr. Morris is the author of a book entitled *Scientific Creationism*, which is published in two separate editions. One edition, called the Public School Edition, contains no reference to the Bible and could be used in our public schools today on an equal-time basis to provide a viable scientific alternative to evolutionism. The other edition, called the General Edition, is intended for use in Christian schools. The first part of the text is exactly the same as the Public School Edition and then it has a final section on the Bible. I will be using both parts of this edition in my presentations. Let me begin by reading from the public school section where Dr. Morris sets forth the aims of the creationist movement.

> ...It is clear that neither evolution nor creation is, in the proper sense, either a scientific theory or a scientific hypothesis. Though people speak of the "theory of evolution" or the "theory of creation," such terminology is imprecise. This is because neither can be *tested*. A valid scientific hypothesis must be capable of being formulated experimentally, such that the experimental results either confirm or reject its validity...A more proper approach is to think in terms of two scientific models, the *evolution model* and the *creation model*. A "model" is a conceptual framework, an orderly system of thought, within which one tries to correlate observable data, even to predict data. When alternative models exist, they can be compared as to their respective capacities for correlating such data. When, as in this case, neither can be proved, the decision between the two cannot be solely objective. Normally, in such a case, the model with the smallest number of unresolved contradictory data, would be accepted as the most probably correct model.
>
> In public schools, both evolution and creation should be taught as equally as possible, since there are children of taxpayers representing both viewpoints in the classes. If people wish *only* evolution to be taught, they should establish private schools for that purpose. [16]

One of the planks in the creationist platform which is often misunderstood, is that evolutionism is itself a religion. Dr. Morris explains just what is meant by the term "religion" in this context:

We are using the term "religion" in a very broad sense, as including any concept of ethics, values, or ultimate meanings. Evolution is, in fact, a religious belief in this sense, and so is atheism. In fact, this is one very cogent reason why creationists object to the exclusive teaching of evolution in the schools, since in effect this amounts to indoctrinating young people in a particular religion with its own system of ethics and values and ultimate meanings.

That evolution is fundamentally religious, is recognized officially by the American Humanist Association:

"Humanism is the belief that man shapes his own destiny. It is a constructive philosophy, a non-theistic religion, a way of life...The American Humanist Association is a non-profit, tax-exempt organization, incorporated in the early 1940's in Illinois for educational and religious purposes." [18]

[Dr. Morris continues:] Many prominent evolutionists such as Julian Huxley, H.J. Muller, Hudson Hoagland, and others, are listed as members of the association. One of the founders is listed as John Dewey, the man more responsible than any other single individual for our modern philosophy of public education. [19]

Let us compare the creation model and the evolution model, on one of the topics for this evening, the existence of God:

...The creation model seems to be the better model, on this point at least. The only objection that could be lodged against it here is that it postulates a supernatural Creator, and the evolutionist often counters with the query: "But, then, who made God?" [As we just heard Carl Sagan do.] But such a question of course *begs* the question. If the evolutionist prefers not to believe in God, he must still believe in some kind of uncaused First Cause. He must either postulate matter coming into existence out of nothing or else matter having always existed in some primitive form. In either case, matter itself becomes its own Cause, and the creationist may well ask: "but, then, who made Matter?"

In either case, therefore, one must simply *believe* - either in an eternal, omnipotent Matter or else in an eternal, omnipotent, Creator God. The individual may decide which he considers more reasonable, but he should recognize this is not completely a *scientific* decision either way. [17]

Let me go on to Fr. Vawter's presentation of the Documentary Theory of Julius Wellhausen. I am always a little surprised and amused to hear so-called "progressive" Catholics set forth as the latest thing, old liberal Protestant theories dating from the turn of the century, which even most liberal Protestants have long abandoned. The reason for the demise of many of these rationalist theories has been the rise of biblical archaeology.

Currently the most exciting discoveries in biblical archaeology are being made at Ebla in Syria. At this ancient site thousands of clay tablets covered with cuneiform writing have been discovered. They have been dated at around 2400 B.C., or about a thousand years *before* the time of Moses.

The so-called *Religionsgeschichte*, the history or evolution of religions, claims that Moses was incapable of writing the Mosaic law code around 1500 B.C., because the high ethical monotheism of the code did not evolve until about 600 B.C., the time of the Babylonian Captivity. Let me read a few excerpts from a recent book on the Ebla discoveries entitled, *Ebla Tablets: Secrets of a Forgotten City*, by Clifford Wilson, a Protestant, who is a distinguished biblical archaeologist:

There is elaborate discussion of case law, with varying conditions recognized for what at first might seem to be the same crime. In the case of a complaint involving sexual relations, if the girl was able to prove that she was a virgin and that the act was forced on her, the penalty against the man was death. Otherwise he would pay a fine that varied according to the circumstances...

The Ebla laws dealing with sex offenses are remarkably close to those found in Deuteronomy 22:22-30. In that passage there is a distinction made according to whether the girl was a virgin and cried for help, or was a willing participant in the act. This is very close to the law at Ebla. [20]

These recent discoveries at Ebla have also made the Mythical Theory of Herman Gunkel completely untenable. Gunkel had claimed that the Hexameron was merely a purified version of a Babylonian creation myth, the *Enuma elish*, because its religious doctrine, creation out of nothing was supposed to be a late development in the religious history of the Jews. This means, of course, that the literary form of the Hexameron was not history as had always been thought, but rather myth, and therefore it contained no historical truth. Now a new creation story has been discovered at Ebla which is earlier than Moses, and also earlier than the *Enuma elish*. This story says that God created the world out of nothing:

A New Creation Tablet   .

Professor Pettinato [the epigrapher working on the tablets], said that the record appeared to be remarkably like that found in the first verses of Genesis. - "In the beginning, God created the heavens and the earth."...He said that the creation tablet was closer to Genesis Chapter 1 than anything yet discovered. It said that there was a time when there was no heaven, and Lugal ("the great one") formed it out of nothing; there was no earth and Lugal made it; there was no light, and he made it. [21]

Dr. Wilson maintains that, rather than the Hexameron being a corrupted version of the *Enuma elish* as Gunkel claimed, it is more likely that this myth is a corrupted version of the Hexameron:

Differences from the Biblical Record

Typical of the differences is the way in which the heavens and the earth were supposed to have been created. In the Babylonian account the god Marduk cuts the goddess Tiamat in two before he proceeds to use her mutilated body in the work of creation. The Bible record is very different from these fantastic and grotesque ideas. There we read of God who is all powerful, the One who created worlds by the word of his power...

According to the Babylonian version, after Marduk was successful the rebel gods feared that he would make them his servants forever. They appealed to him for leniency and gave him homage. They recognized that "his command shall be preeminent above and below." Eventually Marduk ageed to punish only their leader. So the god Kingu, who had incited the goddess Tiamat to revolt, was bound, and the total crime was laid upon him. The punishment included the letting of his blood - he had to cut his own throat. Marduk then created man from Kingu's blood. Thus it was that man, as the offspring of Kingu (made from clay mixed with his blood), could only be evil. He was to be subject to every whim of the gods, a servile creature quite unlike the noble being whom God created, as we read in Genesis...

The more we study the Bible record the more we are impressed that *here* we have the original, and that at best, the Babylonian story is a distortion and a corruption of the original. [22]

So much for my comments on the presentations of Dr. Schonfield and Fr. Staatz. Let me conclude now by turning to the Bible. If you remember, I explained that the final section of the General Edition of *Scientific Creationism* was not intended to be used in the public schools but only in Christian schools. We heard Fr. Vawter claim that it is not God's usual procedure to make direct revelations to man, and therefore He would not have revealed the story of the creation of the world to Adam, who then handed it down to his descendants. But this is a completely gratuitous assertion and the Bible is full of such direct revelations on the part of God:

In accord with the common practice of ancient times, records and narratives were written down on tables of stone, and then handed down from family to family, perhaps finally, to be placed in a library or public storehouse of some sort. It seems most reasonable to believe that the original records of Genesis were written down by eyewitnesses and handed down through the line of patriarchs from Adam through Noah and Abraham and finally to Moses...

There are really two creation accounts, the second (Gen 2:4-3:24) written by Adam, from his viewpoint; the first (Gen 1:1-2:3) could not have been observed by any man at all and must have been written by God Himself, either with His own "finger," as He did also the ten commandments (Ex 3:18), or else by direct supernatural revelation...In a very direct and peculiar way, this constitutes the Creator's personal narrative of heaven and earth. It would be well not to try to explain away its historicity by calling it merely a literary device of some time. Rather, men should bow before its Author in believing obedience, acknowledging that He has clearly spoken in words that are easy to be understood, concerning those things which man could never discover for himself. [23]

In conclusion let me say that we heard Fr. Staatz claim that two discoveries have conspired to make the literal, historical interpretation of the Hexameron obsolete - the theory of the evolution of man and the discovery of the ancient literature of the Near East. I have just demonstrated that the discovery of this literature, the Ebla tablets, for example, have confirmed rather than denied that interpretation, and we will again come to the same conclusion when we consider the theory of the evolution of man when we discuss the sixth day of creation which deals with the origin of man.

Dean Smalley

I have been asked to conclude our meetings by giving a brief summary of the presentations of our four speakers. It was feared that by the time Rev. Swezey completed his presentation some of our students might have forgotten what Dr. Schonfield had to say. But since I am the Dean of the Divinity School here at Cabot, and a liberal Protestant, it would be difficult, if not impossible, for me to remain completely objective in a discussion such as this. So I will try to limit myself to summaries rather than interpretations or commentaries.

Our topics for this meeting on the first day of creation, were the existence of God and the origin of religion.

Dr. Schonfield read the astronomer Carl Sagan's presentation of the humanist position regarding God's existence, which is, of course, that there is no compelling evidence for that existence and therefore religion is of purely natural origin.

Fr. Staatz concentrated mainly on an older scientific theory of the origin and evolution of religion, the *Religionsgeschichte*, which was the basis of the Documentary Theory of Wellhausen and the Mythical Theory of Gunkel. These theories, he said, have demonstrated that the Hexameron is not an historical, but rather a fictional account of the origin of the world, though of course, written for a religious purpose. He claimed that the theory of evolution as applied to the universe and man, and the discovery of the ancient literatures of the Near East, have made both the fundamentalist and concordist interpretations of the Hexameron obsolete.

Both Mrs. Stepan and Rev. Swezey reacted strongly to Dr. Schonfield's statements concerning the existence of God. Mrs. Stepan presented one of Aquinas' arguments from reason for the existence of God, and Rev. Swezey gave the creationist position that both the eternity of God or the eternity of Matter (the only other alternative) must be taken on faith, since neither can be tested scientifically.

Mrs. Stepan and Rev. Swezey also criticized the *Religionsgeschichte*, Mrs. Stepan claiming that the theory was in conflict with recent findings in cultural anthropology, and Rev. Swezey maintaining that it was refuted by recent discoveries in biblical archaeology.

Mrs. Stepan concluded with the Catholic claim that the Church is the official interpreter of the Bible, which it exercises through its

Tradition and Magisterium, while Rev. Swezey held fast to the Protestant principle of *sola Scriptura*, or private interpretation of the Bible.

This concludes the discussion for this evening. Our next meeting will be held at Cheverus College, when we will continue with the first day of creation.

REFERENCES

1   Carl Sagan, *Broca's Brain*,
    Random House, New York, 1979, footnote, p.295.
2   Sagan, *Op. cit.*, p.287.
3   *Idem*, pp.307,308.
4   *Idem*, p.311.
5   Peter Hebblethwaite, s.j., *The Council Fathers and Atheism*,
    Paulist Press, Deus Books, New York, 1967, pp.96,97.
6   *The Wanderer*, Dec 27, 1979, p.4,
    St. Paul, Minn.
7   Bruce Vawter, c.m., *A Path Through Genesis*,
    Sheed and Ward, New York, 1956, p.38.
8   Vawter, *Op. cit.*, pp.48,49.
9   *Idem*, pp.33,35,36.
10 Pope Paul vi, *Ecclesiam Suam*,
    Paulist Press, Glen Rock, n.j., 1964, pp.55,56.
11 St. Thomas Aquinas, *Summa Contra Gentiles*, (*II, 25*),
    Joseph Rickaby, s.j., *Of God and His Creatures*,
    B. Herder, St. Louis, 1905, p.92.
12 St. Thomas Aquinas, *Summa Theologica*, (*I, Q2, a3*),
    Benziger Brothers, New York, 1947, p.13.
13 Msgr. John Steinmueller, *A Companion to Scripture Studies*, Vol. 2,
    Joseph F. Wagner, New York, 1969, p.108.
14 Steinmueller, *Op. cit.*, p.69.
15 Pope Pius xii, *Humani Generis*,
    Weston College Press, Weston, Mass., 1951, pp.45,46.
16 Henry Morris, *Scientific Creationism*,
    Creation-Life Publishers, San Diego, Cal., 1974, pp.9,14.
17 Morris, *Op. cit.*, p.19.

18 *Idem*, footnote, p.196,
    Membership Brochure, *What is Humanism?*
    Humanist Community, San Jose, Cal.
19 *Idem*, p.19
20 Clifford Wilson, *Ebla Tablets: Secrets of a Forgotten City*,
    Creation-Life Publishers, Master Books, San Diego, Cal., 1979, pp.34,35.
21 Wilson, *Op. cit.*, p.4.
22 *Idem*, pp.51-53.
23 *Idem*, pp.205,206.

THE SECOND MEETING

A) The Atomic Theory of Matter
B) Science and Morality

Scene: A lecture room at Cheverus College. The large audience is composed of faculty and students from Cheverus and from Cabot University.

Dean Smalley

Good evening. I would like to express first my thanks to Father Rector and to all our friends at Cheverus College for their gracious hospitality. As I mentioned the last time, we will alternate the meetings between Cabot and Cheverus. Our first meeting was intended primarily to get acquainted with our four speakers and our somewhat unusual format, but tonight we will begin in earnest with *The Six days of Creation.*

The first day of creation deals with the origin of "light," or as we have chosen to phrase it, the origin of matter and energy. Our discussion will begin with the atomic theory of matter and since this theory led directly to the development of the atomic bomb, we thought this would be a good place to discuss the moral responsibility, if any, of the scientists who developed the atomic bomb, and of the scientific community in general.

So let me begin our meeting tonight by reading again the Scriptural account of the first day of creation:

> In the beginning God created the heavens and the earth. The earth was without form and void, and darkness was upon the face of the deep; and the Spirit of God was moving over the face of the waters.
>
> And God said, "Let there be light," and there was light. And God saw that the light was good; and God separated the light from the darkness. God called the light Day, and the darkness he called Night. And there was evening, and there was morning one day (Gen 1:1-5).

Dr. Arthur Schonfield

Our main topic for this evening is the *Origin* of Matter and Energy, but the humanist, of course, since he cannot accept the existence of a God who created matter and energy out of nothing, has to hold that matter and energy have existed from all eternity. Carl Sagan, my spokesman for humanism at our last meeting, does not discuss directly the atomic theory of matter, so let me turn to another prominent humanist, the late Jacob Bronowski. I am sure that many of you watched his remarkable television series, *The Ascent of Man*, which ran a few years ago. Dr. Bronowski, a mathematician and physicist, was one of the directors of the British Humanist Association, and during World War II he worked on the atomic bomb. But after the war he deliberately abandoned physics and took up the study of biology. At the time of his death in 1974, he was engaged in research work in biology at the Salk Institue in La Jolla, California.

Let me begin with a little historical background. The modern atomic theory of matter began in 1897 at the University of Cambridge in England, with J.J. Thomson's discovery of the electron, that tiny particle of matter which carries a negative charge of electricity. The discovery proved that the atom was not the smallest particle of matter as its Greek name *atom*, "indivisible," had implied, but that it could itself be broken down into still smaller parts.

In 1911 Ernest Rutherford, also at the University of Cambridge, discovered a more massive subatomic particle, the proton, which carries a positive charge of electricity. Rutherford then proposed the planetary model of the atom, with the protons in the center like the sun, and the electrons in orbits like planets.

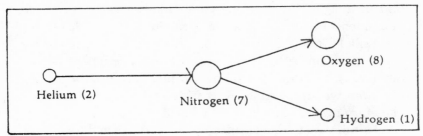

Plate 1 *The Transmutation of Elements*

In 1919 Rutherford achieved for the first time the alchemist's dream, the transmutation or the changing of one element into another. You can see from the diagram on the blackboard that Rutherford was bombarding nitrogen with alpha particles. He had discovered that the alpha particles given off by the radioactive bismuth, are the nucleus of the helium atom which has two protons. As these protons struck the nitrogen atom which has seven protons, one bounced off becoming hydrogen, one proton, while the other remained in the nucleus, thus converting it into oxygen, which has eight protons.

Then in 1932 James Chadwick, also of the University of Cambridge, discovered another subatomic particle, the neutron, which has no electrical charge. The physicists had been trying to split the nucleus of the uranium atom but without success, because the electrical field of the atom repelled electrically charged particles. But now with the neutron, and no electrical charge, they had a particle which could penetrate to the very core of the atom.

Uranium has 92 positively charged protons in its nucleus, and since like charges repel, the nucleus should be flying apart, so it must be held together by a tremendous amount of energy. It was Enrico Fermi in 1934 who first achieved nuclear fission, actually splitting the atom. Using a stream of neutrons, he split uranium 92 into barium 56 and krypton 36. You can see from the numbers that barium and krypton, 56 + 36, add up to 92. This fission released some of the energy which was holding the nucleus together. Here is Dr. Bronowski's summary of this golden age of atomic physics in his *The Ascent of Man:*

> ...Physics in the twentieth century is an immortal work. The human imagination working communally has produced no monuments to equal it, not the pyramids, not the *Illiad*, not the ballads, not the cathedrals. The men who made these conceptions one after another are the pioneering heroes of our age...J.J. Thomson, who overturned the Greek belief that the atom was indivisible; Rutherford who turned it into a planetary system...Chadwick, who discovered the neutron; and Fermi, who used it to open up and transform the nucleus.[1]

Finally in 1934, the Hungarian, Leo Szilard, pointed out that nuclear fission could set off what he called a "chain reaction," which he realized could be developed into a bomb. Albert Einstein had actually predicted the atomic bomb years earlier with his famous equation, $E = mc^2$, energy equals mass times the speed of light squared, which means that mass can be converted into energy, and vice versa. In 1939 Szilard wrote a letter to President Roosevelt which he got Einstein, because of his tremendous prestige, to sign, urging the development of an atomic bomb. Bronowski reproduces a photograph of the letter in *The Ascent of Man:*

> F.D. Roosevelt
> President of the United States...
> Sir:
>
> ...It has been made probable - through the work of Joliot in France as well as Fermi and Szilard in America - that it may be possible to set up a nuclear chain reaction in a large mass of uranium, by which vast amounts of power and large quantities of new radium-like elements would be generated. Now it appears almost certain that this could be achieved in the immediate future.
> This new phenomenon would also lead to the construction of bombs, and it is conceivable - though much less certain -

that extremely powerful bombs of a new type may thus be constructed . A single bomb of this type, carried by boat and exploded in a port, might very well destroy the whole port with some of the surrounding territory...

Yours very truly
Albert Einstein [2]

Roosevelt immediately launched the Manhattan Project, which six years later produced the first atomic bomb. The question now naturally arises - what was the moral responsibility of the scientists who were involved in the production of the bomb - Einstein, Szilard, Fermi, and so on, and of the scientific community in general? Bronowski, who himself worked on the bomb, faces the question squarely, and answers it, I think, about as well as it can be answered:

> But Szilard did not stop. When in 1945 the European war had been won, and he realized that the bomb was now about to be made and used on the Japanese, Szilard marshalled protest everywhere he could. He wrote memorandum after memorandum. One memorandum to Roosevelt failed only because Roosevelt died during the very days that Szilard was transmitting it to him. Always Szilard wanted the bomb to be tested openly before the Japanese and an international audience, so that the Japanese should know its power and should surrender before people died.
>
> As you know Szilard failed, and with him the community of scientists failed. He did what a man of integrity could do. He gave up physics and turned to biology - that is how he came to the Salk Institute - and he persuaded others too [including Bronowski]. Physics had been the passion of the last fifty years, and their masterpiece. But now we knew that it was high time to bring to the understanding of life, particularly human life, the same singleness of mind that we had given to understanding the physical world.
>
> The first atomic bomb was dropped on Hiroshima in Japan on 6 August 1945 at 8:15 in the morning. I had not been long

back from Hiroshima when I heard someone say, in Szilard's presence, that it was the tragedy of scientists that their discoveries were used for destruction. Szilard replied, as he more than anyone else had the right to reply, that it was not the tragedy of scientists: "It is the tragedy of mankind." [3]

Let me conclude by returning to our main topic, the origin of matter and energy. I repeat, that since the humanist cannot accept the existence of God, and therefore the concept of creation out of nothing, he has to hold that matter and energy have existed for all eternity.

Fr. Robert A. Staatz

At our last meeting I said that, once it is clearly understood that the literary form of the Hexameron is not history, but rather myth, a concord or harmony between contemporary science and the Hexameron is obviously impossible. This does not mean, however, that a harmony between science and *theology* concerning the origin of the world and so on is impossible. In fact such a harmony or synthesis has been worked out by the French Jesuit, the late Teilhard de Chardin, whose work, it seems to me, provides a providential bridge between secular humanism and liberal Christianity. Now it is impossible to understand Teilhard's work without knowing a little about his life; so in the course of this dialogue, I would like to insert whenever appropriate, a few comments on his life.

He was born Pierre Teilhard de Chardin in 1881, and when he was eighteen years old he entered the Jesuit Seminary at Aix en Provence. Now, this was the time of the anticlerical governments in France and the Jesuits were obliged to leave the country, Teilhard's group going to England, where he was ordained in 1911. In 1914 Teilhard went off to war. As you know, the French government drafted all priests and religious, many of them serving as combat troops. Teilhard became a *brancardier*, a stretcher-bearer, in the Eighth Tunisian Regiment, a colonial unit composed of Moslem troops but with a French cadre.

Teilhard participated in most of the major engagements of the war, and it is a miracle he ever survived. Among his many decorations for bravery was one he was awarded during the battle of Verdun, when he volunteered to go alone at night to within a few yards of the German trenches to recover the body of his dead captain. Yet Teilhard considered these four terrible years the most formative of his life. The image of the infantry on the attack was his favorite metaphor to describe the onward rush of humanity towards Omega or God.

Let me give a little sample of some of Teilhard's theological speculations on the topic of this evening's discussion, the origin of matter and energy. Teilhard did not think the Thomistic notion of creation *ex nihilo* (creation out of nothing), appropriate for our time. Let me read a few excerpts from a fellow Jesuit, Robert Faricy, in his *Teilhard de Chardin's Theology of the Christian in the World:*

> He calls his theory of creation "creative union" (*l'union créatrice*). "'Creative union' is not exactly a metaphysical doctrine. It is much better described as a sort of empirical and pragmatic explanation of the universe."...He does not consider creation strictly in terms of being, as would be the case if his approach were traditionally metaphysical. Rather, he describes being in terms of union. For him, being in its active sense means to "unite oneself or to unite others"; in its passive sense, being means "to be united or unified by another." As we shall see, "to create" means "to unite," and "to be created" means "to be united." It seems well to point out too that he does not think of creation "as an instantaneous act, but in the manner of a process or synthesizing action." [4]

Our subtopic for this evening is Science and Morality, especially as regards the moral responsibility of the scientific community for the development of the atomic bomb, but Teilhard, who was an incurable optimist, did not regard the atomic bomb and the subsequent development of nuclear power as a great moral disaster. Let me read from a superior biography of Teilhard by the English writer, Robert Speaight, entitled simply *Teilhard de Chardin:*

The present writer recalls one occasion in the summer of 1946. Teilhard had only just returned from China and..the conversation turned on the atomic bomb. If the gas chamber and the Gestapo were one challenge to his optimism, the atomic bomb was another. His essay on the subject had recently appeared in *Études* (Sept 1946). Whereas hitherto man had used the natural forces of matter - fire, steam, and electricity - he now had his hands on the levers of matter itself. He was "a new being" who hardly yet "recognized himself," conscious of a power capable of indefinite development. Teilhard believed that the "sceptre of bloody conflicts" would be exorcised by the "rays of mounting unanimity," and that the effect of the atomic bomb might well be that war would "be doubly and definitively put an end to." The excess of power in our hands make all strife impossible; in comparison with the possibilities of conquest opened up by science, the romantic trappings of war would seem tedious and old-fashioned; and men would grow together by "looking passionately, and together, at the same thing." [5]

Let me turn now from science to the Bible. Since I come before Mrs. Stepan, I will have to wait until the following meeting to offer any comments on her presentation. At our last meeting she stated that the Biblical Commission in 1906 and 1909 had condemned the Documentary Theory of Wellhausen and the Mythical Theory of Gunkel. Yet Mrs. Stepan herself acknowledged that decrees of a commission of Cardinals, even if approved by a Pope, are not infallible, and therefore could be revised at a later date. Now this, in fact, is just what has happened. Let me read from perhaps the foremost biblical scholar in the country today, the Sulpician Raymond Brown, who is the President of the American Biblical Society, and a consultor of the new Biblical Commission. This is from his superb *Biblical Reflections on Crises Facing the Church*, which appeared in 1975. He is quoting from a statement by Athanasius Miller, o.s.b., the secretary of the Biblical Commission concerning the publication of a new edition of the *Enchiridion Biblicum*, "Handbook of the Bible," a collection of Roman documents dealing with Holy Scripture:

"...The *Enchiridion* renders great service first of all to the history of dogmas. It reflects clearly, moreover, the fierce battle that the Church at all times has had to fight, though with varying degrees of intensity, to maintain the purity and truth of the Word of God. Especially in this respect the decrees of the Pontifical Biblical Commission have great significance. However, *as long as these decrees propose views which are neither immediately nor mediately connected with truths of faith and morals, it goes without saying that the scholar may pursue his research with complete freedom* [Brown's emphasis] and may utilize the results of his research, provided always that he defers to the supreme teaching authority of the Church.

"Today we can hardly picture to ourselves the position of Catholic scholars at the turn of the century, or the dangers that threatened Catholic teaching on Scripture and its inspiration on the part of liberal and rationalistic criticism, which like a torrent tried to sweep away the sacred barriers of tradition. At present the battle is considerably less fierce; not a few controversies have been peacefully settled and many problems emerge in an entirely new light, so that it is easy enough for us to smile at the narrowness and constraint which prevailed fifty years ago." [6]

Our present Pope, John Paul II, is himself a firm believer in all the latest developments in biblical criticism. He has recently given a series of allocutions on the first three chapters of Genesis. Let me read a few excerpts from an allocution given by him on September 12, 1979:

From the point of view of biblical criticism, it is necessary to mention that the first account of man's creation is chronologically later than the second. The origin of this latter is much more remote. This more ancient text is defined as *Yahwist* because the term *Yahweh* is used to denominate God. It is difficult not to be struck by the fact that the image of God presented there has quite considerable anthropomorphic traits (among others we read in fact that "...the Lord

God formed man of the dust from the ground, and breathed into his nostrils the breath of life" Gen 2:7).

In comparison with this description, the first account, that is, the one held to be chronologically later, is much more mature both as regards the image of God, and as regards the formulation of the essential truths about man. This account derives from the priestly and *Elohist* tradition, from *Elohim* the term used in that account for God. [7]

Now this is identical to what I gave from Bruce Vawter and to which Mrs. Stepan objected. Let me read another excerpt from an allocution delivered by the Pope the following week, September 19, 1979: (The second and third chapters of Genesis tell the story of Adam and Eve.)

The second chapter of Genesis constitutes, in a certain manner, the most ancient description and record of man's self-knowledge; and together with the third chapter...the whole archaic form of the narrative...manifest its primitive *mythical* character. [8]

So Pope John Paul II clearly holds that the first three chapters of Genesis are a composite of sources, one older and less developed, and the literary form of these chapters is the myth. This is all I have been trying to say.

I think the basic fallacy on which the concordist and fundamentalist interpretations of the Hexameron are based is a false notion of the innerancy or freedom from error of the Bible. Does the Bible really give us absolute truth, or like everything else does it present a mixture of truth and error? To answer this question, I will have to go back once more to the Documentary Theory of Julius Wellhausen. Wellhausen built his theory on an examination of the so-called "doublets" or repetitions in the Pentateuch, a characteristic of Semitic literature. For example, there are two creation stories in Genesis, two Flood stories, and so on. Let us examine just one of these doublets, a story about the patriarchs:

From there *Abraham* journeyed toward the territory of the

Negeb and dwelt between Kadesh and Shur; and he sojourn-
ed in Gerar. And Abraham said of Sarah his wife, "She is my
sister." And Abimelech king of Gerar sent and took Sarah.
But *God* came to Abimelech by night...(Gen 20:1-3a).

The Hebrew word for God is *Elohim*, so Wellhausen reasoned
that this story must have been written by the Elohist or E author,
who preferred that name for God. Now here is the doublet, or
repetition of the story:

> So *Isaac* dwelt in Gerar. When the men of the place asked
> him about his wife, he said, "She is my sister"; for he feared
> to say, "My wife," thinking, "lest the men of the place should
> kill me for the sake of Rebekah";...So Abimelech warned all
> the people, saying, "Whoever touches this man or his wife
> shall be put to death." And Isaac sowed in that land, and
> reaped in the same year a hundredfold. The *Lord* blessed
> him...(Gen 26:6-8,11,12).

The Hebrews substituted the word *Adonai*, "Lord," out of reverence for the sacred name Yahweh, "I am who am," so Wellhausen concluded that this version of the story was by the Yahwist
or J author. Here is Bruce Vawter's analysis of these two stories,
and their implication with regard to the kind of truth we find in
the Bible:

> What is Genesis? Like any other book it is the expression of
> its author's mind. If that author is inspired, then the expres-
> sion is of a mind enlightened by grace, which will therefore
> be unerring. How did the author of Genesis intend to express
> his mind in including the "doublets, repetitions, and discord-
> ances" of his sources in the book which he produced? He was
> as well aware as we that it was likely that a striking event
> which E has associated with Abraham had taken place once
> more down to the last detail with Isaac, as J had it. Neither
> was he in any better position than we to decide which version
> was correct. What is more important is that he could not
> have cared less. The fact that he included both versions, not

only here but countless other times, is eloquent testimony that verifying details of this sort was of no concern to him whatever. If he had included rival traditions that clash over the "who" or "when," he could not have told us better that to him the "who" and the "when" were not important, and that he had a purpose that transcended these trivialities. What that purpose was, we must try to find when we read Genesis. All we need say for the moment is that it is this *use* of his sources, this *purpose* that he had, that is the expression of the author's mind. It is this, therefore, that is the inspired meaning of Genesis, and whatever is foreign to this purpose is not the meaning of Genesis. *What the author intended to teach* is the meaning of Genesis; that is the word of God which is free from error. We can say, therefore, that while Genesis undoubtedly contains errors, it teaches none. [9]

Bruce Vawter is saying that the inspired authors were evidently confused as to just who was involved in this story, Abraham or Isaac. But the authors in this particular case have no intention of teaching us historical truth, but rather religious truth, namely, God's providential care of a chosen soul.

Let me conclude my presentation tonight with another reading from Raymond Brown on the latest developments in the problem of the inerrancy of the Bible. This is again from his *Biblical Reflections on Crises Facing the Church:*

The final decree of Vatican II on Divine Revelation (the Constitution *Dei Verbum*)...in many...biblical matters...repeated the *status quo* achieved under Pius XII, and in regard to the inspiration of the Scriptures it simply reiterated past positions. But one can detect a significant movement with regard to inerrancy. Inerrancy is a correlary of inspiration: it has been repugnant to Christians to posit error in the Bible for which God has an author's role and responsibility. Only gradually have we learned to distinguish that while all Scripture is inspired, all Scripture is not inerrant. The first step in narrowing the scope of inerrancy is to recognize that the concept is applicable only when an affirmation of truth is involved. In the Bible there are passages of poetry, song, fiction, and fable where the matter of inerrancy does not even arise. A second step is to recognize that not every affirmation of truth is so germane to God's purpose in inspiring the Scriptures that He has committed Himself to it. Already in *Providentissimus Deus* (1893) Pope Leo XIII acknowledged that the scientific affirmations of the Bible were not necessarily inerrant, since it was not God's purpose to teach men science. Eventually the same principle was applied to historical affirmations, but the last frontier had been religious affirmations. Job's denial of an afterlife (Job 14:14-22) makes it difficult to claim that all religious affirmations in the Bible are inerrant. Vatican II has made it possible to restrict inerrancy to the essential religious affirmations of a biblical book made for the sake of our salvation. [10]

In conclusion let me repeat Bruce Vawter's statement on the inerrancy of Scripture: "What the author intended to teach is the meaning of Genesis, this is the word of God which is free from error. We can say therefore, that while Genesis undoubtedly contains errors, it teaches none." This principle will be crucial for our understanding of the Hexameron.

Mrs. Maria Stepan

I would like to begin tonight by giving a little outline of the method I will be following during the course of this dialogue. First I will offer comments on Dr. Schonfield's then on Fr. Staatz's presentations from this particular meeting, then on Rev. Swezey's presentation from the preceeding meeting, and finally I will conclude with my own comments on the topics of the day.

Dr. Schonfield refused to speculate on the *origin* of matter and energy, saying that since the humanist finds no compelling evidence for the existence of God, he is forced to conclude that matter and energy have existed for all eternity. But this attitude is not scientific to say the least.

An interesting recent development concerning one of the current scientific theories on the origin of the universe, the Expanding Universe Theory, concerns the original state of matter in the first few seconds after what is popularly known as the "Big Bang." This is the so-called "anthropic principle" and is postulated not only by believing scientists but by many agnostics and atheists as well. The principle states that the slightest changes in the amount of mass and energy would have resulted in a universe in which no life could exist. In other words the universe appears to have been made for man to live in, thus indicating that the origin of the universe was not a random event, but was presided over by a directing Intelligence. One of the proponents of the "anthropic principle" is the Benedictine, Fr. Stanley Jaki who holds doctorates in both theology and physics. Let me read an excerpt from his *Cosmos and Creator* which appeared in 1980. This is from a review by the Franciscan, Fr. Owen Bennett entitled *Cosmos: A Trap or a Home?* which appeared in the *Homiletic and Pastoral Review* in December of 1983:

The specific particular character of the universe thus evolved has a further most striking specificity: it is a universe for human life! On this Jaki comments:

"[This] specific cosmic evolution is dependent on conditions restricted to within narrow limits. One of them is the original ratio of photons to protons, neutrons and electrons. If that ratio had been slightly less than the value given above, much perhaps all hydrogen would have turned into helium. In that case the universe would have been deprived of all organic life. Another of those conditions relates to the total number of those particles, that is, to the total mass of the universe. If that mass had been slightly more than indicated by the actual rate of expansion and other observations, the expansion would have, on account of the greater gravitational attraction, been too slow to permit the cosmic cooking of the elements which must produce them also in their actual, most peculiar relative percentages. With markedly more matter originally present, the expansion (and the cosmic cooking) would not have taken place at all. Had that mass been slightly less, the expansion would have been much too fast to

maintain temperatures and pressures necessary for that
cosmic cooking. The universe can indeed be said to have had
a very narrow escape in order to become what it actually is.
Indeed it may be said that the universe weighs as much as it
does, because we humans are here: a most weighty consideration, which is encountered in recent cosmological literature under the label of the anthropic principle. The universe
is indeed anthropocentric in a far deeper sense than the one
which was discredited by the Copernican revolution." [11]

This is of course just what is said in the Bible: "For thus saith the
Lord that created the heavens. God himself that formed the earth,
and made it, the very maker thereof: he did not create in vain: he
formed it to be inhabited" (Isaiah 45:18).

Let me go on now to Dr. Bronowski's treatment of our subtopic
of Science and Morality, especially as regards the development of
the atomic bomb. Fr. Jaki gave the Gifford Lectures at the
University of Edinburgh from 1974 through 1976, which he
entitled *The Road of Science and the Ways to God.* Here is his
comment on Dr. Bronowski's claim that the scientific community
was not responsible for the tragedy of Hiroshima:

For the past three hundred years science, or rather the
method of science, has been presented as bringing utopia to
earth, but it was only during the last generation that utopia
seemed to have been delivered to everyone's doorstep in the
form of sophisticated gadgets that even the most sanguine
scientists never dreamed of half a century before. Yet at the
same time, science increased man's destructive capabilities in
a measure which brought a sense of horror to every doorstep.
The decade of bewilderment, which the 1960's became, was
the product of a conflict between a heavenly promise and a
hellish threat both coming largely from the very same source.
Worshippers of science gladly swallowed J. Bronowski's
claim that science was not responsible for Hiroshima, and
they applauded the words of retiring Nobel laureate physicist, I.I. Rabi, that "science is the *only* valid underlying
knowledge that gives guidance to the *whole* human adven-

ture and that those who are not acquainted with science do not possess the *basic* human values that are necessary in our time." Those who did not worship science, to say nothing of those who were ignorant of it, could only be made antagonistic by such sophomoric encomiums heaped upon it. [12]

I come now to Fr. Teilhard de Chardin, Fr. Staatz's "bridge" between secular humanism and liberal Christianity. Now Fr. Teilhard's so-called "synthesis" between science and theology has been rejected by both the scientific community and the Church. Speaking for the scientific community, let me read from *This View of Life* by the late George Gaylord Simpson, a professor of paleontology at Harvard University, who was a close personal friend of Teilhard, and one of his literary executors:

> Teilhard's beliefs as to the course and causes of evolution are not scientifically acceptable, because they are not in truth based on scientific premises and because, to the moderate extent that they are subject to scientific tests, they fail those tests. Teilhard's mystic vision is not thereby invalidated, because it does not in truth derive from his beliefs on evolution - quite the contrary. There is no possible way of validating or testing Teilhard's mystic vision of Omega [God]. Any assurance about it must itself be an unsupported act of mystic faith...The attempt to build an evolutionary theology mingling mysticism and science has only tended to vitiate the science. I strongly suspect that it has been equally damaging on the religious side, but here I am less qualified to judge. [13]

During his life Teilhard was forbidden to publish by the Church, but in his will he left his manuscripts to his secretary who turned them over to his humanist friends, like Professor Simpson and Sir Julien Huxley who promptly published them. In 1962 during the reign of Pope John xxiii, the Holy Office responded with a *Monitum* or warning against these works, which has never been withdrawn:

Several works of Fr. Pierre Teilhard de Chardin, some of which were published posthumously, are being edited and are gaining a good deal of success.

Prescinding from a judgment about those points that concern the positive sciences, it is sufficiently clear that the above mentioned works abound in such ambiguities, and indeed even serious errors, as to offend Catholic doctrine.

For this reason, the most eminent and most reverend Fathers of the Supreme Sacred Congregation of the Holy Office exhort all Ordinaries, as well as superiors of Religious Institutes, rectors of seminaries, and presidents of universities, against the dangers presented by the works of Fr. Teilhard and his followers. [14]

Fr. Staatz went on to give a rebuttal of my presentation at our first meeting in which he quoted Fr. Raymond Brown to the effect that decisions of the Biblical Commission issued during the reign of Pope St. Pius x had been abrogated in 1955. Fr. Staatz gave the impression that this had been done by an official Vatican document which was signed by the secretary of the Biblical Commission, Fr. Athanasius Miller, o.s.b. Fr. Miller actually made these remarks in a magazine article, hardly the place for an official Vatican pronouncement, to say the least!

Fr. Brown was, as Fr. Staatz says, appointed as a consultor to the Biblical Commission, but for one year only, 1972. Why was his appointment not renewed? Let me turn again to Msgr. Steinmueller (a consultor to the Biblical Commission for over twenty years) from his *Sword of the Spirit*:

I was a consultor of the first Pontifical Biblical Commission from 1947 (after the publication of *Divino Afflante Spiritu*) to 1971, and I never heard any intimation that the decrees of the Commission were ever revoked. At the most they were clarified (cf. Letter to Cardinal Suhard of Paris, 1948). Recently some Catholic scholars have asserted that these decrees were implicitly revoked by *Divino Afflante Spiritu* (1943), and that this is confirmed by two articles written in 1955 by A. Miller and A. Kleinhans, who seemed to restrict the scope of the decrees to matters of faith and morals...The articles referred to were *unauthorized* and were condemned by the voting Cardinal members of the Commission. A. Miller and A. Kleinhans were to be brought before the Holy Office because of the articles, but were saved from this ordeal through the personal intervention of Cardinal Tisserant before the Holy Father. It was my friend Fr. Miller, o.s.b., who told me the whole story before his return to Germany. [15]

Fr. Staatz also claimed in his rebuttal of my first presentation, that Pope John Paul II rejected the Mosaic authenticity of the Pentateuch and quoted from an allocution of the Holy Father in which he used the term "Elohist" in speaking of the first chapter of Genesis, the Hexameron, and the term "Yahwist" in speaking of the second and third chapters, the story of Adam and Eve. Now this in no way denies the substantial Mosaic authorship of those texts.

I had mentioned that in 1906 the Biblical Commission had condemned the Documentary Theory of Wellhausen, but at the same time it said that it could be granted without prejudice to the Mosaic authenticity of the Pentateuch, that Moses himself possibly had used written and oral sources in his production of that work. It is legitimate, therefore to refer to these possible sources as "Elohist" or "Yahwist," where those names of God are used, as long as in the process the substantial Mosaic authorship of the Pentateuch is not denied, which the Holy Father does not do, and which Fr. Vawter does.

I should mention here in passing, for whatever it might be worth, that Israeli scientists have recently run the book of Genesis through a computer and concluded that it was written by *one* author, not the three or four claimed by the liberals.

Now the Mosaic authenticity of the Pentateuch is not just a minor literary dispute. Msgr. Steinmueller says that it is also a serious theological problem, leading directly to the question of the inerrancy of the Bible, and even to the claim by some liberal Catholics that Our Lord did not know that He was the Messiah, or even that He was God!

The Mosaic authenticity of the Pentateuch is not merely a literary and purely historical or archaelolgical problem; it is also to a certain extent a theological question. Those passages which are directly ascribed to Moses by Sacred Scripture must be believed by *divine faith* to have Moses as their author, and the substance of the other parts of Pentateuch is *theologically certain* to be of Mosaic origin. Hence, it would be an *error in faith* to deny the Mosaic origin of those passages of the Pentateuch which are directly attributed to him, and it would be at least *temerarious* to deny the Mosaic origin of those parts which constitute the substance of the Pentateuch.

Some of these passages are spoken by Christ Himself: Matt 8:4 (cf. Lev 14:2-32 on leprosy), Matt 19:8 (cf. Deut 24:1-4, on divorce), Mark 7:10 (cf. Ex 20:12, 21:17, Lev 10:9, Deut 5:16, on honoring parents), Mark 12:26 (cf. Ex 3:2,6 on God of the patriarchs). Christ explicitly asserts that Moses in his writings wrote of Him (John 5:45-47). These words of Christ cannot mean His accomodation to the general opinion of His contemporaries, which held that the entire Pentateuch was composed by Moses, for the admission of any such accomodation implies that Christ tolerated error. [16]

Fr. Staatz then went on to read from another allocution of Pope John Paul II, in which the Holy Father referred to the "mythical" aspect of the story of Adam and Eve. Fr. Staatz claimed that the Holy Father was therefore denying the historicity of the story. The term "myth," in the popular sense, means an extravagant story that is certainly not historical, but when the term is used in its technical sense, as the Holy Father is using it here, it does not mean something that denies history, but rather something that transcends it. The Holy Father appends a series of footnotes to the allocution, giving several of the current technical definitions of myth, none of which deny the historicity of a particular story. Actually, the Holy Father uses the term "mythical" only once in referring to Adam and Eve, and then uses the term "prehistory," which Msgr. Steinmueller also prefers to myth. In the succeeding allocution (*L'Osservatore Romano*, Oct 1, 1979), the Holy Father explains just what he means by "theological prehistory." He uses the term to refer to Adam and Eve as they were in the state of innocence, because, he says, "history" proper did not begin until after the Fall. This is because "history" is inseparable from *Heilsgeschichte*, "salvation history." After Adam and Eve fell, God immediately promised them a future Redeemer: "I shall put enmities between thee and the woman, and thy seed and her seed; she shall crush thy head, and thou shalt lie in wait for her heel (Gen 3:15, Douay-Rheims).

Fr. Staatz continued with Fr. Vawter's treatment of the inerrancy of the Bible. We saw that Julius Wellhausen had built his Documentary Theory on what are called "doublets" or repetitions, a characteristic of Semitic literature. Now just because two stories are somewhat similar does not necessarily mean that they are a doublet. The two stories of Abraham and Isaac, referred to by Fr. Vawter, are two similar but separate incidents. It is completely gratuitous to say that they are the same incident with the names confused. Fr. Vawter went on to say that what was important in inspiration was not what the author actually said, but what was in his mind - what was his purpose or intention in writing - this was what was inspired and did not contain error, while what he actually *said* might contain error. Pope Leo xiii in his encyclical *Providentissimus Deus* long ago warned of the dangers of this method of limiting inspiration:

> *Inerrancy of Holy Scripture.* It may also happen that the sense of a passage remains ambiguous, and in this case good hermeneutical methods will greatly assist in clearing up the obscurity. But it is absolutely wrong and forbidden either to narrow inspiration to certain parts of Holy Scripture, or to admit that the sacred writer has erred. As to the system of those who, in order to rid themselves of these difficulties, do not hesitate to concede that divine inspiration regards the things of faith and morals, and nothing beyond, because (as they wrongly think) in a question of the truth or falsehood of a passage we should consider not so much what God has said as the reason and purpose which he had in mind in saying it - this system cannot be tolerated. [17]

Fr. Vawter writing in 1956 claimed that the Bible contained historical errors, though no religious errors, but he left the door wide open. Fr. Brown writing only twenty years later in 1975, confidently asserted that the Bible contained not only scientific and historical errors, but religious errors as well. Let me begin with his so-called scientific errors. Fr. Brown used as his authority for this statement, believe it or not, the encyclical *Providentissimus Deus* of Pope Leo xiii. Pope Leo had actually said that the Bible does not teach us the essential nature of the visible universe, but rather describes it as it "sensibly appears." Now just because the Bible uses *popular* expressions hardly means that it contains scientific errors. Even Fr. Vawter recognized this in *A Path Through Genesis*, when he said that anyone who claimed he denied the heliocentric theory because he said "the sun set," rather than "the earth set," would be "three times a fool."

We have heard what Fr. Vawter would consider an historical error - the completely gratuitous assertion that the Yahwist and Elohist authors were confused as to whom the incident at Gerara had actually happened, Abraham or Isaac. I have already dealt with this claim.

Fr. Brown also said that the Bible contained religious errors, and used as an example Job's doubt about the after-life. Job said, "If a man die, shall he live again?" (Job 14:4). But Job had said this in the midst of his terrible trials, when he was on the verge of despair. He later repented of these utterances and made a beautiful profession of faith in the Redeemer to come and in the resurrection of the body. To use this as an example of a religious error in the Bible is just ridiculous. Fr. Brown might as well have used the high priest Caiphas' statement, "He has uttered blasphemy" (Matt 26:65).

Fr. Brown gave as his authority for the statement that the Bible contains scientific, historical, and religious errors, the Second Vatican Council. He said: "Vatican ii has made it possible to restrict inerrancy to the essential religious affirmations of a biblical book made for the sake of our salvation." This is a paraphrase of a statement that was the subject of a long and bitter dispute among the Council Fathers, because some of them feared that this statement would be misused in exactly the way that Fr.

Brown has misused it. Fr. John McKee tells the story of this dispute in his excellent *The Enemy Within the Gate:*

> ...The original text was not "for the sake of our salvation" but "pertaining to our salvation" and 184 Council Fathers asked that the phrase be dropped for the precise reason that it might be taken as restricting inerrancy to faith and morals. The Theological Commission dragged its feet, and on October 8, 1965, a group delivered a memorandum to the Pope, claiming openly that the phrase had been deliberately inserted to restrict inerrancy in a way contrary to Catholic teaching. After an investigation, the Pope sent observations on this and other matters to the Theological Commission. He said that the matter involved "great responsibility for him towards the Church and towards his own conscience." The Commission was asked to drop the expression "truth pertaining to salvation" from the text. After the discussion and voting, the Commission adopted the text as we now have it.
>
> To see what had, or had not, been effected we compare the two texts:

Early Text	*Final Text*
"The books of Scripture must be acknowledged as teaching...without error the truth pertaining to salvation."	"The books of Scripture firmly, faithfully and without error, teach that truth which God for the sake of our salvation, wished to see confided to the Sacred Scriptures." [Flannery translation]

When one compares the two versions, one sees that a tightening has taken place to placate the Pope and the traditionalist section of the Council, but one detects still some foot-dragging on the part of the liberals. The text could have been sharper and met more fully the wish of the Vicar of Christ. If the Council had dropped the dangerous phrase as requested, instead of replacing it with an improved one, there could have been no misrepresentation. As it is, we know in what sense the Bishop of Rome gave his seal to this decree...any phrase which may seem ambiguous must be interpreted in line with tradition. [18]

So much for the presentations of Dr. Schonfield and Fr. Staatz. I would also like to make a few comments on Rev. Swezey's presentation during our first meeting. I will be running a meeting behind in whatever comments I might have on Rev. Swezey since he always comes after me. I must confess that I am also at a loss to explain the position of the Catholic bishop and the appearance of Fr. Vawter in behalf of the evolutionist cause. I personally see nothing wrong with the case for scientific creationism intended for use in the public schools which Rev. Swezey presented. Surely the First Amendment to the Constitution was never intended to exclude God and creation from the public schools. I also fail to see what the bishop and Fr. Vawter hoped to gain in terms of the current ecumenical movement with Protestants. To date this movement has largely been between liberal Catholics such as Fr. Brown, and liberal Protestants, and has borne very little fruit. Perhaps the ecumenical movement would be more fruitful if it were between conservative Catholics and conservative Protestants who both believe, at least, that the Bible is free from error.

However, I do have one comment to make on the passage that Rev. Swezey read which was intended for use only in Christian schools. While it is of course possible that God wrote the Hexameron with His "finger," or failing that, directly revealed it to Adam, who then *wrote* it down, I think that this is an example of the exaggerated reverence that some biblical Protestants have for the *written* word of God. In the Catholic Church great weight is also given to Tradition, and I think that it is more probable that God directly revealed the story of creation to Adam, who then handed it down *orally* to his children and grandchildren, and that it wasn't actually written down until some generations later. God can just as easily protect an oral tradition as a written document.

Let me go on now to my own comments on the first day of creation. Catholics believe that the Church has been appointed by God to be the official interpreter of the Bible, and that this is done through Tradition, the teachings of the Fathers and Doctors, and the Magisterium of the Church, that is, the pronouncements of the various Popes and Councils. So accordingly let me begin with the Magisterium of the Church. For the title of our meeting tonight we chose *The Origin of Matter and Energy*. The Church teaches that matter and energy have not existed from all eternity as the humanists claim, but were created by God out of nothing at the very beginning of time. This teaching is what is called a "defined doctrine of the faith," and it was so defined at the First Vatican Council in 1870:

> If anyone does not admit that the world and everything in it, both spiritual and material, have been produced in their entire substance by God out of nothing, let him be anathema. [19]

And from Tradition here is St. Thomas Aquinas in his *Summa Theologica* commenting on the first day of creation:

> It is said (Gen 1:2a) *The earth was void and empty or invisible and shapeless* according to another version [Septuagint], by which is understood the formlessness of matter, as Augustine says...on account of its being impossible for Moses to make the idea of such matter intelligible to ignorant people, except under the similitude of well-known objects. Hence he used a variety of figures in speaking of it, calling it in very truth water or earth. At the same time it has so far a likeness to earth, in that it is susceptible of form and to water in its adaptability to a variety of forms...
>
> By the words *Spirit of God* Holy Scripture usually means the Holy Ghost, who is said to *move over the waters*...that is to say, over the formless matter signified by water, even as the love of the artist moves over the materials of his art, that out of them he may form his works. [20]

So St. Thomas thinks that all the matter in the universe was created by God out of nothing on the first day, but in a formless state, and on succeeding days He made all the creatures of the world from this primordial matter. We will see when we come to our discussion of the second day of creation, that this interpretation can easily be harmonized with some of the contemporary scientific theories on the origin of the universe. St. Thomas concludes with the Holy Spirit brooding over that formless matter, because one day from that same matter will come Mary, His bride, whom He will overshadow making her fruitful with the Word of God.

Rev. De Verne Swezey

When I first began my campus ministry some years ago, I found that I had very little success in trying to interest students in biblical Christianity, so overwhelmed were thy by the continuous barrage of secular humanism. But after I discovered creationism, that is, that there is a viable scientific alternative to evolutionism, I have had a little more success. But more recently I have taken advantage of the split in the humanist camp, that is, the split between what is usually called establishment humanism and counter-culture humanism, or what I prefer to call secular humanism and sacral humanism. It is not generally realized that the counter-culture movement is a religious movement, though unfortunately not a Christian one. It is caught up in all kinds of religions - Hindu, Buddhist, American Indian, etc., which could be summarized simply as pantheism. This movement was briefly described by Dr. Bronowski in his *The Ascent of Man*, and castigated as a "contemptible failure of nerve."

However, counter-culture humanism has an excellent critique of establishment humanism which I think all Christian apologists should take advantage of, in somewhat the same way that St. Paul took advantage of the split between the Sadducees and the Pharisees concerning the resurrection of the body. Liberal Christians subject the Bible to intense criticism and then take the teachings of science on faith, that is simply on the word of the scientists. It should be the other way around. The Bible should be taken simply on faith, and science subjected to critical analysis, especially when it pretends to give answers to "ultimate questions" such as the existence of God and the origin of religion.

Let me read a few excerpts from one of the most prominent spokesmen for the counter-culture movement, Theodore Roszak (unfortunately a lapsed Catholic), the author of the very influential *The Making of a Counter-Culture*. This is from his *Where the Wasteland Ends* which came out in 1972:

> The religious renewal we see happening about us - especial-
> ly among disaffiliated young people, but by no means only
> among them - seems to me neither trivial nor irresponsible,
> neither uncivil nor indecent. On the contrary, I accept it as a
> profoundly serious sign of the times, a necessary phase of our
> cultural evolution, and - potentially a life-enhancing influence
> of incalculable value. I believe it means we have arrived, after
> long journeying, at an historical vantage point from which we
> can see at last where the wasteland ends and where a culture
> of human wholeness and fulfillment begins. We can recognize
> that the fate of the soul is the fate of the social order; that if
> the spirit within us withers, so too will the world we build
> about us. Literally so. What, after all, is the ecological crisis
> that now captures so much belated attention but the
> inevitable extroversion of a blighted psyche? Like inside, like
> outside. In the eleventh hour, the very physical environment
> suddenly looms up before us as the outward mirror of our
> inner condition: for many, the first discernible symptom of
> advanced disease within. [21]

With that little introduction to the counter-culture movement itself, let us see what Theodore Roszak says about our subtopic of Science and Morality. *The Ascent of Man* and *Where the Wasteland Ends* came out in 1972, and yet amazingly Roszak has an almost exact prediction of Bronowski's position regarding the moral responsibility of the scientific community for the atomic bomb:

> Those who begin to desert scientific culture in disgust at its
> incorrigible reductionism are correct to believe that the scien-
> tific community is incapable of eradicating the vice. Ethical
> resolutions and passionate appeals to principle can have little
> effect. They will always seem to compromise the "freedom of
> inquiry" and "intellectual adventure" scientists have been
> taught to prize above all else...Most scientists will find it

simpler (and more advantageous to their careers) to resort to Pilate's strategy and wash their hands, vaguely laying the blame for any "misuse" of knowledge on the technicians, the state, the public, on everyone in general...and no one in particular. Do not discussions of social responsibility in science always finish, after much ritualistic soul-searching, in such quandries? In any event, a timid cry for prudence will never drown out the bravado of the "quest for truth." [22]

While the counter-culture offers an excellent negative critique of contemporary scientism, it has little to offer in a more positive way. For a more positive approach I will go first to the creationist movement and then to the Bible itself. Let me turn now to the creationist model for the origin of matter and energy. This is again from Dr. Henry Morris' *Scientific Creationism*, and from the section intended for use in the public schools:

...The creationist utilizes the scientific law of *cause and effect*. This law, which is universally accepted and followed in every field of science, relates every phenomenon as an effect to a cause. No effect is ever quantitatively "greater" or qualitatively "superior" to a cause. An effect can be lower than its cause but never higher.

Using causal reasoning, the theistic creationist notes that:

The First Cause of limitless Space	*must be infinite*
The First Cause of endless Time	*must be eternal*
The First Cause of boundless Energy	*must be omnipotent*
The First Cause of universal Interrelationships	*must be omnipresent*
The First Cause of infinite Complexity	*must be omniscient*
The First cause of Moral Values	*must be moral*
The First Cause of Spiritual Values	*must be spiritual*
The First Cause of Human Responsibility	*must be volitional*
The First Cause of Human Integrity	*must be truthful*
The First Cause of Human Love	*must be loving*
The First Cause of life	*must be living*

We conclude from the law of cause and effect that the First Cause of all things must be an infinite, eternal, omnipotent, omnipresent, omniscient, moral, spiritual, volitional, truthful, loving, living Being! Do such adjectives describe Matter? Can random motion of primeval particles produce intelligent thought, or inert molecules generate spiritual worship? To say that Matter and its inate properties constitute the ultimate explanation for the universe and its inhabitants is equivalent to saying that the law of cause and effect is valid only under present circumstances, not in the past. [23]

Let me conclude by turning again to the final section of the General Edition of *Scientific Creationism*, which is intended for use only in Christian schools. Here are Dr. Morris' comments on the Scriptural account of the first day of creation which deals with the origin of "light," or as we have it, the origin of matter and energy:

> Another point important to recognize is that creation was "mature" from its birth. It did not have to grow or develop from simple beginnings. God formed it full-grown in every respect, including even Adam and Eve as mature individuals when they were first formed. The whole universe had an "appearance of age" right from the start. It could not have been otherwise for true creation to have taken place. "Thus the heavens and the earth were finished, and all the host of them" (Gen 2:1).
>
> This fact means that the light from the sun, moon, and stars was shining upon the earth as soon as they were created, since their very purpose was "...to give light on the earth" (Gen 1:17). As a matter of fact, it is possible that these light-waves traversing space from the heavenly bodies to the earth were energized even *before* the heavenly bodies themselves in order to provide the light for the first three days. [24]

Now of course the classic objection to the Scriptural account of the origin of light is - "But where did the light on the first day come from, if the sun, moon, and stars were not created until the fourth day?" Here is Dr. Morris' reply to this objection:

> The light for the first three days obviously did not come from the sun, moon, and stars, since God did not make them and place them in the heavens until the fourth day (Gen 1:16-19). Nevertheless, the light source for the first three days had the same function ("to divide the light from the darkness") as did the heavenly bodies from the fourth day onward (Genesis 1:4,18). This "division" now results from the sun and moon and the earth's axial rotation. For practical purposes, therefore, the primeval light must essentially have come from the same directions as it would later when the permanent light sources were set in place. [25]

In conclusion let me repeat a point I would like to emphasize frequently during the course of our dialogue: Liberal Christians subject the Bible to intense criticism, and then take the teachings of science on faith, that is, simply on the word of the scientists. It should be the other way around. The Bible should be taken simply on faith, and science subjected to critical analysis, especially when it pretends to give answers to the "ultimate questions."

Dean Smalley

Let me conclude our meeting tonight by again making a brief summary of our four presentations. If you remember from the last time, I decided in view of my liberal Protestant bias, to refrain as much as possible from giving interpretations or commentaries, but to confine myself to brief summaries.

The first day of creation deals with the origin of matter and energy, and our two topics for this evening were: The Atomic Theory of Matter, and Science and Morality.

Dr. Schonfield used the late Jacob Bronowski, one of the directors of the British Humanist Association, to present his position regarding our two topics. After a brief review of the history of the atomic theory Dr. Bronowski concluded that the scientific community was not responsible for the tragedy of Hiroshima.

Fr. Staatz considers the famous scientist-theologian, Teilhard de Chardin, a "providential bridge" between secular humanism and liberal Christianity. Teilhard refused to accept the current pessimistic views regarding science and morality. Concerning the inerrancy of the Bible Fr. Staatz claimed that the Bible like everything else, contains a mixture of truth and error. He said that the Second Vatican Council had limited the inerrancy of the Bible to only "those essential religious affirmations...made for the sake of our salvation."

Mrs. Stepan began with the so-called "anthropic principle" as presented by the physicist and theologian, Stanley Jaki. This principle maintains that the universe from its very beginning had a certain predisposition towards life and seems to have been made for man to live in, indicating the directing hand of God rather than random processes. She also claimed that Teilhard de Chardin's "synthesis" between science and theology has been rejected by both the scientific community and by the Church. She then stated that Pope Leo XIII in his encyclical *Providentissimus Deus* had long ago condemned Fr. Vawter's method of limiting the inerrancy of the Bible, and contrary to Fr. Brown, Vatican II had *not* endorsed this limitation.

Rev. Swezey used the social critic Theodore Roszak to attack Dr. Bronowski's position regarding the atomic bomb in particular, and the lack of moral responsibility in general, on the part of the scientific community. Rev. Swezey concluded with a strictly literal interpretation of the biblical phrase "let there be light," saying that the light of the first day could have come miraculously from the same places that would later be occupied by the sun, moon, and stars on the fourth day.

Our next meeting will again be held at Cabot University, and we will go on to discuss the second day of creation.

REFERENCES

1 Jacob Bronowski, *The Ascent of Man*,
   Little, Brown and Co., Boston, 1973, pp.349,351.
2 Bronowski, *Op. cit.*, p.371.
3 *Idem*, p.370.
4 Robert Faricy, s.j., *Teilhard de Chardin's Theology of the Christian in the World*, Sheed and Ward, New York, 1967, pp.108,109.
5 Robert Speaight, *Teilhard de Chardin*,
   Collins, London, 1967, p.267.
6 Raymond Brown, s.s., *Biblical Reflections on Crises Facing the Church*,
   Paulist Press, New York, 1975, pp.110,111.
7 Pope John Paul ii, General Audience, Sept 12, 1979,
   L'Osservatore Romano, Sept 17, 1979.
8 Pope John Paul ii, General Audience, Sept 19, 1979,
   L'Osservatore Romano, Sept 24, 1979.
9 Bruce Vawter, c.m., *A Path Through Genesis*,
   Sheed and Ward, New York, 1956, pp.26,27.
10 Brown, *Op. cit.*, p.115.
11 Stanley Jaki, o.s.b., *Cosmos and Creator*,
   Scottish Academic Press, 1980,
   U.S.A., Regnery Gateway Editions, New York, pp.40,41.
   Quoted in: *Cosmos: A Trap or a Home?* Owen Bennett, o.f.m., conv.,
   Homiletic and Pastoral Review, New York, December, 1983, p.52.
12 Stanley Jaki, o.s.b., *The Road of Science and the Ways to God*,
   University of Chicago Press, Chicago, 1978, p.329.
13 George Gaylord Simpson, *This View of Life*,
   Harcourt, Brace and World, New York, 1964, p.232.
14 Msgr. Leo Schumacher, *The Truth About Teilhard*,
   Twin Circle Publishing Co., New York, 1968, p.11.
15 Msgr. John Steinmueller, *The Sword of the Spirit*,
   Stella Maris Books, Fort Worth, Tex., 1977, pp.7,8.
16 Msgr. John Steinmueller, *A Companion to Scripture Studies, Vol. 2*,
   Joseph F. Wagner, New York, 1969, p.23.
17 *Rome and the Study of Scripture*,
   Abbey Press, St. Meinrad, Ind. 1964, pp.23,24.

18 Fr. John McKee, *The Enemy Within the Gate*,
    Lumen Christi Press, Houston, Tex., 1974, pp.264-266.
19 The Jesuit Fathers of St. Mary's College, *The Church Teaches*,
    B. Herder Book Co., St. Louis, 1955, p.153.
20 St. Thomas Aquinas, *Summa Theologica*, (*I, Q66, a1, ad2,3; I, Q74, a3, ad3*),
    Benziger Brothers, New York, 1947, pp.329,330,358.
21 Theodore Roszak, *Where the Wasteland Ends*,
    Doubleday and Co., Anchor Books, Garden City, N.Y., 1973, p.xvii.
22 Roszak, *Op. cit.*, pp.232,233.
23 Henry Morris, *Scientific Creationism*,
    Creation-Life Publishers, San Diego, Cal., 1974, pp.19,20.
24 Morris, *Op. cit.*, pp.209,210.
25 *Idem*, p.210.

THE SECOND DAY

The Origin of the Universe

THE THIRD MEETING
A) The Oscillating Universe
B) The Law of Entropy

Scene: Cabot University

Dean Smalley

Good evening and welcome again to Cabot University. We begin tonight our discussion of the second day of creation, which deals with the origin of the universe. We have scheduled two meetings for this day, the first dealing with the Oscillating Universe and the Law of Entropy, and the second with the Age of the Universe. I will begin our meeting tonight by reading the Scriptural account of the second day:

> And God said, "Let there be a firmament in the midst of the waters, and let it separate the waters from the waters." And God made the firmament and separated the waters which were under the firmament from the waters which were above the firmament. And it was so. And God called the firmament heaven. And there was evening and there was morning a second day (Gen 1:6-8).

Dr. Arthur Schonfield

The origin of the universe is another of Carl Sagan's "ultimate questions," and the chapter in *Broca's Brain* dealing with this great issue is entitled *Gott and the Turtles*. Sagan, characteristically, begins his presentation with a funny story:

> Some ancient Asian cosmological views are close to the idea of an infinite regression of causes, as exemplified in the following apocryphal story: A Western traveler encountering an Oriental philosopher asks him to describe the nature of the world:
> "It is a great ball resting on the flat back of the world turtle."

69

"Ah yes, but what does the world turtle stand on?"
"On the back of a still larger turtle."
"Yes, but what does he stand on?"
"A very perceptive question. But it's no use, mister; it's turtles all the way down." [1]

In 1913 the American astronomer Vesto Slipher discovered that the light coming to the earth from the distant galaxies was shifted to the red end of the spectrum. By means of an instrument called a spectrometer, Slipher broke up the incoming light into the colors of the rainbow. Scattered through these colors are dark lines known as Fraunhofer lines, which indicate the chemical makeup of a particular star. If the dark lines are at the red end of the spectrum, this is known as a "red shift," and if they are at the blue end, a "blue shift." The shift is indicative of a phenomenon known as the "Doppler Effect" which is more familiar to us from the physics of sound. If a truck approaches blowing its horn, the notes sound high, but as it passes, they become low. So too if the dark lines are shifted to the blue end of the spectrum (equivalent to the high notes), the star is approaching, and if to the red end (equivalent to the low notes), the star is receding.

In 1927, after extensive confirmation of Slipher's discovery, the American astronomer Edwin Hubble proposed his Expanding Universe Theory. Since the galaxies in the universe, including our own Milky Way Galaxy, are moving further and further apart as indicated by the red shift, there must have been a time in the distant past when all the galaxies were together in one solid mass. This mass must have exploded, an event which the English astronomer, Fred Hoyle humorously referred to as the "Big Bang," a phrase which has become a part of our vocabulary.

Einstein's famous equation, $E = mc^2$, which we have seen predicted the atomic bomb, states that energy equals mass times the speed of light squared, or in other words, that mass can be converted into energy. But equations can be reversed, so energy can be converted into mass, and at the birth of our universe there was energy alone from which all the mass in the universe was formed.

One popular explanation for the phenomenon of the expanding

universe was the Steady State Theory of Sir Fred Hoyle. Hoyle maintained that, as the universe expanded, the matter at its outer limits was annihilated but was continuously replaced by new matter created at the center; so the universe was always in a "steady state," the total amount of matter neither increasing nor decreasing. The universe then, had no beginning, and would never end. Our own galaxy would one day disappear over the edge of the universe, but eventually would be replaced by a new galaxy being formed at the center.

But in 1965 two American astronomers, Arno Penzias and Robert Wilson, discovered what is known as the "background radiation" of the universe. Outer space instead of being absolute zero as astronomers had predicted, was actually about three degrees above absolute zero. This infinitesimal "heat" is thought to be a remnant of the energy left over from the Big Bang, and this discovery forced even Sir Fred Hoyle, who had maintained that there was no Big Bang, to abandon the Steady State Theory.

Now there are two possibilities for the future of our expanding universe. Either the universe will continue to expand forever, and eventually die what is called a "heat death," or it will one day fall back on itself and end in a Big Crunch. After this Big Crunch will there be another Big Bang? Indeed, will the universe go Bang, Crunch, Bang, for all eternity? This possibility was first proposed as a serious scientific theory in 1931 by two astronomers, the Englishman Sir James Jeans and the American Robert Millikan. Here is Carl Sagan:

> ...An observer would see expansion eventually replaced by contraction, and galaxies slowly and then at an ever increasing pace approaching one another, a careening, devasting smashing together of galaxies, worlds, life, civilizations, and matter until every structure in the universe is utterly destroyed and all the matter in the cosmos is converted into energy: instead of a universe ending in a cold and tenuous desolation, a universe finishing in a hot and dense fireball. It is very likely that such a universe would rebound, leading to a new expansion of the universe and, if the laws of nature remain the same, a new incarnation of matter, a new set of condensations of galaxies and stars and planets, a new evolution of life and

intelligence. But information from our universe would not trickle into the next one and, from our vantage point, such an oscillating cosmology is as definitive and depressing an end as the expansion that never stops. [2]

Despite the gloomy end lying in wait for an oscillating universe, it is still preferred by the majority of scientists, to the expanding-forever version. If there were just one Big Bang, it would make no sense, at least scientifically speaking, since science cannot study a singular event.

Now whether the universe will end in a "heat death" or a Big Crunch depends on the total amount of matter in the universe. If the total mass is below a certain critical amount, the universe will continue to expand forever, but if above that amount, it will one day contract.

In a remarkable scientific paper published in the December 15, 1974 issue of the *Astrophysical Journal*, a wide range of observational evidence is brought to bear on the question of whether the universe will continue to expand forever (an "open" universe) or whether it will gradually slow down and recontract (a "closed" universe), perhaps as part of an infinite series of oscillations. The work is by J. Richard Gott III and James E. Gunn, then both of the California Institute of Technology, and David N. Schramm and Beatrice M. Tinsley, then of the University of Texas. In one of their arguments, they review calculations of the amount of mass in and between galaxies in "nearby" well-observed regions of space, and extrapolate to the rest of the universe; they find that there is not enough matter to slow the expansion down...

The amount of missing matter required to make the universe ultimately collapse is substantial. It is thirty times the matter in standard inventories such as Gott's. But it may be that dark gas in the galactic outskirts, and the astonishingly hot gas glowing in X-rays between the galaxies, together constitute just enough matter to close the universe, prevent an expansion forever - but condemn us to an irrevocable end in a cosmic fireball 50 billion or a hundred billion years hence.

The issue is still teetering...Our inventories of mass are still far from complete. But, as new observational techniques develop, we will have the capacity of detecting more and more of any missing mass; and so it would seem that the pendulum is swinging towards a closed universe.

It is a good idea not to make up our minds prematurely on this issue. It is probably best not to let our personal preferences influence the decision. Rather, in the long tradition of successful science, we should permit nature to reveal the truth to us. But the pace of discovery is quickening. The nature of the universe emerging from modern experimental cosmology is very different from that of the ancient Greeks who speculated on the universe and the gods. If we have avoided anthropomorphism, if we have truly and dispassionately considered all the alternatives, it may be that in the next few decades we will, for the first time, rigorously determine the nature and fate of the universe. And then we will see if Gott knows. [3]

Sagan, again characteristically, couldn't resist concluding with a pun on the name of Gott (God). Let me go on now to our second topic for this evening, the Law of Entropy. It has been claimed that the Law of Entropy precludes an Oscillating Universe. This law as it was originally formulated by Rudolf Clausius stated that the amount of available energy in the world was growing less and less. But Clausius based his theory on a false notion of the nature of heat. It is now realized that the Law of Entropy is not an absolute, but rather a statistical law, which means it is not applicable in every situation. Now Carl Sagan does not discuss entropy, so let me turn back to Jacob Bronowski and his *The Ascent of Man:*

> In 1850 Rudolf Clausius...said that there is energy which is available, and there is also a residue of energy which is not accessible. This inaccessible energy he called entropy, and he formulated the famous Second Law of Thermodynamics: entropy is always increasing. In the universe, heat is draining into a sort of lake of equality in which it is no longer accessible.
> That was a nice idea a hundred years ago, because then

heat could still be thought of as a fluid. But heat is not material any more than fire is, or any more than life is. Heat is a random motion of the atoms. And it was Ludwig Boltzman in Austria who brilliantly seized on that idea to give a new interpretation of what happens in a machine, or a steam engine, or the universe.

When energy is degraded, said Boltzman, it is the atoms that assume a more disorderly state. And entropy is a measure of disorder: that is the profound conception that came from Boltzman's new interpretation. Strangely enough, a measure of disorder can be made; it is the probability of the particular state - defined here as the number of ways it can be assembled from its atoms...

Of course, disorderly states are much more probable than orderly states, since almost every assembly of the atoms at random will be disorderly: so by and large any orderly arrangement will run down. But "by and large" is not "always." It is not true that orderly states *constantly* run down to disorder. It is a statistical law, which means that order will *tend* to vanish. But statistics do not say "always." Statistics allow order to be built up in some islands of the universe (here on earth, in you, in me, in stars, in all sorts of places) while disorder takes over in others. [4]

As you know, the idea of a universe continuously creating and destroying itself is common to many Eastern religions, most familiarly to Buddhism. The Englishman, Nigel Calder, is another fine popularizer of science lore; and shortly before Bronowski's series *The Ascent of Man,* he put on an excellent TV production entitled *Violent Universe* - some of you might remember it. Let me conclude with Calder's interesting and humorous presentation of the Oscillating Universe:

In the Far East, as an historian of astronomy tells me in Tokyo, there is really little interest in the origin of the universe, because of the pervasive Buddhist belief in cyclical patterns of events...

The questions scientists ask and the hypotheses they

entertain are influenced by philosophical attitudes of their society, but their discoveries can be iconoclastic. Especially in research into the origins of things - of the universe, of the earth, of life, and of man - the scientist intrudes into the domain traditionally proper to the Divine Creator. There is a well-known formula for a stand-off: science deals with facts, religion with faith, and never the twain shall meet. It is a simplification that saves a good deal of argument in the still hours of the night. Scientists rarely claim expertise in theology, and churchmen have learned by hard experience not to do so in science. When they picked fights with Galileo and Darwin, they were bound to come off worse. The historical trend is nevertheless unmistakable. Science has progressively eroded the area in which divine intervention is necessary or even admissable. Religions that once offered to explain everything, and claimed commonplace natural phenomena as deliberate acts of God, are now confined in their mundane scope to those areas wherein scientists are still groping for under-standing - particularly the workings of the human mind. Even there, the prospect is plain enough: before the end of the century we should know in detail how the brain works, how we think and why we feel.

The evidence grows that everything after the creation of our Galaxy - including the origin of the earth and of life - is explicable as a chancy but not mysterious series of physical and chemical processes. Any opportunity for supernatural explanations of the material world is therefore driven right back to the creation of the matter of the universe - to be literal, out at least eight billion light years from here, where we lose sight of events. Is there a constructional job for God, so far away, so long ago?...

If...the universe goes through an endless cycle of explosion, collapse and explosion, creation as such can be pushed infinitely far back in time - bad for Moses, but bully for the Buddha. [5]

Fr. Robert A. Staatz

I have copied this illustration on the blackboard from Bruce Vawter's *A Path Through Genesis*. Let me begin my presentation tonight with his commentary on the Scriptural account of the second day of creation:

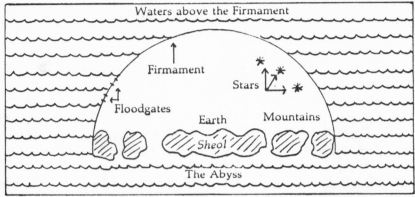

Plate II   *Biblical Cosmos according to Fr. Vawter*

If you will look at the illustration...you will see how an ancient Semite thought of the world in which he lived, and understand therefore the description of v.6ff. The earth was of course flat, with a mountain here or there, and some rather large ones at the end of the earth. The sky was a firmament, a solid bowl set over the earth. It had to be solid: how else would the waters above it fail to pour down and entirely flood the earth? That there were waters above the solid firmament was an easy deduction: how else explain the rain, which happened when water made its way through windows in the firmament (the "floodgates of the heavens" in 8:2) to fall on the earth?...Because of these ideas, the author has pictured the beginning of the world as a separation of the waters by means of the great firmament which God has raised above the earth. Scientifically speaking, this is obviously a pathetic notion of the universe. As we can see, it is based entirely on appearances. The earth does *look* flat, it does *appear* to meet the sky at the horizon. The sky does *seem* like an inverted blue bowl overhead. All this was enough for the

Hebrew, who never thought it worthwhile to inquire much further, even if he had the means of doing so...

Everything the author intended to tell us is true. God did create the sky, the seas, and the dry land...The sky is not a solid bowl, as the author believed; but it looks like one, and that is all he has said. [6]

So obviously there can be no concord or harmony between the Scriptural and the scientific account of the origin of the universe. But again this does not mean that a harmony cannot be made between theology and science concerning the origin and evolution of the universe - which brings me again to the subject of Teilhard de Chardin. Teilhard, however, rejects the popular oscillating or closed universe, because he considers such a universe meaningless. Let me read again from Robert Faricy, a fellow Jesuit, in his *Teilhard de Chardin's Theology of the Christian in the World:*

Toward the end of his life Teilhard writes that the more the years pass, "the more I recognize in myself and around me the great secret preoccupation of modern man; it is not so much to dispute possession of the world as to find some means to escape from it. The anguish of feeling, inside this bubble of the universe, not just spatially but ontologically shut in!" "Fear of being lost in a world so vast...that man seems to have lost all significance. Fear of being reduced to immobility. Fear of being unable to find a way out." A universe that is closed, hermetically sealed, is a universe that is meaningless for man, bewildering and menacing and finally stifling of enthusiasm for life and for action. A world that is closed and meaningless is a world in which human endeavor has no lasting value. A man needs to be sure that something of his endeavor is lasting, that something in all that he does has some truly permanent value. [7]

Teilhard well knew that the idea of an oscillating universe was common to both secular humanism and to Buddhism. Because of this he considered these religions less relevant for modern man, and therefore less true, than the Christian religion, rightly understood:

> ...The truth of a religion is how well that religion harmonized
> with the view of a universe that is progressing along a path of
> increasing complexity-consciousness toward an autonomous
> and transcendent Center of convergence. The religion that
> best fits this perspective, the "truest" religion, will be the
> religion the most relevant to human existence and to human
> endeavor, the religion that gives a maximum of meaning to
> life and action.
>   Teilhard finds inadequate the oriental religions and modern
> neo-humanist "religions of progress" (including Commun-
> ism). Very briefly, neither of these two groups of religions is
> really *activating*; neither adequately activates man in the
> direction of evolution, toward God-Omega. The oriental
> religions tend to remove man from an active participation in
> evolution; they tend not to encourage human endeavor but to
> discourage and even eliminate it. Neither are the "religions of
> progress" really activating in the long run; they leave no "way
> out" for the universe. They are closed systems and regard the
> universe as a closed system; they do not give assurance
> against the possibility of total death for mankind. The
> "religions of progress" are hollow with the "sickness of the
> dead end," and so - finally - they too, in spite of their claims,
> discourage human endeavor. [8]

Let me go on now to Teilhard's own views on the origin and
evolution of the universe, which seem to me to combine the best of
both contemporary science and modern theology. If you
remember from our last meeting, Teilhard did not think the
Thomistic notion of creation *ex nihilo*, relevant for our scientific
age. He preferred to think of creation as an ongoing process of
unification. Correlative to God's existence is a void, which he calls
an "infinite multiplicity." This concept gives Teilhard some
completely new insights into the famous "problem of evil." Here
again is Robert Faricy:

> ...If creation is seen as a long process of unification, beginning

with an infinite multiplicity and proceeding through the ages along an axis of increasing organization toward a final synthesis in Christ, then, according to Teilhard, the problem of evil is no longer a real problem. In the ancient cosmos that was thought to have come ready-fashioned from the hands of the Creator, it is natural that the reconciliation between a partially bad world and the existence of a God who is both good and all-powerful appeared difficult. But in a cosmos in a state of evolution, of becoming, the problem disappears. It is not because He lacks omnipotence, but by the very structure of the void itself - considered as an infinite multiplicity - that God in creating, can proceed in only one manner: by a progressive unification. Through a gradual process of attracting elements to Himself, by arranging and unifying little by little through a utiliization of the random combinations that occur in quantities of large numbers, God draws things toward greater unity and toward Himself. At first these elements are almost infinitely numerous, very simple, and with negligible consciousness. Gradually, units appear that, although less numerous, are more organized. Finally, man appears, highly complex and gifted with human consciousness. In a process of this kind, it is inevitable that every success be paid for by a certain amount of failure or waste. In pre-life, this waste takes the form of disharmony or decomposition. Among living things, it takes the form of suffering and death. And in the moral order, in the realm of human freedom, this waste and failure appears as sin. There is no order in the process of formation that does not imply disorder at every stage of the process. There is nothing in Teilhard's idea of the inevitability of waste, failure, disorder, that would imply a less than omnipotent Creator. The fact is simply this: because unorganized multiplicity is subject to the play of chance in the arrangements that lead to greater unification, it is absolutely impossible that its progress toward unity be unaccompanied by failure and disorder. Evil occurs by statistical necessity. [9]

It is on this notion of "infinite multiplicity" that Teilhard bases his interpretation of the difficult doctrine of hell; an interpretation with which I heartily concur. This is from Teilhard's biographer, Robert Speaight:

> He did not shrink from the doctrine of eternal punishment. The aggregation of souls and the consummation of matter composing the tissue of the *terre nouvelle* was also a segregating process. Matter which had not overcome its multiplicity would be rejected and men might be rejected with it. Hell was not only *below*; we had the word of Christ himself that its darkness was also *beyond*. Teilhard clung to his right to believe that it was eternally uninhabited. But the Christian choice presupposed the Christian risk; and Hell however we conceived it, might be considered "a structural element of the universe." [10]

Teilhard thought of the universe as a great cone, with a base he called "infinite multiplicity" converging to an apex of "Omega" or God. As the universe converges it becomes more complex and as a result more conscious, until finally in man, matter becomes self-conscious. Teilhard called this progress, the "law of complexity-consciousness." The evolutionary progress of the universe only makes sense in terms of the goal to which it is being drawn - Omega. This is again from Robert Faricy:

> We can consider the total process of evolution to be in the form of a cone; the evolutionary process, then, is moving, converging, to the summit of the cone, the Omega point. The Omega point, according to Teilhard's analysis, is the final point in the evolutionary process and so necessarily a part of that process, somehow within it. On the other hand, the Omega point is autonomous and transcendent, somehow divine. For Teilhard the Omega point, insofar as it is tran-scendent of evolution, is God. Omega is not in his view a simple future point of convergence, but a now-existing God. This modifies our conception of evolution. Before, all that was evident was a seemingly spontaneous progress of evolu-tion toward higher levels of consciousness; the cause of evolu-

tion's progress along the curve of complexity-consciousness was not at all apparent. We can see now that the universe makes evolutionary progress because it is *drawn* by a transcendent God. [11]

Some of Teilhard's jargon such as "infinite multiplicity" and "complexity-consciousness" is admittedly difficult but necessary, since he was venturing into an area where no one had been before. To Teilhard there was no such thing as "brute matter." Beginning with the unpredictability of a subatomic event, Heisenberg's Principle, to the ability of chemical molecules to "recognize" one another, to the playfulness of a cat, finally to man's self-consciousness, matter progressed from greater degrees of complexity to greater degrees of consciousness.

Let me go on now to our second subtopic, the so-called Law of Entropy. Teilhard's ideas on entropy are a good illustration of his synthesis of the best of modern science and the new theology:

> ...Teilhard often describes sin as a return to multiplicity, as movement away from unity and organization. He obviously does not mean that sin is something quantitative; he is using an analogy taken from the scientific concept of entropy, the gradual movement of a more organized system to a lower state of organization and energy. [12]

I am sure that Rev. Swezey will bring out that the creationists think that the idea of entropy (from order to disorder) and of evolution (from disorder to order), are contradictory concepts. But it was Teilhard's great genius to see how these two notions could be successfully harmonized. Let me turn again to his biographer Robert Speaight. *Le Phénomène Humain* is considered Teilhard's most important work:

> ...Teilhard's "fundamental pioneering achievement" - codified, so to speak, in *Le Phénomène Humain* - was to have made sense "out of the two most famous, but apparently contradictory, scientific ideas to come out of the nineteenth century...the theory of biological evolution on the one hand and

the second law of thermodynamics" - or the law of increasing entropy - "on the other." The latter held out no better prospect to mankind than ultimate annihilation. Against this, Teilhard's law of increasing complexity-consciousness - his perception of an alternative trend in evolution - was "far more than an unreasoned hope for the future"; it was scientifically verifiable - and its verification from a strict observation of phenomena was the theme of *Le Phénomène Humain*.

In conclusion, let me say again, that the description of the origin of the universe in the Bible cannot be taken in the strictly literal sense, nor can it be harmonized with current scientific ideas on the origin and evolution of the universe. But it is possible, as Teilhard de Chardin has so convincingly shown, to harmonize the new theology and contemporary scientific theory.

Mrs. Maria Stepan

Let me begin tonight with Dr. Schonfield's presentation of the origin of the universe. Dr. Schonfield mentioned that science cannot study a singular event like one Big Bang, and therefore prefers an infinite series of Big Bangs, the so-called Oscillating Universe. But this is not the whole story, since the fact that the universe began in time, no matter how long ago, that it is therefore not eternal, points irresistably to God, a fact that the secular humanists refuse to acknowledge.

The Oscillating Theory maintains that the universe has been expanding since the so-called "Big Bang," but that one day it will turn around and eventually go "Crunch," and then go Bang again, and this Bang, Crunch, Bang, will continue for all eternity. Sagan sees the universe as a cosmic perpetual motion machine that will never run down. Now, I have a wonderful analysis of the irrationality of this theory by Dr. Arno Penzias. Dr. Penzias received the Nobel Prize for astronomy in 1978 for his discovery of the background radiation of the universe. St. Thomas says that you can't convincingly prove from reason that the universe was created out of nothing, this must rather be taken on faith, but the Expanding Universe Theory at least postulates that the universe had a beginning in time, the "Big Bang," and that one day it will end. Either the universe will continue to expand forever and die a "heat death," or else it will turn around and eventually go "Crunch," never to expand again. For this reason the humanists prefer the Oscillating Theory, which claims that the universe had no beginning and will never end. Dr. Penzias, however, a believing Jew, thinks that the Expanding Universe Theory can easily be harmonized with the story of creation as told in the book of Genesis.

Let me read briefly from the *World of Science, 1979*, an annual supplement put out by the *Illustrated World Encyclopedia*. This is from an article by Malcolm W. Browne entitled *Scientists Expect New Clues for the Origin of the Universe:*

"The thing I am most interested in now," Dr. Penzias said in an interview, "is whether the universe is open or closed. If it is open - and the data seems to indicate that it is open - this is precisely the universe that organized religion predicts, to put it in crude terms." A closed universe, one that explodes, expands, falls back on itself and explodes again, repeating the process over and over eternally would be a pointless universe.

The astronomer continued: "A theologian friend of mine who is a priest told me once he could not conceive of Calvary happening twice. He said his faith as a Christian would be shaken if it could be proven to him that the universe, with its finite number of particles, could be reconstituted an infinite number of times. It would mean that every event - the creation of man, this conversation we are having, everything - would be repeated again and again an infinite number of times, simply by random chance. That is the meaning of infinity. In other words a closed universe would be as pointless as the throw of dice. But it seems to me that the data we have right now clearly show that there is not nearly enough matter in the universe, not enough by a factor of three, for the universe to be able to fall back on itself ever again."

"My argument," Dr. Penzias concluded, "is that the best data we have are exactly what I would have predicted had I nothing to go on but the five books of Moses, the Psalms, the

Bible as a whole." [14]

Remember Dr. Schonfield began with Carl Sagan holding Broca's brain and pondering the meaning of life. If the Oscillating Universe is true, he is doomed to hold that brain an infinite number of times and ponder the meaning of life for all eternity. The finite number of particles in the universe will be reshuffled in continuous Bangs and Crunches an infinite number of times. This also means that the particular assembly of a relatively few particles called Carl Sagan will turn up again by chance an infinite number of times. This is what you get, if all that exists is a finite amount of matter plus an infinite amout of time plus chance. So Sagan answers his own question: What is the meaning of life? If there is no God, life is as meaningless as an Oscillating Universe.

Let me turn now to Fr. Staatz and his picture on the blackboard of the universe as he claims it is presented in the Bible. It never seems to occur to any of these liberal scholars like Fr. Vawter that an expression like the "floodgates of heaven," for example, could be used in the metaphorical sense. Usually the liberals don't want to take anything in Genesis, Adam and Eve, for example, in the literal sense, but suddenly everything becomes strictly literal. One of the great weaknesses of the liberals is that they seem to think that the Bible was written only for the men of ancient times; but the Bible is not only a human but also a divine Book, and it was written for our own as well as ancient times. It was written both for men who judged the world by appearances only, and also for those who probe more deeply into the nature of things.

So I completely disagree with the liberal claim that it is impossible to make a harmony between legitimate contemporary science and the Bible. We have just heard Dr. Schonfield and Carl Sagan say that at the birth of our universe, the so-called Big Bang, there was at first just energy which was then converted into mass, the reversal of Einstein's famous equation $E = mc^2$. Isn't this exactly what the Bible says about the first day of creation? "Let there be light," or in other words, "Let there be energy." Indeed, Sheldon Glashow, a professor of physics at Harvard University, claims in his "Grand Unified Theory," that in the few first split seconds after the Big Bang all there was in the cosmos was photons, light particles. The Bible is meant to be relevant for the men of all ages, not just for the men for whom it was originally written - this is the miracle of it. This point is well made by Fr. P.J. Flood, a Professor of Scripture at St. Peter's College in Glasgow:

> As has been well said, God tempered the expressions in the Hexameron that they should always be true, both when men judge from appearance only and when they inquire into the ultimate nature of things. Since there is truth in both of these views of the world's formation. God was unwilling to forestall by revelation the natural development of the human mind, but wished that at no period of intellectual discovery should his inspired Scripture be convicted of error. [15]

Let me go on to Fr. Teilhard de Chardin's ideas on the origin and evolution of the universe. We heard that Teilhard thought of the universe as a great cone with a base of "infinite multiplicity" converging to an apex, which he called "Omega" or God. In other words the universe, according to Teilhard, is not expanding but rather contracting. Let me repeat briefly Dr. Schonfield's explanation of the so-called "red shift" and its implications with regard to our universe. Here is an excerpt from a book entitled *The Red Limit: The Search for the Edge of the Universe*, by a young science reporter, Timothy Ferris:

> The historical scaffolding under Hubble's discovery dated back to the early nineteenth century, when Christian Doppler, a physicist teaching in Vienna, found that the wavelength of lines in the spectrum of a light source ought to shift if the source were moving toward or away from the observer, just as the pitch of an automobile horn sounds higher - shorter wavelength - if the car is approaching and lower - longer wavelength - if it is speeding away. The spectrum is said to be "Doppler shifted" by velocity. Spectral lines could be measured with considerable accuracy, so this meant the velocities of remote, bright objects, namely stars, could be too. James Keeler at Lick Observatory quickly succeeded in finding a Doppler shift in the spectrum of the bright star

Arcturus; it had a blue shift, indicating it and the sun were drawing closer in the course of their common sweep of our galaxy. [16]

So, since as Slipher discovered, the light from the distant galaxies (not the nearby stars in our own galaxy), is shifted to the red end of the spectrum, this indicates that these galaxies are moving away from us. In Teilhard's cone universe, on the other hand, all the galaxies are converging and should therefore be shifted to the blue end of the spectrum. I suppose Teilhard's disciples will claim that his "cone" is only a metaphor, but the whole appeal of his so-called "synthesis" is that it is supposed to be based on hard, not metaphorical science.

I have said before, the Church has been appointed by God to be the official interpreter of the Bible, and she does this through her Tradition and Magisterium. So let me begin my own interpretation of the second day with Tradition, namely from St. Thomas Aquinas. First here he is in his *Summa Contra Gentiles*, rejecting the ancient pagan notion of an oscillating universe:

The effect is like its cause. But the resurrection of Christ is the cause of our resurrection; and Christ rising from the dead dieth now no more (Rom 6:9). Hence it is said: *The Lord shall cast out death forever (Isa 25:8): Death shall be no more (Rev 21:24).*

Hereby entrance is denied to the error of certain Gentiles of old, who believed that times and temporal events recurred in cycles. For example, in that age one Plato, a philosopher in the city of Athens, and in the school that is called Academic, taught his scholars thus, that in the course of countless revolving ages, recurring at long but fixed intervals, the same Plato, and the same city, and the same school, and the same scholars would recur, and so would be repeated again in the course of countless ages. [17]

And here is St. Thomas' own interpretation of the second day of creation from his *Summa Theologica:*

Whether then, we understand by the firmament the starry heaven, or the cloudy region of the air, it is true to say that it divides the waters from the waters, according as we take water to denote formless matter, or any kind of transparent body, as fittingly designated under the name of waters. [18]

We have seen that St. Thomas understands by "waters" formless matter, which God created on the first day and from which on succeeding days He formed all the creatures of the universe. We have seen how the first day can easily be harmonized with the Big Bang. Could not this separation of the waters of the second day, the separation of the formless matter, also be harmonized with the Expanding Universe? I am not claiming that the Bible is teaching science, or that the Expanding Universe is necessarily true, but that the Bible is susceptible of a variety of interpretations, and is intended by God to be relevant for the men of all ages.

As for the Magisterium of the Church, I have already stated that it is a defined dogma of the faith, from the First Vatican Council, that the universe was created by God at the very beginning of time, and therefore not eternal, as the Oscillating Theory claims. Let me turn now to an allocution of Pope Pius xii entitled *The Proofs of the Existence of God in the Light of Modern Natural Science* which he delivered to the Pontifical Academy of Science in 1951. Pope Pius is speaking here of our second topic the Law of Entropy, and in the process rejecting both the Oscillating and the Steady State Theories:

But not only has modern science broadened and deepened our knowledge of the reality and extent of the mutablity of the universe; it offers us precious indications also about the directions according to which natural processes work. While only one hundred years ago, especially since the discovery of the Law of Conservation, it was thought that natural processes were reversible, and consequently, according to the principles of strict causality - or better, determination - of nature, an ever-recurring renewal and rejuvenation of the universe was thought possible; with the Law of Entropy discovered by

Rudolf Clausius, man was led to know that spontaneous natural processes are always coupled with a decrease of free and available energy; that is to say, that in an enclosed material system, it must lead finally to a stoppage of all processes at the macroscopic level. This fatal destiny, that only perhaps too-gratuitous hypotheses like that of continual supplementary creation [the Steady State Theory] endeavor to keep from the world, but which on the contrary leaps out of positive scientific experimentation, eloquently postualtes the existence of a Necessary Being. [19]

The fact that the universe will one day end illustrates it's complete contingency or dependency, and points to a Necessary Being - to God. If the universe will one day end, it must therefore have had a beginning. Here is Pope Pius speaking of that beginning:

One cannot deny that a mind which is enlightened and enriched by modern scientific knowledge and which calmly considers the problem is led to break the circle of matter which is totally independent and autonomous - as being either uncreated or having created itself [the Oscillating and Steady State Theories] and rise to a creating Mind. With the same clear and critical gaze with which it examines and judges the facts, it discerns and recognizes there the work of creative Omnipotence, whose strength raised up by the powerful *fiat* uttered billions of years ago by the creating Mind, has spread through the universe, calling into existence, in a gesture of generous love, matter teeming with energy. It seems truly that modern science, leaping back over millions of centuries, has given witness to that primordial *Fiat lux* ["Let there be light."], when out of nothing erupted matter and a sea of light and radiations until the particles of the chemical elements formed and clustered into millions of galaxies. [20]

Pope Pius xii is not endorsing the Big Bang or the Expanding Universe Theory, nor the fantastic age of the universe built into those theories - that is not his function. The Expanding Universe

Theory is certainly far from being a proven fact. The Pope is merely showing that a reasonable scientific theory - and I see no harm in granting that to this theory - should lead an unbelieving scientist of good will to God. Now, this is apparently just what has happened in the case of Dr. Robert Jastrow, the head of NASA's Goddard Institute for Space Studies, who had previously identified himself as an agnostic. Here is the conclusion of his discussion of the Expanding Universe Theory from his excellent *God and the Astronomers*, which appeared in 1978:

> This is an exceedingly strange development, unexpected by all but theologians. They always accepted the word of the Bible: *In the beginning God created heaven and earth.* To which St. Augustine added, "Who can understand this mystery or explain it to others?" But we scientists did not expect to find evidence for abrupt beginning because we have until recently such extraordinary success in tracing the chain of cause and effect backward in time.
>
> Now we would like to pursue that inquiry farther back in time, but the barrier to progress seems insurmountable. It is not a matter of another theory. At the moment it seems as though science will never be able to raise the curtain on the mystery of Creation. For the scientist who has lived by his faith in the power of reason, the story ends like a bad dream. He has scaled the highest peak; as he pulls himself over the final rock, he is greeted by a band of theologians who have been sitting there for centuries. [21]

Rev. De Verne Swezey

The creationist Dr. Henry Morris begins his presentation on the origin of the universe with a discussion of the First and Second Laws of Thermodynamics, which he says are violated by the various evolutionary models of the universe. This is again from the public school section of *Scientific Creationism:*

> It is well to note at this point the implications of the First and Second Laws of Thermodynamics with respect to the

origin of the universe. It should be stressed that these two laws are *proven* scientific laws, if there is such a thing. They have been experimentally tested, measured and confirmed thousands of times, on systems both extremely large and extremely small, and no scientist today doubts their full applicability in the space-time coordinates accessible to us. Therefore the cosmic implications of the two laws are profound.

1) The First Law (Law of Energy Conservation) states that nothing now is either "created" or destroyed. It therefore teaches quite conclusively that the universe did not create itself; there is nothing in the present structure of natural law that could possibly account for its own origin.

2) The Second Law (Law of Energy Decay) states that every system left to its own devices always tends to move from order to disorder, its energy tending to be transformed into lower levels of availability, finally reaching the state of complete randomness and unavailability for further work. When all the energy of the cosmos has been degraded to random heat energy, with random motion of molecules and uniform low-level temperature, the universe will have died a "heat death."

3) The fact that the universe is not dead yet is clear evidence that it is not infinitely old. Since it will die in time, if present processes continue, time cannot have been of infinite duration. Our present universe is a *continuum* of space, mass, and time, so if one of these entities has a beginning the other two must have begun concurrently.

4) The Second Law requires the universe to have had a beginning; the First Law precludes its having begun itself. The only possible reconciliation of this problem is that the universe was created by a Cause transcendent to itself. [22]

It is obvious then that both the Steady State and Oscillating

Theories are in violation of these two basic scientific laws. The Steady State Theory in violation of the Law of Conservation, maintains that matter can create itself out of nothing, and can also annihilate itself, while the Oscillating Theory in violation of the Law of Entropy, maintains that matter can go from a state of maximum disorder, the Big Crunch, to one of increasing order, the Expanding Universe.

The length to which some of these humanists go to get away from a God who creates the universe out of nothing is fantastic. A typical example of this is the latest variation of the Expanding and Steady State Theories, a combination of them both, the Inflationary Theory of MIT's Alan Guth. In this so-called "theory," all the matter in the universe before the Big Bang creates itself out of nothing. Let me read a few excerpts from a review which appeared in the June 1983 issue of *Discovery* entitled *The World according to Guth* by science reporter Dennis Overbye:

...More radical theorists are ready to create the universe out of nothing. Their inspiration comes from quantum theory, in which the uncertainty principle predicts that random fluctuations in empty space can produce real particles; theorists suspect that, in the yet-to-be-discovered theory of quantum gravity, space-time itself can arise from random fluctuations in a primordial nothingness. This requires the universe itself to be, in some sense, nothing...

Guth finds this idea intriguing. In his theory as the universe inflates with a nearly constant energy density, its total energy (from which the stars and galaxies are eventually made) increases. The universe, concludes Guth, got its mass-energy for free. "It is tempting," he says, "to imagine creating the universe from literally nothing. Such ideas are speculation squared, but on some level they are probably right."...

Coleman and Guth were in a Harvard lecture hall one April afternoon as a young Tuft's professor, Russian *emigré* Alex Vilenkin, presented his version of genesis. According to him, the universe as a young bubble had tunneled like a metaphysical mole from somewhere else to arrive in space and time. That someplace else was "nothing." Aterward the three physicists sat in the hall and had a conversation that Lewis Carrol might have enjoyed, about nothing. "What is nothing? asked Coleman, pressing his fingers together in front of his face. "Nothing," said Vilenkin, "is no space, no time." Coleman pondered that for a while. "There is an epoch without time; it is eternity," he said finally. "So we make a quantum leap from eternity into time." His words hung unchallenged in the darkening air until it was time to go home. Guth, a fan of nothing, congratulated Vilenkin, put on his bicycle helment, went outside to pedal home. There he received the ultimate comeuppance for a man who had inflated the universe. His tire was flat. [23]

Well I am glad that at least Overbye has a sense of humor, but men like Guth *et al.*, are certainly not practising science, but rather doing harm to their God-given intellects by such irrational speculations.

Let me go on to the counter-culture movement. I have explained how I like to take advantage of this movement in my campus ministry, since it has such an excellent critique of establishment scientism. I would like to read a few paragraphs from another popular spokesman for the counter-culture, Jeremy Rifkin, in his *Entropy: A New World View*. If you remember, we just heard Dr. Bronowski claim that Ludwig Boltzman had successfully disproved the universal applicability of the Law of Entropy:

Adding embarassment to fantasy, Ludwig Boltzman jumped into the fray, determined to rescue classical physics from the steady encroachment of the Entropy Law. Boltzman's "h-Theorem" is a remarkable sleight-of-hand designed to accomodate the Second Law while at the same time undermining its clout. Boltzman acknowledged the validity of the second law up to a point. He was willing to admit that in a closed system entropy increases, but was unwilling to claim that it was an absolute certainty. He preferred the word *probably* to *certainty* and in doing attempted to turn the second law into a probability or statistical law. What Boltzman was saying is that while it's unlikely that energy would move from a colder to a hotter state, it was not impossible. It's important to be clear on what Boltzman was arguing because it is still taken seriously by many scientists. Sir Arthur Eddington gets right to the point about the likelihood of Boltzman's probability theorem ever working, even once in the real world. He proposes a vessel with two equal parts separated by a partition. The first compartment contains air, the second compartment a vacuum. The partition between the two compartments is opened, allowing the air to spread evenly through the vessel. Eddington allows that at some future time there is always the chance that all those billions upon billions of molecules of air diffused through the entire vessel will in their individual random movements all end up in the right-hand side of the compartment once again at exactly the same time. As to how probable such an occurrence is, Eddington concludes:

"If an army of monkeys were strumming on typewriters they 'might' write all the books in the British Museum. The chance of their doing so is decidely more favorable than the chance of the molecules returning to one half of the vessel." [24]

Jeremy Rifkin says that the Law of Entropy is not just a mathematical abstraction but something we all experience every day, and to deny its universality is unreasonable, to say the least:

This conforms to our everyday sense of the world around us. Left on their own, things do not tend spontaneously to move to more and more ordered states. Anyone who has ever had to take care of a house, or work in an office, knows that if things are left unattended they soon become more and more disorderly. Bringing things back into a state of order requires the expenditure of additional energy. For example, consider a deck of playing cards that is organized by number and suit. The deck is in a state of maximum order or minimum entropy. Fling the deck to the ground and the cards will scatter into a random disordered state. Picking each card off the floor and then arranging them one by one back into their original ordered state will take the expenditure of more energy than was used to scatter them in the first place...

Albert Einstein once mused over which of the laws of science deserved to be ranked as the supreme law. He concluded by making the following observation:

"A theory is more impressive the greater is the simplicity of its premises, the more difficult are the kinds of things it relates, and the more extended its range of applicability, therefore, the deep impression which classical thermodynamics [the First and Second Laws] made on me. It is the only physical theory of universal content which I am convinced, that within the framework of applicability of its basic concepts will never be overthrown." [25]

Let me turn once again to the final section of *Scientific Creationism*, which we have seen is intended only for use in Christian schools. Here is Dr. Morris' own interpretaion of the biblical account of the second day of creation:

The World That Then Was (II Pet 3:6)

It must be recognized that this primordial-created world was different from the present world in many ways. There were in that world "...waters which were above the firmament" (Gen 1:7), and this corresponds to nothing in the present world. The word "firmament" (Hebrew *raquia*, meaning "stretched-out thinness") is essentially synonymous with "heaven" (note Gen 1:8), and thus means simply "space," referring to space in general or to specific space, as the context requires. In this case, the firmament was essentially the atmosphere, where the birds fly (Gen 1:20). The waters above it must have been in the form of a vast blanket of invisible water vapor, translucent to the light from the stars, productive of a marvelous greenhouse effect which maintained mild temperatures from pole to pole, thus preventing air-mass circulations and the resultant rainfall (Gen 2:5). It would certainly have had the further effect of efficiently filtering harmful radiations from space, markedly reducing the rate of mutations in living cells, and, as a consequence, drastically decreasing the rate of aging and death. [26]

This vast water canopy then, was the occasion of the great longevity of the patriarchs from Adam to Noah. But during the time of Noah this canopy fell down at God's command, causing the great Flood. Dr. Morris than goes on to interpret the First and Second Laws of Thermodynamics in biblical terms:

The Fall, the Curse, and the Laws of Thermodynamics...

Sin came into the world when man first doubted, then rejected, the Word of God, in the garden of Eden. And death came into the world when sin came into the world. God was forced to tell Adam "...cursed is the ground for thy sake...for dust thou art and to dust thou shalt return" (Gen 3:17-19). The basic physical elements ("dust" of the "ground") were thus placed under the Curse, and all flesh constructed from these elements was also cursed.

The classic passage of the New Testament on this subject is Romans 8:20-22:

"For the creation was made subject to vanity, not willingly, but by reason of him who hath subjected the same in hope. Because the creation itself also shall be delivered from the bondage of corruption [or, more literally, "decay"] into the glorious liberty of the children of God. For we know that the whole creation groaneth and travaileth in pain until now."

This universal "bondage of decay" can be nothing less than the universal principle which scientists have finally formalized as the Second Law of Thermodynamics. By the same token, God's "rest" at the end of his work of creating and making all things (Gen 2:1-3), together with the providential sustenance of His creation ever since (Neh 9:6), must constitute the universal principle now known as the First Law of Thermodynamics, the Law of Conservation of Mass-Energy.

Scientists have demonstrated the universality of the two laws, but they are unable to discover *why* they work. The answer to the question - why should energy always be conserved and entropy always increase? - can only be found in these Biblical records. There are numerous other Biblical allusions to the First Law (Colossians 1:16,17; Hebrews 1:2,3; II Pet 3:5,7; Psalms 148:5,6; Isaiah 40:26; Ecclesiates 1:9,10; 2:14,15 etc.) and to the Second Law (Psalm 102:25-27; Isaiah 51:6; I Pet 1:24,25; Hebrews 12:27; Romans 7:21-25; Revelations 21:4; 23:3, etc.). It is significant that these two universal (and all-important) principles, discovered and formally recognized little more than a century ago, have been implicity in the Biblical revelation for thousands of years. [27]

In conclusion let me say again that the various evolutionary models of the origin of the universe conflict with two of the most basic laws of physics, the First and Second Laws of Thermodynamics, while the creation model not only conforms to, but actually predicts these two laws.

Dean Smalley

It is time again for me to give a brief summary of our four presentations. The second day of creation deals with the origin of the universe, and our two subtopics for this evening were the Oscillating Universe and the Law of Entropy.

Dr. Schonfield said that Carl Sagan considers the origin of the universe one of the "ultimate questions," and its most likely answer is the Oscillating Universe. However, since this theory is in apparent conflict with the Law of Entropy, Dr. Sconfield explained how this law is not now considered an absolute, but rather a statistical law, which means it is not applicable in all circumstances.

Fr. Staatz said that the Oscillating Universe is a dead end and thus gives no incentive for progress, as does Teilhard de Chardin's notion of a universe evolving toward Omega or God. Fr. Staatz once again claimed that the concordist interpretation of the Hexameron by Mrs. Stepan (harmonizing the Bible and contemporary science), and the fundamentalist or literalist interpretation of Rev. Swezey, were unacceptable since the literary form of the Hexameron is the myth.

Mrs. Stepan said that Fr. Staatz's denial of the possibility of a harmony between contemporary science and the Bible was based on a false notion of the Bible. The Bible, she said, was not written for the men of ancient times alone, but for the men of modern times as well. She proposed her own harmony between contemporary science and the first and second days of creation, saying that the Big Bang could easily be harmonized with the "Let there be light (energy)" of the first day, and the Expanding Universe with the "And God...separated the waters" (considered by St. Thomas a metaphor for "formless matter") of the second day. Mrs. Stepan, however, stated that she was not saying that the Bible was teaching science, or that the Big Bang and the Expanding Universe were necessarily true, but that the Bible was susceptible of a variety of interpretations, and thus relevant for the men of all times.

Rev. Swezey maintained that the evolution model of the universe violates two of the most basic laws of physics, the First and Second Laws of Thermodynamics, while the creation model actually predicts these two laws. He said that while science tells *how* these two laws work, the Bible tells *why* they work, the First Law because of God's conservation of the universe, and the Second because of God's curse placed on the world after the Fall of our first parents. Mrs. Stepan tries to harmonize the Bible and science, while Rev. Swezey seems to claim that the Bible is actually teaching science.

This concludes our discussion for this evening, and we will meet again next week at Cheverus College.

REFERENCES

1   Carl Sagan, *Broca's Brain*,
     Random House, New York, 1979, pp.292,293.
2   Sagan, *Op. cit.*, pp.297,298

3   *Idem*, pp.298-300.

4   Jacob Bronowski, *The Ascent of Man*,
     Little, Brown and Co., Boston, 1973, pp.347,348

5   Nigel Calder, *Violent Universe*,
     Viking Press, New York, 1969, pp.135-137.

6   Bruce Vawter, c.m., *A Path Through Genesis*,
     Sheed and Ward, New York, 1956, pp.40,41.

7   Robert Faricy, s.j., *Teilhard de Chardin's Theology of the Christian in the
     World*, Sheed and Ward, New York, 1967, pp.74,75.

8   Faricy, *Op. cit.*, pp.80,81.

9   *Idem*, pp.143,144.

10   Robert Speaight, *Teilhard de Chardin*,
     Collins, London, 1967, p.146.

11   Faricy, *Op. cit.*, pp.77,78

12   *Idem*, footnote, p.148

13   Speaight, *Op. cit.*, pp.274,275.

14   Malcolm W. Browne, *Scientists Expect New clues to the Origin of the
     Universe*, World Science, 1979, Year Book,
     Illustrated World Encyclopedia, New York, 1979, p.68

15   P.J. Flood, *Evolution and Sacred Scripture, Claves Regni*, June 1932
     Quoted in: E.C. Messenger, *Theology and Evolution*,
     Sands and Co., London, 1949, p.25.

16   Timothy Ferris, *The Red Limit*,
     Wilson, Morrow and Co., New York, 1977, pp.45,46.

17   St. Thomas Aquinas, *Summa Contra Gentiles, CXXXII*,
     Joseph Rickaby, s.j., *Of God and His Creatures*,
     B. Herder, St. Louis, 1905, p.406.

18   Aquinas, *Summa Theologica*, (*I, Q68, a3*), p.341.

19   Pope Pius xii, *The Proofs of the Existence of God in the Light of Modern
     Natural Science, L'Osservatore Romano*, Nov 23, 1951, p.1.

20   Pope Pius xii, *Op. cit.*, p.2.

21   Robert Jastrow, *God and the Astronomers*,
     W.W. Norton and Co., New York, 1978, pp.25,26.

22   Henry Morris, *Scientific Creationism*,
     Creation-Life Publishers, San Diego, 1974, pp.25,26.

23   Dennis Overbye, *The World according to Guth*,
     Discovery, June 1983, Time Inc., New York, p.199.

24   Jeremy Rifkin, *Entropy: A New World View*,
     Viking Press, New York, 1980, pp.39,41,42.

25   Rifkin, *Op. cit.*, pp.42,43.

26   Morris, *Op. cit.*, pp.210,211.

27   *Idem*, pp.212,213.

THE FOURTH MEETING
The Age of the Universe

Scene: Cheverus College

Dean Smalley

Good evening. Once again I would like to thank Father Rector and all our friends here at Cheverus College for their gracious hospitality. Tonight will be our concluding meeting on the second day of creation which deals with the origin of the universe, and our topic for this evening is the Age of the Universe. I will begin as usual by reading the Scriptural account of the second day:

> And God said, "Let there be a firmament in the midst of the waters, and let it separate the waters from the waters." And God made the firmament and separated the waters which were under the firmament from the waters which were above the firmament. And it was so. And God called the firmament Heaven. And there was evening and there was morning a second day (Gen 1:6-8).

Dr. Arthur Schonfield

At our preliminary meetings the speakers agreed to use easily available and popular books in their various presentations to encourage student participation. One of the best known popularizers of science lore is Isaac Asimov, and I would like to begin our discussion tonight by reading from one of his many books, this one entitled *The Universe*. Asimov begins with the age of the earth. Even as late as the beginning of the nineteenth century most scientists were still under the spell of the fundamentalist interpretation of the Bible and assumed that the earth was only around 6000 years old.

But the first half of the nineteenth century had seen an

99

important revolution in attitude. In 1785, the Scottish geologist James Hutton (1726-1797) had published a book entitled *Theory of the Earth* in which he studied the slow changes that the earth's surface underwent - the layering of sediment, the erosion of rocks, and so on. He suggested the "uniformitarian principle" which held that whatever changes were going on today had been going on at essentially the same rate throughout the past. According to this principle, it would take enormous stretches of time to produce all the thicknesses of sediments that could be found, all the erosion that could be observed, all the buckling and other forced changes to which the earth's surface had been subjected.

Hutton did not persuade his readers at the time, but between 1830 and 1833, another Scottish geologist, Charles Lyell (1797-1875), published *The Principles of Geology*. In this book, Hutton's work was summarized, popularized, and backed up by additional evidence. This eventually turned the trick, and geologists began to interpret the earth's history in terms of hundreds of millions of years. [1]

It is important to remember Hutton's "uniformitarian principle," namely that whatever changes are going on today also occured at the same rate in the past. Towards the end of the nineteenth century the physicists entered the picture with Antoine Becquerel's discovery of radioactivity:

As uranium gives off its radiations, its atoms change their nature, becoming other kinds of atoms which also give off radiations and change nature again. Eventually, the uranium changes no further.

The rate at which uranium changes in this manner follows a simple rule, well known to chemists as a "first-order reaction." This means that if the rate of change is determined over a short interval of time, it can be predicted, quite accurately, over any longer interval. It could be shown, for instance, that half of any quantity of uranium would break down and change to lead in 4.5 billion years. This tremendous time interval is called the "half-life" of uranium-238 (the most common form of the uranium atom.).

Suppose now, that you consider a rock containing uranium compounds. Inside it, the uranium is constantly breaking down and turning into lead. If the rock remains solid and unbroken, the lead atoms formed cannot possibly escape but must remain intermingled with the uranium. The uranium compounds may have been pure to begin with, but they become increasingly contaminated by lead. Since the rate at which nuclear reactions proceed is not effected by the puny changes in temperature and pressure encountered on the earth, we know that the exact quantity of lead accompanying the uranium depends on the length of time the rock has remained solid (and on the quantity of lead present originally) and not on any unprecitable environmental changes to which it may have been subjected. [2]

By this new method it was soon established that our earth is approximately four and a half billion years old. From the age of the earth let us go on to the age of the universe which lies in the domain of astronomy.

In 1979 the scientific community and the world in general, celebrated the centenary of the birth of Albert Einstein. Of the many televison progams about Einstein at that time, my favorite was by Nigel Calder, whom we have met before, entitled *Einstein's Universe*. Here is Calder's presentation of Hubble's discovery of the Expanding Universe:

In the 1920's and 1930's, Edwin Hubble sat at the 100 inch telescope on Mount Wilson near Los Angeles night after night, year after year. For his painstaking research into the motions of the galaxies, he invented ways of estimating distances of galaxies and used Doppler's effect to judge their speeds. The light of a distant galaxy was always red-shifted - reduced in frequency - indicating that the galaxy was moving away from our own Galaxy, the Milky Way, at a high speed. This was remarkable enough; it implied a general expansion of the universe. Even more remarkable was the rule he discovered about the relationship of speed and distance. In

"Hubble's Law" the speed of the galaxies was in simple proportion to their distance: double the distance and the galaxies were going away twice as fast. By 1929, Hubble had established his law out to a distance of six million light-years. ...There was a big snag. Hubble estimated the maximum age of the universe since the expansion - the "Hubble time" - at two billion years. Assuming that gravity had slowed down the galaxies since the expansion began, the universe had to be younger than that. But there was already solid evidence that the earth was several billion years old and many stars seemed much older. How could the earth be older than the universe?

For this good reason, the Big Bang Theory was treated with considerable reserve until the 1950's, when Hubble's former pupils began to discover flaws in his scale of distances. Since then the Hubble time has been revised upwards; nowadays it is generally taken to be about 10-15 billion years ago, which accomodates the ages of the oldest known stars (about ten billion years) and of the earth (now put at 4.55 billion years).[3]

In 1917 Albert Einstein published his General Theory of Relativity, and without his realizing it at the time, his equations actually predicted the Oscillating Universe:

When physicists and astronomers play at being God they try to imagine an overall "design" for the universe which encompasses the origin and fate of all the atoms, stars, and galaxies within it, yet avoids trivia like the origin of the sun and the earth. Nobody ever played this game more skillfully than Albert Einstein or botched it so badly. He lost his nerve at the critical moment in 1917 when the oracle of his mathematics confided to him a cosmic story that he found altogether too sensational to believe...Leaving the details aside, we can say that Einstein's pristine theory of gravity shouted an extraordinary possibility. The maximum diameter of the universe may depend on its total energy and nothing else...

In amazingly simple mathematics, the theory fills out the

story of what I call the Simple Universe. It starts very small and spontaneously grows in diameter extremely rapidly. Thereafter the rate of expansion of the universe diminishes steadily as it approaches its maximum diameter. Then it stops growing and begins to collapse. It shrinks faster and faster, until once again it is extremely small, and all its contents are destroyed in a Big Crunch. Einstein's equations provided a modern version of Genesis and Revelation.

The most uncanny feature of the story is that not only the maximum diameter of the universe but the entire time-scale of events is fixed by the amount of energy in it...By Einstein's simplest formulae, [the universe] is due to expand to a maximum diameter of about 40 billion light-years. Its total lifespan from its explosive genesis to its comprehensive doomsday is, by this reckoning, about 63 billion years. From other information we can estimate that we are living at a time one-sixth of the way through the universe's life cycle, when it is still expanding rapidly. These estimates were not available to Einstein in 1917, but the general story was there, in his equations. [4]

This is basically the same as Carl Sagan's argument which I read the last time, only instead of presenting it in terms of the total mass of the universe, Calder is using the total energy. The two are interchangeable. The Oscillating Universe Theory is accepted by most scientists, and it is now thought that the universe goes through periods of expansion and contraction about every sixty billion years. It is at least ten billion years since the Big Bang occurred, and we have about fifty billion years to go until the Big Crunch.

But suppose there is so much energy in the universe that it continues to expand forever, or in other words, what if there was only one Big Bang? What existed before that Big Bang? A prominent American astronomer when asked this question replied, "I refuse to speculate." This attitude however is certainly not scientific and Nigel Calder does not refuse to speculate. Here are his interesting and amusing comments on this most profound problem:

What came before the Big Bang? According to strict logic, thou shalt not ask that question. If time began with the Big Bang, the word "before" has no meaning. But the human imagination will not be bound by logic and the question is an entirely natural one to ask. Indeed it is the point of convergence of all scientific, philosophical, and religious thought. To put it bluntly: did God just say "Let there be light!" (meaning gamma rays) and the Big Bang ensued? Or did the energy come from somewhere else? Like "before," "somewhere else" has no strict meaning, yet we can all sense the intention of the question...

One solution to the problem offers itself. If ours is a Simple Universe or something like it, that will eventually recollapse into the Big Crunch, then you can quite easily imagine a new universe being born out of the ashes of the old one, in a new Big Bang...and so on *ad infinitum*. There are technical problems about such a yo-yo universe [the Law of Entropy], but it has an agreeable sort of plausibility. At the very least it gives a hint to the curious that the question of what came "before" our universe may not be quite unanswerable. Yet the answer may be "nothing." As John Wheeler has remarked, it costs nothing to make a Simple Universe, in the sense that the energy put into its creation is fully recovered in its collapse. Conceivably universes are two a penny, and ours is just one among many that arise spontaneously.

To pretend that there is no religious element in this curiosity about the cosmos would be idle. I have before me the writings of a Catholic theologian who explicitly favors the interminably expanding universe, which he sees as being in keeping with "faith in the Creator, and in a creation once-and-for-all." Hindus and Buddhists, Marxists and many agnostics would prefer the yo-yo universe: the Easterners because it accords with their idea of endless cycles, and the others because they tell themselves that it removes the problem of initial creation to a comfortable distance - out of sight. Their preferences are, of course, beside the point when it comes to evaluating the scientific evidence, but I mention them because they help to illuminate the passion and dedication with which scientists try to predict the long-term future of the universe. Religion as such may not come into it, but the religious urge to find meaning in life certainly does. [5]

Fr. Robert A. Staatz

The Anglican Archbishop Ussher, using the Hebrew text of the Bible, claimed the universe was created in 4004 B.C. Ussher also thought that the "days" of the Hexameron should be understood in the strictly literal sense of a twenty-four hour period. But his interpretation of biblical time, still held by many fundamentalists, including Catholic fundamentalists, has been rejected by the Magisterium of the Church. Here is a decision of the Biblical Commission handed down in 1909:

> *Yom* - Whether the word *Yom* (day), which is used in the first chapter of Genesis to describe and distinguish the six days, may be taken in the strict sense as the natural day, or in a less strict sense as signifying a certain space of time; and whether free discussion of this question is permitted to interpreters.
>
> *Answer*: - In the affirmative. [6]

As might have been expected, some conservative Catholic biblical scholars have tried to interpret the phrase "a certain space of time" in terms of millions of years, and thus construct a concordance or harmony between the biblical six days and scientific discoveries on the age of the universe. But from our discussion of the literary form of the Hexameron, we have seen that such an attempt is impossible.

Bruce Vawter is recognized as *the* authority on the book of Genesis in the Church today, and is the author of the article on the subject in *A New Catholic Commentary on Holy Scripture*. Let me read his comments on "concordism" from this excellent article:

> Prompted by the laudable intention of defending the inerrancy of the Scriptures, another form of interpretation called

concordism, appeared with the advent of the modern scientific discovery. Concordism tried to safeguard inerrancy without turning its back on indubitable scientific facts by positing a harmony between biblical and scientific thought. It is true that the Biblical Commission in 1909 made a gesture towards the concordists by stating that there was nothing contrary to faith in taking *Yom* (day) to refer to an indefinite period of time. However...the Commission on the same occasion rejected the basic premise of concordism in its affirmation that "it was not the mind of the sacred author in the composition of the first chapter of Genesis to give scientific teaching about the internal constitution of visible things and the entire order of creation, but rather to communicate to his people a popular notion in accord with the current speech of the time and suited to the understanding and capacity of man."...

The basic error that lies behind these sallies into bad science and bad exegesis is a confusion as to the nature and the purpose of inspiration. The words of Genesis 1 are divinely inspired, but they are the *inspired words of an ancient Israelite speaking to the men of his age as one of them in their language*. For him to have anticipated the discoveries of modern science, divine revelation would have been a necessity, and there is not the slightest indication that any such revelation was given, just as there is no reason that it should have. [7]

This point concerning the proper interpretation of the Hexameron is so important that it is worth repeating. Here it is again given in a slightly different manner by the Benedictine Ignatius Hunt in his popular *Understanding the Bible*:

The purpose of the Priestly account in Gen 1:1 to 2:4a in setting forth God's creative work in a six-day mold was not to teach that God actually created everything in six twenty-four-hour days, nor was it to teach that he created in six "periods" of thousands of years (a concordist explanation that is even further from the sacred writer's intention!), *but* to show that

God is the maker of everything and that man should observe the Sabbath. The six twenty-four-hour days are an artificial device used by the writer to stress Sabbath observance...To set forth a rigorously scientific account of how creation actually took place was obviously not the author's purpose, and hence does not fall under inerrancy in that way. We show fairness and reasonableness in judging modern writers. Is there any reason why this same fairness and reasonableness should not be shown to the biblical writers, who were no less human?

...Our concern in all these matters is to take the Bible as it is, not to make it what we would like it to be. The Bible...is not a science manual, just as it is not history in the modern sense of "history for history's sake." [8]

Ignatius Hunt concludes with our specific problem for tonight, the age of the universe:

> The creation account in Genesis loses nothing of its everlasting importance and meaning when understood in its genuine literal meaning. Its impact may strike the reader of the twentieth century as forcibly as the reader of the sixth-fifth centuries B.C. With the benefit of intervening Christian revelation and our recovery of much of the oriental background, we may even profit more from the account today than the readers of old.
>
> Speaking before the Pontifical Academy of Science on November 22, 1951, Pope Pius XII referred to the material universe as being between five and ten billion years old! [9]

One of the reasons Pius XII gave as the scientific basis for this conclusion, was the recession of the spiral nebulae or galaxies. These nebulae, he said, are known to travel at speeds of up to 25,000 miles per second. We can imagine a backward flight of the galaxies like a motion picture in reverse, returning to the common spot where the cosmic processes began. Thus knowing the speed at which they travel plus their distance from this common point of convergence, the astronomers have estimated that these processes began some five to ten billion years ago. Now I know that these figures must sound a little shocking to my conservative colleague, so let me read directly from Pope Pius XII:

> The examination of numerous nebulae pursued especially by Edwin E. Hubble at Mount Wilson Observatory, led to the significant result - however much tempered with reservations - that the distant systems of galaxies tend to move farther apart from each other with such velocity that the distance between two such nebulae doubles in 1300 million years. If we look back on the time required for this process of the "Expanding Universe" we see that from one to ten billion years ago the matter of all the spiral nebulae found itself compressed in a relatively small space, at the time the cosmic processes began. [10]

As we can see, these figures are derived from Hubble's original estimate of the age of the universe, which Dr. Schonfield has shown to be in error, and has since been revised upwards by Hubble's disciples to around twenty billion years. The Holy Father concludes this part of his allocution with these comments:

> Although these figures may seem astounding, nevertheless, even to the simplest of the faithful, they bring no new or different concept from the one they learned in the opening words of Genesis: "In the beginning...," that is to say, at the beginning of things in time. The figures we have quoted clothe these words in a concrete and almost mathematical expression, while from them there springs forth a source of consolation for those who share the esteem of the Apostle for that divinely inspired Scripture, which is always useful "for teaching, for reproving, for correcting, for instructing." [11]

In conclusion let me say again that any interpretation of the Bible which conflicts with established scientific data, is no true interpretation. The scientific community is unanimous in assigning an age of around twenty billion years to our universe. In 1951 Pope Pius XII accepted the then current scientific estimate for the age of the world, and that should be enough for most Catholics.

Mrs. Maria Stepan

I would like to begin tonight by commenting briefly on Nigel Calder's quote from a Catholic theologian who, he says, explicitly favors an interminably Expanding Universe as being in keeping with "faith in the Creator." We Catholics are not committed to any particular scientific theory concerning the end of the world, but only to the fact that the world is not eternal and will one day end. The end might well be miraculous, and not come about by any natural means. The expanding forever version, however, does seem more likely at the moment, scientifically speaking, since there is apparently not enough mass to close the universe, and thus cause it to collapse. But if the missing mass is discovered, and it does seem likely that the world will one day end in a Big Crunch, this would be just as acceptable to Catholics as long as there is only one Crunch, although fifty billion years in the future is hard to take seriously. As a matter of fact, such an end of the world seems more Scriptural than the expanding forever version - "and the stars shall fall from heaven, and the powers of heaven shall be moved" (Matt 24:29).

The Australian Wallace Johnson, a Catholic layman, has recently published a book entitled *The Crumbling Theory of Evolution* in which he attempts to summarize primarily for Catholics, the scientific case for creationism which has been developed largely by Protestant creationist scientists over the past few years. He deals at length with the scientific arguments of the creationists for a young earth, but he thinks the most telling argument is one that surfaced after his book came out. Let me play a few minutes of a tape of a lecture he delivered recently in Brisbane, Australia:

Creation in 4004 B.C. - what a laugh! Bishop Ussher and his Bible believers have long been figures of fun for our scientific age. But now the laughing should stop. Dr. John Eddy, solar physicist, has been making detailed observations of the sun. Observations which in some interpretations are throwing into doubt basic theories of the age of the sun. Well that much I got into my book* - the next bit I didn't. Here it is. Dr. Eddy as an evolutionist says he expects that the sun is four and a half billion years old. However, he also says this. I quote: "I suspect that we could live with Bishop Ussher's age of the world and sun. I don't think [listen to this], I don't think we have much in the way of observational evidence to conflict with that." Put another way he is saying that the theories of billions of years of cosmic evolution have not much scientific data to support them. This leader in the field of solar physics is as good as saying that the Book of Genesis is unshaken by the facts of science. If only that could be told to our students! [13]

Let me now examine Fr. Staatz's presentation on the age of the universe. I am always amused to hear liberal Catholics enthusiastically endorsing the decision of the Biblical Commission on *Yom* (day) when they reject all the other decisions handed down at the same time. Also Fr. Hunt's claim that Pope Pius XII accepted a universe billions of years old is simply not true. Pope Pius was mainly interested in showing how a legitimate scientific theory should lead an unbelieving scientist of good will to God. He considered the Expanding Universe such a theory, even though it has built into it such a fantastic age of the universe; he was neither endorsing the Expanding Universe Theory nor the age of the universe that the theory proposes. Let me read just one of the many qualifications he gave during the course of the allocution:

It is very true that as far as creation in time, the facts so far ascertained do not constitute an absolute proof concerning simple creation, as are those reached from both metaphysics and from revelation. The facts pertaining to natural science, to which We have referred, are still in need of further research and confirmation and the theories built on them are in need of new proofs and development, in order to offer a secure base for argumentation which by itself stands outside the realm of the natural sciences. [14]

Let me go on now from Dr. Schonfield and Fr. Staatz to Rev.

* Wallace Johnson, *The Crumbling Theory of Evolution*, Queensland Binding Service, Brisbane, Australia, 1982, Available in the U.S.A. from: Keep the Faith Inc., P.O. Box 254, Montvale, N.J.

Swezey's presentation at our last meeting. I was glad to hear Dr. Morris say that creation out of nothing cannot be proven scientically, but must be taken on faith. This is also the opinion of St. Thomas:

> By faith alone do we hold, and by no demonstration can it be proved, that the world did not always exist...The reason for this is that the newness of the world cannot be demonstrated on the part of the world itself. For the principle of demonstration is the essence of a thing. Now everything according to its species is abstracted from *here* and *now*; whence it is said that universals are everywhere and always. Hence it cannot be demonstrated that man, or heaven, or a stone were not always. Likewise neither can it be demonstrated on the part of the efficient cause, which acts by will. For the will of God cannot be investigated by reason, except as regards those things which God must will of necessity; and what He wills about creatures is not among these...But the divine will can be manifested by revelation on which faith rests. *Hence that the world began to exist is an object of faith, but not of demonstration or science.* And it is useful to consider this, lest anyone, presuming to demonstrate what is of faith, should bring forth reasons that are not cogent, so to give occasion to unbelievers to laugh, thinking that on such grounds we belive such things that are of faith. [15]

But I think that the title of Dr. Morris' book *Scientific Creationism* does give the unfortunate impression that creation can be demonstrated scientifically. I would like to suggest therefore, that creationism versus evolutionism, is not the best of dichotomies, since creation is a religious term and evolution supposedly is a scientific term. I think that something like Fixism versus Evolutionism might be more appropriate, and we will see later when we discuss the theory of evolution that the older notion of Fixism is still a viable scientific alternative to Evolutionism. On the other hand, I think that creationism versus humanism is a good dichotomy, since as Dr. Morris has shown, humanism is also a religious term.

I would like to go on now to my own comments on our topic for this evening, the age of the universe. We have heard that the Anglican Archbishop Ussher, proposed on the basis of an analysis of the dates given in the Hebrew Bible, that the universe was created in 4004 B.C. Let me turn to the English Dominican, Hugh Pope, who in 1913 brought out a book with a title which today sounds very old-fashioned, *The Catholic Student's "Aids" to the Bible*. Amusingly, Fr. Pope has *"Aids"* in quotation marks, as though he wasn't quite sure that they would prove so to his students. His commentary on Archbishop Ussher's computations is understandably a little tedious, so I have summarized it in this table on the board:

1)	From the Creation to the Flood	1656
2)	From the Flood to the Death of Thare	427
3)	From the Death of Thare to the Death of Joseph	286
4)	From the Death of Joseph to the Exodus	144
5)	From the Exodus to the Foundation of the Temple	480
6)	From the Foundation of the Temple to the Destruction of Jerusalem	423
7)	From the Destruction of Jerusalem to the Birth of Our Lord	588
		4004

Plate III   Biblical Chronology according to Archbishop Ussher

Let me just read Fr. Pope's comments on the first period, from the Creation to the Flood:

This system is known as that of Archbishop Ussher; it is founded upon the existing Hebrew text. But difficulties arise with regard to each period. Thus for the period between Adam and the Flood the Septuagint [the Greek version of the Old Testament] gives 2242 years; this is due to the fact that the Septuagint adds 100 years to the ages of the patriarchs at the birth of their first-born sons. On the other hand the Samaritan Pentateuch only assigns 1307 years to this period...

It is evident that we have here very different systems of chronology, it is not only a question of mere textual variants, but of systematic procedure; and we have no reason for supposing that the Septuagint and the Samaritan variants are due to mere idiosyncracies on the part of translators or copyists; these variants rather seem to indicate that they had a very different Hebrew text before them.

At the same time it is well to bear in mind that the Biblical Chronological system is in no sense a scientific one; that its details are often conflicting; that starting as it does from the beginning when there can have been no means of dating events - it is possibly only meant as a guide to the memory and not as a clue to history. On the other hand none of the dates assigned by scholars to the events of this early period can be regarded as more than approximate and should not be regarded as solid means of testing the biblical statements. These latter, indeed, are as ancient as any other system of chronology which has been handed down to us. [16]

Let me read from another source for the age of the world - the *Roman Martyrology*. This is a list of the saints and martyrs for each day of the year which is still read every day in many religious houses. Here is the reading for Christmas day:

In the year, from the creation of the world, when in the beginning God created heaven and earth, five thousand one hundred and ninety-nine...Jesus Christ, the eternal God, and Son of the Eternal Father, desirous to sanctify the world by His most merciful coming, having been conceived of the Holy Ghost, and nine months having elapsed since His conception, is born in Bethlehem of Juda, having become Man of the Virgin Mary. [18]

The decision of the Biblical Commission on *Yom* (day) stated that the "days" of the Hexameron need not necessarily be understood in the strictly literal sense of 24 hours, but could be understood in a broader sense of a "certain period of time." This decision is not settling the problem of the age of the world, but merely leaving it open. A Catholic is free, as a matter of private opinion, to hold either Archbishop Ussher's 4004 B.C., the *Roman Martyology's* 5199 B.C., or the tentative billions of years of Pope Pius XII (with all his qualifications), but none of these opinions can be taught authoritatively as a matter of faith.

Personally, and I can only speak for myself here, I prefer the biblical age of the world as given in the *Roman Martyrology*. This version is based on the Greek Septuagint which is probably more reliable than the Massoretic Hebrew text used by Archbishop Ussher. So while I can't affirm this preference with any great authority, it is not just a sentimental preference, since the creationist movement has produced solid scientific arguments for a young earth.

Rev. De Verne Swezey

Let me begin my presentation on the age of the universe with the phenomenon we have heard so much about at these meetings, the "red shift." We have seen that both the Expanding and the Oscillating Theories are based on this phenomenon. These theories assume that the red shift is a Doppler shift. But what if the red shift is not a Doppler shift? The assumption that the speed of light is always constant is based on observations of light traveling for only relatively short distances. What if the light coming in from the distant galaxies has slowed down on its long journey? This would also explain the red shift, and would mean that the universe is not expanding, but rather static. It would also mean that the galaxies are not as far from us as had been thought, and of course, it would remove the basis for the currently accepted age of the universe. This is what is known as the "tired light" hypothesis, and is espoused by a minority of astronomers, among whom is Gerald Hawkins who is well known for his astronomical speculations on the Stonehenge Monument. Let me read a brief excerpt from a standard text on astronomy, *Exploration of the Universe*, by George Abell:

Are the Red Shifts Really Doppler Shifts?

Not all scientists accept the interpretation of the red shift as an indication of an expanding universe. They argue that the observed red shifts in the spectra of distant galaxies may not be Doppler shifts at all, but may be caused by some unknown effect on light as it travels over large distances. It has been suggested, for example, that photons may lose energy or "tire" as they traverse space; since the energy of a photon is inversely proportional to its wavelength, the "tired light" hypothesis could explain the red shifts of the lines of the spectra of remote objects. [17]

The "tired light" hypothesis should be capable of experimental verification, what with the space shuttle, artificial satellites, laser beams, etc., and especially these amazing atomic clocks that can measure time to less than one billionth of a second.

Let me go on now to the creationists and the age of the universe. Here again is Dr. Henry Morris from the section of *Scientific Creationism* intended for use in the public schools.

...The creation model does *not*, in its basic form, *require* a short time scale. It merely assumes a period of special creation sometime in the past, without necessarily stating when that was. On the other hand, the evolution model does *require a long* time scale. The creation model is thus free to consider the evidence on its own merits, whereas the evolution is forced to reject all evidence that favors a short time scale.

Although the creation model is not necessarily linked to a short time scale, it is true that it does fit more naturally in a short chronology. Assuming the Creator had a purpose in His creation, and that purpose centered primarily in man, it does seem more appropriate that He would not waste aeons of time in essentially meaningless caretaking of an incomplete stage or stages of His intended creative work.

In any case, the creation model permits us to look seriously at those natural processes which seem to favor a young earth and a recent creation. We shall see later...that there exist many such processes. Unfortunately, most people do not know this, since we were all indoctrinated as children in school with one model of origins exclusively. Only those processes which seem to favor an exceedingly old earth and old universe were included in our instruction. Teachers should now be careful to include a fair presentation of *both* types of processes - those which seem to support the evolution model by their consistency with a very old earth, and those which seem to favor the creation model by pointing to a recent origin of the earth and the universe. [18]

That the red shift method of measuring the age of the universe is highly subjective, and therefore of doubtful scientific value, is evident from Hubble's original conclusion that the universe was younger than the earth! So let me go on now from the age of the universe to the age of the earth. We have heard from Isaac Asimov that the method of measuring the age of the earth is based on the decay rate of radioactive uranium into lead. Dr. Morris, who is a professional geologist, has an excellent critique of this method of measuring the age of the earth:

> There is no way of being sure that the radiogenic daughter products of uranium...decay were not present in the minerals when they were first formed. This possibility is most evident in the case of modern volcanic rocks. Such rocks formed by lava flow from the earth's interior mantle commonly contain uranium minerals, and these, more often than not, are found to have radiogenic, as well as common, leads with them when the lava first cools and the minerals crystallize.
>
> Sidney P. Clementson, a British engineer, has recently made a detailed study of such modern volcanic rocks and their uranium "ages," as published in Soviet geophysical journals and other papers, and has shown that in all such cases the uranium-lead ages were vastly older than the true ages of the rocks. Most of them gave ages of over a billion years, even though the lava rocks were known to have been formed in modern times. This is clear, unequivocal evidence that, as Clementson says: "Calculated ages give no indication whatever of the age of host rocks."...
>
> Since, in those cases of igneous rocks whose age is actually

known, the uranium method gives ages which are aeons too large, and since their uranium minerals are normally found in igneous rocks formed by the same kind of processes, therefore it is very probable that their uranium "ages" also will be aeons too large for the same reasons. Why should uranium ages be assumed correct when applied to rocks of unknown age when they are always tremendously in error when calculated on rocks of known age? [19]

I should think that it would also be possible experimentally to either verify or reject the alleged constant rate of radioactive decay. Would it not be possible to subject uranium bearing rocks whose "apparent age" has been measured, to all kinds of pressure, heat, radiation, etc., over an extended period of time, to simulate various cataclysmic conditions, and then remeasure their apparent age?

Dr. Morris then discusses many scientific dating methods that indicate a young earth. Let us look at just one among many - the decay rate of the earth's magnetic field. All these dating methods, such as the uranium-lead method, are based on what is called a "uniformitarian" assumption, namely, that physical processes operated at the same rate in the past as they do today:

A...very important geochronometer is based on the strength of the earth's magnetic field. This evidence is found in a remarkable study by Dr. Thomas G. Barnes, Professor of Physics at the University of Texas in El Paso. Dr. Barnes is the author of many papers in the fields of atmospheric physics and of a widely used college textbook on electricity and magnetism. He has pointed out that the strength of the magnetic field (that is, its magnetic moment) has been measured carefully for 135 years, and has shown, through analytical and statistical studies, that it has been decaying exponentially during that period with a most probable half-life of 1400 years.

This would mean that the magnetic field was twice as strong 2800 years ago, and so on. Only 7000 years ago it must have been 32 times as strong. It is almost inconceivable that it could have been much stronger than this. Thus, 10,000 years ago, the earth would have had a magnetic field as strong as that of a magnetic star! This is highly improbable to say the least...

Thus, 10,000 years seems to be an outside limit for the age of the earth, based on the present decay rate of its magnetic field. Any objections to this conclusion must be based on rejection of the same uniformitarian assumption which evolutionists wish to retain and employ on any process from which they can thereby derive a great age for the earth. [20]

Let me turn now to the section of *Scientific Creationism* which is intended for use only in Christian schools. Here is Dr. Morris' discussion of the difficulties involved in determining the exact age of the universe by means of the Bible:

The genealogical lists in Genesis 5 give the age of each man in the line from Adam to Abraham at the birth of the son who is next in line. When these are added, they give a total of 1656 years from Adam to the Flood. A similar list for the post-diluvian patriarchs in Genesis 11 gives 368 years from the Flood until Abraham migrated into Canaan. Abraham's time is well within the period of recorded history. Although a number of detailed chronological questions for the post-Abrahamic period are not settled, there is general agreement that Abraham's migration occurred no earlier than 2000 B.C.

Therefore, the date of the creation, as obtained by simple addition of the figures given in the Bible, was about 2040 years prior to Abraham's journey from Haran to Canaan, or around 4000 B.C....

Dates as these are considered by modern anthropologists to be quite absurd. These scholars believe man to have been on the earth for at least a million years...

The sharp disagreement of the Genesis chronologies of human pre-history, with these speculations of evolutionary anthropology. is a matter of serious concern. This problem has led to various theories about imaginary "pre-Adamite" men and has been one of the main reasons why so many modern theologians have relegated Genesis 1-11 to the realm of mythology, rejecting its historical content altogether. [21]

Dr. Henry Morris thinks that there are only three acceptable solutions, biblically speaking, to this admittedly difficult textual problem:

1) *Accuracy of Transmission*

For those who take these chapters historically, there seems to be three possible approaches to consider: first, it may be possible that the numbers in Genesis 5 and 11 have been corrupted by faulty transmission. The Massoretic text, on which the figures cited above were based, differs from the Septuagint 1466 years to the period calculated above from creation to Abraham.

This would only extend man's creation back to about 5500 B.C. at most, and this is only a drop-in-the-bucket compared to the demands of evolutionary chronology.

2) *Genealogical Gaps*

...To the extent that *sound* archaelogical research may *require* dating of early settlements at dates earlier than the traditional Ussher chronology allows, the Bible does indicate the possibility of *minor* gaps in genealogies (especially between the Flood and Abraham) which may correlate with such dates.

3) *Revision of Secular Chronology*

On the other hand, it should be realized that the archaeological dating of prehistoric human sites is a highly uncertain process, involving a great number of unverifiable assumptions (as in the radiocarbon technique) and subjective evaluations (as in pottery correlations). All of which to some degree are based on evolutionary presuppositions. In the absence of actual *proof* to the contrary, the date of creation...[is] quite reasonably placed within the past several thousand years. [22]

Dean Smalley

It is time for me to conclude our discussion by attempting to summarize our four presentations. The second day of creation deals with the origin of the universe and our topic for this evening was The Age of the Universe.

Dr. Schonfield presented the scientific arguments for a universe approximately twenty billion years old based on the phenomenon of the red shift. But of course this means, he said, only the time since the Big Bang, since the majority of scientists think that the universe is eternal.

Fr. Staatz rejected the age of the world based on the biblical chronology of Archbishop Ussher, since, he said, this age ignored the non-historical literary genre of the first chapters of Genesis. He claimed that Pope Pius xii had accepted, at least tentatively, the age of the universe claimed by modern science.

Mrs. Stepan said that the Pontifical Biblical Commission had left the age of the world open, and that therefore Pius xii was not authoritatively teaching that the universe is billions of years old, but merely showing how a legitimate scientific theory like the Expanding Universe, should lead an unbelieving scientist of good will to God. She said that a Catholic is free to hold the age of the universe as proposed by Archbishop Ussher derived from the Hebrew, that given in the *Roman Martyrology* based on the Greek Septuagint, or the modern scientific theory. She expressed a personal preference for the age given in the *Martyrology*, but said that it couldn't be taught with any great authority.

Rev. Swezey considered the scientific method of arriving at the age of the universe highly subjective, as evidenced by Hubble's original proposal that the universe was younger than the earth! He claimed that there were equally valid scientific methods that give a younger age for the universe, such as the "tired light" hypothesis, and also a younger earth, such as the decay of the earth's magnetic field. He saw no reason therefore, to reject the commonly accepted biblical chronology, give or take a few thousand years.

This concludes our discussion for this evening, and we will meet again next week at Cabot University.

REFERENCES

1   Issac Asimov, *The Universe,*
    Walker and Co., Avon Books, New York, 1979, p.119.

2   Asimov, *Op. cit.,* p.122.

3   Nigel Calder, *Einstein's Universe,*
    Viking press, New York, 1979, pp.118,119.

4   Calder, *Op. cit.,* pp.122,123.

5   *Idem,* pp.136,137.

6   *Rome and the Study of Scripture,*
    Abbey Press, St. Meinrad, Ind., 1964, p.124.

7   Bruce Vawter, c.m., *Genesis,*
    Fuller, Johnson and Kearns, *A New Catholic Commentary on Holy Scripture,*
    Thomas Nelson and Sons, London, 1969, pp.176,177.

8   Ignatius Hunt, o.s.b., *Understanding the Bible,*
    Sheed and Ward, New York, 1962, pp.14,15.

9   Hunt, *Op. cit.,* p.48.

10 Pope Pius xii, *The Proofs of the Existence of God in the Light of Modern Natural Science, L'Osservatore Romano,* Nov 23, 1951, p.1.

11 Pope Pius xii, *Op. cit.,* p.2.

12 J.W.G. Johnson, *Evolution: The Hoax That's Destroying Christendom,*
    Tape distributed by: Keep the Faith Inc.,
    P.O. Box 254, Montvale, n.j.

13 St. Thomas Aquinas, *Summa Theologica,* (I, Q46, a2),
    Benziger Brothers, New York, 1947, p.243.

14 Hugh Pope, o.p., *The Catholic Student's "Aids" to the Bible,*
    Benziger Brothers, New York, 1913, pp.19,20.

15 *The Roman Martyrology,*
    Newman Bookshop, Westminster, Md., 1947, p.296.
16 George Abell, *Exploration of the Universe,*
    Holt, Rinehart and Winston, New York, 1964, p.582.
17 Henry Morris, *Scientific Creationism,*
    Creation-Life Publishers, San Diego, Cal., 1964, pp.136,137.
18 Morris, *Op. cit.*, pp.143,144.
19 *Idem*, pp.157,158.
20 *Idem*, pp.247,248.
21 *Idem*, pp.248-250.

THE THIRD DAY

The Origin of Life

The Separation of the Dry Land from the Waters

"This is one of the most powerful images of God that the art of any age has ever created. It is known that Michaelangelo was an assiduous reader of the Holy Scriptures, and in this fresco the poetry, the essential style of the first book of the Bible, find a most faithful pictorial rendering...The foreshortening of the figure throws into relief the wonderful creative, blessing hands, while the mild, majestic face translates in visible form the words of Genesis with which the account of each day is closed - 'And God saw that it was good.'"

D. Redig de Campos, *Cappella Sistina*

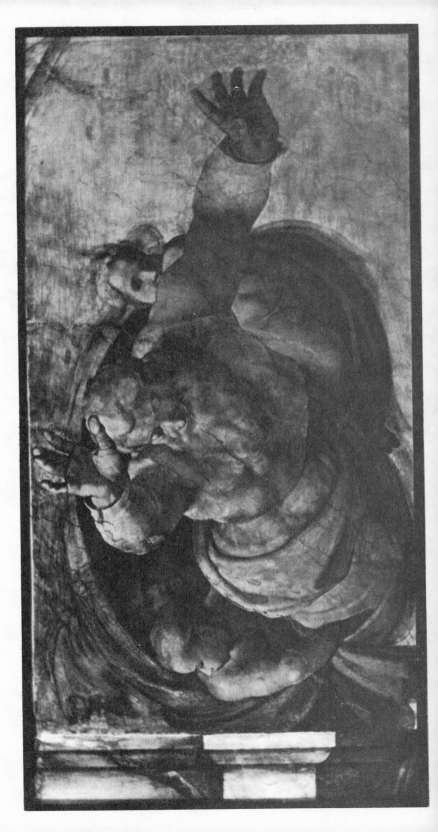

THE FIFTH MEETING
From Spontaneous Generation to Abiogenesis

Dean Smalley

Good evening, and welcome again to Cabot University. Tonight we will discuss the third day of creation, which deals with the origin of life. We have scheduled only one meeting for this day which we have humorously entitled *From Spontaneous Generation to Abiogenesis*. Here is the Scriptural account of the third day:

> And God said, "Let the waters under the heavens be gathered together into one place, and let the dry land appear." And it was so. God called the dry land Earth and the waters that were gathered together he called Seas. And God saw that it was good. And God said, "Let the earth put forth vegetation, plants yielding seed, and fruit trees bearing fruit in which is their seed, each according to its kind upon the earth." And it was so. The earth brought forth vegetation, plants yielding seed according to their kinds, and trees bearing fruit in which is their seed, each according to its kind. And God saw that it was good. And there was evening and there was morning, a third day (Gen 1:9-13).

Dr. Arthur Schonfield

Jacob Bronowski in his *The Ascent of Man* begins his discussion of one of our "ultimate questions," the origin of life, with a humorous presentation of the old notion of spontaneous generation.

> When the theory of evolution implied that some animal species came into being more recently than others, critics most often replied by quoting the Bible. Yet most people believed that creation had not stopped with the Bible. They

thought that the sun breeds crocodiles from the mud of the Nile. Mice were supposed to grow of themselves in heaps of dirty old clothes; and it was obvious that the origin of blue-bottles is bad meat. Maggots must be created inside apples - how else did they get there? All of these creatures were supposed to come to life spontaneously, without the benefit of parents.

Fables about creatures that come to life spontaneously are very ancient and are still believed, although Louis Pasteur disproved them beautifully in the 1860's. [1]

Dr. Bronowski did not describe Pasteur's refutation of spontaneous generation, but concentrated instead on his discovery of what is called molecular dissymetry. Let me review this subject briefly. The human face is symmetrical, that is, it can be divided in half and is the same on both sides. But the hands are unsymmetrical, or dissymetrical, that is, the right and left hands are different, in that they cannot be superimposed one on the other. The amazing thing that Pasteur discovered is that the chemicals in inanimate or non-living nature are always symmetrical, while those in animate or living nature are always unsymmetrical. It is as if in non-living nature there were both left and right-handed gloves, while in living nature there were just left-handed gloves.

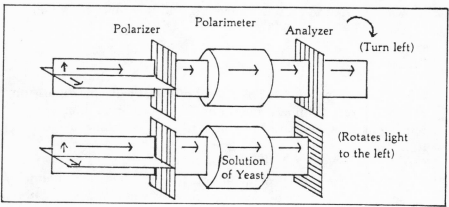

Plate iv   Molecular Dissymetry

I have put an illustration on the blackboard of an instrument called a polarimeter which Pasteur used in his discovery of molecular dissymetry. A beam of light is shone through the polarizer, a sheet of crystalline tourmaline. In the drawing, for the sake of simplicity, I have indicated the light vibrating only up and down and sideways, although actually it vibrates in all directions. As the beam of light passes through the polarizer, it comes out vibrating in only one direction. The crystal lattice of the tourmaline acted like a picket fence, and allowed the up and down vibrations to slip between the slats, but blocked the sideways vibrations. The now polarized light continues through a glass container in which there is a solution of, say yeast, and passes through a second polarizer called an analyzer. If the analyzer is rotated to the left or counterclockwise and the crystalline slats block the polarized light, the solution is said to be optically active to the left, indicating that the chemical molecules in the solution are left-handed in structure, like a left-handed glove. Were a different solution to block the light if the analyzer was rotated to the right or clockwise, it would be said to be optically active to the right, indicating that the molecules were right-handed in structure, like a right-handed glove.

By the use of this instrument Pasteur demonstrated that any solution which contained living matter is always left-handed, or in other words, living things are always unsymmetrical. In the TV version of *The Ascent of Man*, Bronowski was in Pasteur's laboratory seated at Pasteur's own polarimeter:

Right hand, left hand, that was the deep clue that Pasteur followed in his study of life. The world is full of things whose right-handed version is different from the left-handed version: a right-handed corkscrew as against a left-handed, or a right snail against a left one. Above all, the two hands; they can be mirrored one in the other, but they cannot be turned in such a way that the right hand and the left hand become interchangeable. That was known in Pasteur's time to be true also of some crystals whose facets are so arranged that there are right-hand and left-hand versions...

Pasteur made wooden models of such crystals (he was

adroit with his hands, and a beautiful draughtsman) but much more than that, he made intellectual models. In his first piece of research he had hit on the notion that there must be right-handed and left-handed molecules too; and what is true of the crystals must reflect a property of the molecule itself. And that must be displayed by the behavior of the molecules in any unsymmetrical situation. For instance, when you put them into a solution and shine a polarized (that is, an unsymmetrical) beam of light through them, the molecules of one kind say, by convention the molecules Pasteur called right-handed) must rotate the plane of polarization of the light to the right. A solution of crystals all of one shape will behave unsymmetrically towards the unsymmetrical beam of light produced in a polarimeter...

The remarkable fact is that a chemical solution from living cells does just that. We still do not know why life has this strange chemcial propensity. But the property established that life has a special chemical character, which has maintained itself throughout its evolution. For the first time, Pasteur had linked all the forms of life with one kind of chemical structure. From that powerful thought it follows that we must be able to link evolution with chemistry. [2]

Let me go on now to *abiogenesis*, a Greek term coined by Thomas Henry Huxley, meaning "life from non-life." Huxley's mentor Charles Darwin was a Deist, who believed that God had created the world, but had then let natural forces, such as evolution, take over. However, he could not see how life could have evolved from non-life by chance alone, so he brought God back in, as a sort of *Deus ex machina*, to create life; then he sent Him back again into space or somewhere. But in Germany, Darwin's other great ally, Ernst Haeckel, an atheist, claimed that life had evolved from non-lfe by chance alone at the bottom of the sea in what he called the *Urschleim*, or "protoplasmic sludge."

In 1868 a British naval vessel, the *Challenger*, which was equipped with a deep sea dredge, dragged up some mud from the bottom of the ocean. Huxley, after examining the mud, announced that it was moving, indeed was alive! He named it *Bathy-*

bius haeckeli, "Haeckel's deep mud." However, other scientists on examining the mud said that the movement Huxley had observed was merely trapped gas bubbles. Huxley tried to hang on, but after nine years reluctantly withdrew his claim. But in the meantime he had managed to convince Darwin that God was not needed to explain the origin of life. In 1871 Darwin wrote:

> It is often said that all the conditions for the first production of a living organism are now present which could ever have been present. But if (and oh! what a big if!) we could conceive in some warm little pond, with all sorts of ammonia and phosphoric acid salts, light, heat, electricity, etc. present, that a protein compound was chemically formed ready to undergo still more complex changes, at the present day such matter would be instantly devoured or absorbed, which would not have been the case before living creatures were formed. [3]

In 1924 the Russian Alexander Oparin said that while Darwin's "warm pond" model was substantially correct, it was missing one basic element. In the absence of green plants, there would have been no free oxygen. The primitive atmosphere of the earth must have consisted mainly of methane, ammonia, water vapor, and so on. In a weak solution of these chemicals, now humorously called the "primordial soup," the basic chemicals of life, the amino acids which make up the proteins, and the bases which make up the DNA were formed in little bubbles he called "coacervates." We will deal with these basic chemicals of life in more detail when we discuss the origin of species on the fifth day.

It wasn't until 1955 that an American, Stanley Miller, tested Oparin's hypothesis. He put Oparin's primitive atmosphere, the methane, ammonia, and so on, into a flask and heated it for several days. On examining the residue which remained, Miller found that it indeed contained amino acids. Here is Dr. Bronowski:

> ...To talk sensibly about the beginning of life we have to be very realistic. We have to ask an historical question. Four thousand million years ago, before life began, when the earth was very young, what was the surface of the earth, what was

its atmosphere like?

Very well, we know a rough answer. The atmosphere was expelled from the interior of the earth, and was therefore somewhat like a volcanic neighborhood anywhere - a cauldron of steam, nitrogen, methane, and other reducing gases, as well as some carbon dioxide. That is crucial, because oxygen is produced by the plants and did not exist in a free state before life existed.

These gases and their products, dissolved weakly in the oceans, formed a reducing atmosphere. How would they react next under the action of ultra-violet light - which is very important in every theory of life because it can penetrate in the absence of oxygen. That question was answered in a beautiful experiment by Stanley Miller in America round about 1950. He put the atmosphere in a flask - the methane, the ammonia, the water, and so on - and went on, for day after day, and boiled and bubbled them up, put an electric charge through them to simulate lightning and other violent forces. And visibly the mixture darkened. Why? Because, on testing, it was found that amino acids had been formed in it. That is a crucial step forward, since amino acids are the building blocks of life. From them the living proteins are made, and proteins are the constituents of all living things. [4]

Then in the 1970's the English scientist, Lesley Orgel, who worked with Dr. Bronowski at the Salk Institute in California, tried freezing Oparin's "primordial soup," and produced one of the four bases which make up the master molecule, DNA:

We used to think, until a few years ago, that life had to begin in those sultry, electric conditions. And then it began to occur to a few scientists that there is another set of extreme conditions which may be as powerful, that is, the presence of ice. It is a strange thought; but ice has two properties which make it very attractive in the formation of simple, basic molecules. First of all, the process of freezing concentrates the material, which at the beginning of time must have been very dilute in the oceans. And secondly, it may be that the crystalline structure of ice makes it possible for molecules to line up in a way which is certainly important at every stage of life.

At any rate, Lesley Orgel did a number of elegant experiments of which I will describe the simplest. He took some of the basic constituents which are sure to have been present in the atmosphere of the earth at any early time: hydrogen cyanide is one, ammonia is another. He made a dilute solution of them in water, and then froze the solution over a period of several days. As a result, the concentrated material is pushed into a sort of tiny iceberg to the top, and there the presence of a small amount of color reveals that organic molecules have been formed. Some amino acids, no doubt; but, most important, Orgel found that he had formed one of the four fundamental constituents in the genetic alphabet which directs all life. He had made adenine, one of the four bases in DNA. It may indeed be that the alphabet of life in the DNA was formed in these sort of conditions and not in tropical conditions. [5]

So in conclusion let me say that abiogenesis, or the origin of life from non-life by chance alone, first proposed by Huxley and Darwin, and later developed by Oparin, can now be demonstrated experimentally, at least in part. In two quite simple laboratory experiments by Miller and Orgel, the two basic chemicals of life, amino acids, which make up the proteins, and the bases which make up the DNA, were produced under conditions which must have been duplicated in nature countless times over the millenia by sheer chance.

Fr. Robert A. Staatz

I would like to begin my presentation tonight with the Scripture, and then go on to the scientific account of the origin of life. I turn again to the Benedictine Ignatius Hunt and his *Understanding the Bible*:

It is quite likely (and this is no isolated instance) that the story as we know it was worked over from a more primitive form. Thus we note that the third and sixth days are each "overloaded," including two works in place of one. This does not unduly mar the symmetry of the six days, however, and it has long been pointed out how the first day (light) corresponds to the fourth (the heavenly luminaries: sun, moon, stars, as distributors of the light); the second day (water is divided by the firmament) corresponds to the fifth (water and air creatures); and that the third day (separation of dry land *and* plant life) corresponds to the sixth (living creatures upon the earth *and* man). This is not a "scientific" ordering of creation. It is largely "mnemonic," i. e. helpful to memorization, and is based upon ancient oriental ideas common to other peoples besides the Hebrews. Thus we have light before the sun (for the sun was regarded not so much as a light-giver as a place where light gathers); we have the stress upon primeval water and darkness - signs of chaos and disorder. We shall recall from an earlier chapter that the idea of the firmament, a solid, inverted bowl-like covering, high-up over the earth, holding aloft vast stores of water - that could be released by opening the "gates of heaven" (cf. Gen 7:11) - was common in the ancient orient. The earth too, was regarded as saucer-shaped, floating on water and held up by pillars that sank down in the abyss below. These and other indications should make us realize that this is not a "scientific" account. Nor is it entirely correct to describe the narrative as "popular," at least *if* we imply that the writer could have written scientifically had he wished to do so. God does not ordinarily infuse such advanced knowledge into the minds of his inspired instruments - especially when it has little to do with the primary purpose of the Sacred Writings. St. Thomas laid down the sound principle that the "sacred writers went by what sensibly appeared." [6]

The story of the Hexameron is told in the first chapter of Genesis 1:1-31, and the numbers in this scheme, for instance the (3) after "Light," refers to the verses. There are eight "Works," three of "Separation" and five of "Adornment." There are two series of three days each, and the first, second, and third day of each series correspond with one another, thus our third day corresponds with the sixth. On the third day God "adorned" the earth with plants, and on the sixth day He further "adorned" the land with animals and especially with man. So we see that the Bible is not trying to teach us anything about the origin of life, but merely that all life comes from God.

Day	Work	Work of Division	Day	Work	Work of Adornment
1	Light (3)	Separation of light from darkness (4-5)	4	Luminaries	Firmament with sun, moon, stars (16-18)
2	Firmament (6)	Separation of upper from lower waters (7)	5	Fish and birds (20-22)	Waters with fish, air with birds (21-23)
3	Earth-plants (9-12)	Separation of sea from land (9-12)	6	Animals - men (24-27)	Earth with animals, man (24-31)

Plate v   Poetic Schema of the Hexameron

To find out something then, about the origin of life, we have to go to science, not the Bible. So let me turn to Fr. Owen Garrigan, who is a professor of chemistry at Seton Hall University and the author of *Man's Intervention in Nature*, one of the volumes in *The Twentieth Century Encyclopedia of Catholicism*:

Religious people generally think of life as having been created by an act of direct intervention by God rather than by his putting the potentiality for life into chemical matter. The assumption has been that a special act on God's part is necessary for a thing to begin to live. Such a view would make chemical evolution a curiosity without purpose. Further experiments on the details of chemical evolution may one day make the special-intervention view absurd. It does not seem necessary to put the restraint of direct intervention upon the omnipotence of God. After all, direct and indirect intervention are distinct only in man's mind. The terms were invented to help man understand God's creative work. They should be discarded when they no longer help or when they actually hinder Man's understanding of the nature of God's infinitely simple acts...

New, and it seems, compelling reasons lead us back full circle to the idea of the Greeks, that the earth, itself inanimate by so many tests of life, is the mother of all the living. For from the earth - from the simple elements found in the thin crust of this planet's mass - has risen that complex, self-reproducing system that merits the name of life. Not as improbably as we might have thought a few decades ago, chemical complexity tends to increase. There is built into matter a chemical driving force, a reactivity that under certain, not improbable, conditions, moves simple materials to explore the possibilities of more complex combinations, venturing into the region of life itself...

The evidence, incomplete though it is, suggests that the process of *biopoesis* [the making of life] did proceed via chemical evolution to form a self-reproducing, mutating being. And this living product, subject to the pressures of its environment, continues to evolve by means of reproduction, mutation, and natural selection. The product of chemical evolution has just those chemical properties that enable it to progress as the subject of biological evolution. [7]

So, if you can stand it one more time, by a comparison of the Scriptural account of the origin of life, and the scientific account of that origin, we see that a concordance between the two is clearly impossible. But again, this does not mean that a harmony between science and theology is impossible, which brings me to the subject of Teilhard de Chardin. Teilhard, if you remember, says that matter is characterized by what he calls the "law of "complexity-consciousness." The more complex the structure, the more the consciousness. This means that structures like the amino acids and the bases which make up DNA, the basic chemicals of life, must already have some form of rudimentary consciousness. This is not yet experimentally verifiable, but logically has to be there. The transition from non-life to life, then, in Teilhard's synthesis, is

not the great problem it was to earlier theologians, but a completely natural development of the forward and upward movement of
evolution. Here again is the Jesuit Robert Faricy in his *Teilhard de
Chardin's Theology of the Christian in the World*:

> Teilhard's postulate concerning the law of complexity-con-
> sciousness does not just assume that this law is universal. It
> further states that matter presents itself in more and more
> complex groups with corresponding higher levels of con-
> sciousness. This is not to postulate any teleological property
> or metaphysical finality in matter or in the universe as a
> whole. It is simply to state that, over long periods of time and
> through various chance combinations that take place inevita-
> bly among very large populations, matter becomes arranged
> in more highly complex forms that have higher degrees of
> consciousness. In this perspective, life is seen as the outcome
> of a general physico-chemical process "in virtue of which
> cosmic matter, by its very existence and structure...presents
> itself to our experience as actuated by a movement of qualita-
> tive infolding (or arrangement, if you prefer) upon itself."
>   This "infolding arrangement" is in the direction of higher
> complexity; it results with the passage of time in cells, plants,
> animals. Life, far from being an oddity or an evolutionary
> aberration, is the result of millions of years of progress along
> the axis of complexity. "So as to overcome the improbability
> of arrangements leading to units of ever increasing complexi-
> ty, the involuting universe, considered in its pre-reflective
> zones, proceeds step by step by dint of billion-fold trial and
> error." This process of groping, together with the mechanism
> of reproduction and heredity, results in the various species of
> living things. [8]

What makes Teilhard's explanation of the origin of life so
similar to that of humanists like Dr. Bronowski, yet so different, is
that Teilhard knows where the long journey of evolution is
heading. It is converging to a point which Teilhard calls "Omega,"
which he identifies with God.

Mrs. Maria Stepan

Let me begin my presentation tonight by commenting on Jacob Bronowski's explanation of *abiogenesis* or the chemical evolution of life. I would like to read a few excerpts from an excellent book, which unfortunately has not yet been translated into English, *Hasard et Certitude*, "Chance and Certainty," by a French Catholic layman, George Salet. Salet begins his discussion of the origin of life with Alexander Oparin, whose theories Dr. Schonfield explained in some detail. Here is Salet quoting directly from Oparin's *Origin of Life*:

"In the ordinary laboratory synthesis of organic substances, we always obtain a mixture of equal parts of the two forms of dissymetrical molecules (which we call a racemic mixture)...this is *why the probability of the formation of the one or the other of the two active forms is exactly the same.* [Salet's emphasis]

"Such great numbers of molecules take part in chemical reactions that statistical laws apply perfectly. And it is always highly improbable that an excess could be formed of either one or the other of the two opposites. Indeed, we do not as a rule observe any such excess under natural conditions in the absence of life, nor under laboratory conditions, e.g. in *the experiment of Miller...both alanine and other amino acids appeared in racemic form.* In living beings, on the other hand, the amino acids that go to make up *natural proteins are exclusively left-handed in configuration.*

"This property of the protoplasm of producing and storing only one of the possible optically active forms is an indication of the dissymetry of living matter. While it is absent from *inanimate nature, dissymetry is characteristic of all living things.*

"The fact was already noted by Pasteur who spoke of it as the great characteristic feature which perhaps alone establishes the only well marked line of demarcation which can at present be drawn between the chemistry of non-living and of living matter." [Oparin, *Origin of Life*] [9]

The amino acids which Stanley Miller found in his flask were in a racemic or symmetrical mixture, that is, they were half left-handed and half right-handed as always occors in inanimate nature. So this does not provide, in spite of Dr. Bronowski's claim, experimental proof for the theory that life arose from non-life by chance alone, on the contrary, it disproves it. Salet continues with a humorous presentation of a hypothetical rabbit made of right-handed molecules:

> The amino acids synthesized by a rabbit are left-handed because its DNA is of a determined dissymetrical form which perpetuates itself from generation to generation by replication. Let us now consider any biochemical process, let us say DNA duplication. It is known that most of these processes are capable of being carried out *in vitro* [in a test tube] if the necessary precursors and enzymes are available. It is certain, then, that if we could substitute for every dissymetrical molecule found in the chemist's test tube, its other *enantiomorph* ["opposite shape"], the process would continue just as well.
>
> *If then it were possible to replace every dissymetrical molecule in the body by its other enantiomorph (which is the same as imagining another rabbit identical to the mirror image of the first) the rabbit we would get would be perfectly viable.* As a matter of fact there exist only left-handed rabbits, but it is impossible to find the least reason why there could not exist right-handed rabbits...We must however say that, as long as animals know only how to synthesize a part of the amino acids able to support life, all the right-handed rabbits would die of starvation surrounded by the vegetable world as it is today. [10]

A right-handed rabbit would be perfectly capable of life; there is no chemical difference between it and a left-handed rabbit. But all the plants in the world are left-handed, and could not be assimilated by a right-handed rabbit. A right-handed rabbit could only eat a right-handed carrot, and there are none.

The mystery then is this: if life were the natural evolution of inanimate matter, because this matter is symmetrical, there could only have appeared *racemic mixtures*, in which the two optically active forms always exist in equal proportions. We must then push the matter to its logical extreme. If life results from the evolution of matter *according to the laws of matter, there would be racemic mixtures* of alanine [one of the 20 amino acids], racemic mixtures of protobionts [the hypothetical ancestor of the simple cell], racemic mixtures of simple cells, and racemic mixtures of rabbits. The right-handed rabbit had an apparition probability rigorously identical to the probability of the left-handed rabbit. How is it that you can't find even one? [11]

In Oparin's "primordial soup," if it ever existed, when the amino acids and the bases supposedly formed in little bubbles, the "coacervates," they would have formed in racemic or symmetrical mixtures, as they did in the experiments of Miller and Orgel. But as a matter of fact all of the amino acids and bases that appear in animate nature are left-handed or unsymmetrical. The mathematical chances for the appearance of a right-handed living cell are identical to those of the left-handed cell. So the fact that there are none indicates that the origin of life was directed not by chance but by an Intelligence.

Dr. Bronowski called molecular dissymetry the "thumbprint of life," but it could better be called "the thumbprint of the Creator." These new discoveries about the chemical bases of life have brought us right back to the third day of creation - "And *God* said, 'Let the earth put forth vegetation'" (Gen 1:11). George Salet would rephrase the Scripture, with a smile I am sure, "And God said, 'Let the earth put forth (the left-handed) vegetation.'" Dr. Bronowski on the other hand wanted to phrase it - "And the *earth* brought forth the left-handed vegetation"; God was not needed. But Salet has shown that if this were true, it would have been - "And the earth brought forth the left-handed and the right-handed vegetation." So God has left His "thumbprint" on all living things, for all men of good will to find Him.

Another amazing thing about the left-handed make-up of all

living things, is that after the death of a living organism all the amino acids gradually begin to rearrange themselves until they are in a racemic mixture - "Dust thou art and into dust thou shalt return" (Gen 3:19).

I would like to take issue once again with Fr. Staatz and his ongoing claim that it is impossible to make a harmony between the Scriptural account of the third day of creation and contemporary science. But first let me reread the first two verses of the third day:

> And God said, "Let the waters under the heavens be gathered together into one place, and let the dry land appear." And it was so. God called the dry land Earth, and the waters that were gathered together he called Seas. And God saw that it was good (Gen 1:9,10).

If I seriously proposed just a few years ago that at one time all the land masses of the earth were gathered together into one place because the Bible says so, I would have been subject to ridicule by both scientists and liberal Catholics alike. But today it is considered reputable science to say that at one time all the land masses of the earth were indeed gathered together into one place, now called *Pangea*, "all the land." This is the so-called "Continental Drift Theory" which was first proposed by the German geologist Alfred Wegener in 1912. Let me read a brief summary of this theory from a student reference book entitled *The Book of Popular Science*:

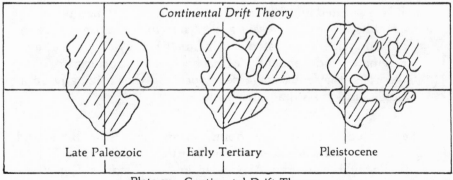

Continental Drift Theory

Late Paleozoic   Early Tertiary   Pleistocene

Plate vi   Continental Drift Theory

Soon after the mapping of the Atlantic ocean, some four hundred years ago, geographers noted that the western coast-lines of Europe and Africa seemed to match the opposite coastlines of Eastern North and South America. By just "moving" these continents together, so to speak, one could fit them along these coasts. But it was not until 1858 that a map was published demonstrating the excellence of the fit; it was suggested that the continents in question had once been united. The idea this time took hold. By about 1900, a number of geologists proposed that certain lands of the Southern Hemisphere - major parts of Africa, Madagascar, Australia, Antartica, and South America - were joined in a huge supercontinent called Gonwanaland (named after the Gonwana region of central India). However, the vast majority of orthodox geologists refused to take these ideas very seriously. But from 1912 into the 1920's, the German scientist Alfred Wegener advanced a powerful theory of continental drift. He proposed that in a time of earth history about 200 to 300 million years ago, the so-called Upper Paleozoic, all the present continents were united in a single tremendous land-mass called *Pangea*. At that time, *Pangea* started to break up slowly into its component continents which eventually moved into the configurations they have today...

Many of Wegener's...ideas are sound and have continued to provide a firm basis for later drift theories. In fact, a number of them had been noted even before Wegener wrote. It was pointed out that many rock beds, rock structures (such as faults, or cracks), fossils and even living organisms were so alike on widely separated continents that they could not have originated independently of each other. According to drift theorists, they must have developed together originally on a single land mass that later broke up. [12]

Let me continue on this point, harmonizing the Bible and science, by reading an excerpt from an article entitled *How Life on Earth Began* by George Alexander in the *Reader's Digest* for August 1982. George Alexander goes briefly through the theory of

Oparin and the experiments of Miller and Orgel, adding the latest development from NASA's Ames Research Center in California, where it has been recently proposed that metal-bearing clays could have played a crucial role. The article concludes:

> And God said, "Let the waters bring forth abundantly the moving creature that hath life," the King James Bible tells us. "And the Lord God formed man of the dust of the ground."
>
> As the Bible proclaimed, and as many primitive societies have intuited life began in the mud at the ocean's edge, and the mother molecules emerged out of a handful of clay a long time ago. We are just beginning to learn how. [13]

George Alexander is saying that the Scriptural and the scientific account of the origin of life can easily be harmonized. This is also the position of both St. Augustine and St. Thomas Aquinas, as I will show. If the Hexameron is not an historical account, but merely a purified version of an ancient pagan myth as the liberals claim, how is such a harmony possible?

Let me go on now to my own presentation on the origin of life. I would like to read a few excerpts from *An Introduction to the Philosophy of Animate Nature* by the Holy Ghost Father, Henry Korin, a scholastic philosopher in the tradition of St. Thomas:

> The question to be considered here is not how living bodies originate now. With respect to the present, everyone admits biogenesis ["life from life"] as a law; i.e., not a single instance is known of a living body which did not come into existence through a process of generation from another living body. The experiments of Pasteur and others have conclusively shown that in all instances where life seemed to originate from inanimate matter, microscopically small organisms gave rise to new living bodies.
>
> Our problem is concerned with the possibility of living bodies originating from inanimate matter. To a certain extent this problem refers to the future insofar as the question can be raised whether or not laboratory experiments will ever succeed in producing a living organism, no matter how

primitive, from inanimate matter. It refers to the past insofar as all available evidence points to the fact that once life on earth was physically impossible, so that at some time in the distant past living bodies must have made their first appearance on earth. Because observation of this first appearance is evidentally impossible, the question how this life originated may be studied philosophically by an investigation of any position that is not in accordance with reason. In this way it perhaps will be possible to arrive at the conclusion that only one position offers a greater probability than others. [14]

	The Origin of Life
Creationists	1) Produced by God as the sole organizing cause of matter
St. Augustine	2) Produced by God acting through causes intrinsic to matter.
St. Thomas Aquinas	3) Originated under the influence of secondary causes extraneous to matter.
Humanists	4) Produced from matter without influence of extraneous causes.
Teilhard de Chardin	5) Has always existed.
Fred Hoyle	6) Came from other planets.

Plate vi   Possible Origins of Life according to Philosophy

This is an outline of six possible explanations for the origin of life by Fr. Korin. Let us run through them briefly:

1) *Produced by God as the sole organizing cause of matter.* This would seem to be the position of our fundamentalist friends. Let us quote directly from Fr. Korin:

The first living bodies were produced by God's positive intervention in the existing order of nature. Suspending the laws of nature, He directly produced in inanimate matter the conditions which made matter proximately disposed for actuation by a soul. This soul was educed from the potency of matter, except in the case of man whose soul was directly created by God...

There cannot be any doubt that God had the power directly to organize matter in such a way that it is immediately disposed for actuation by a soul. However, it would seem unreasonable to attribute directly to God what can be brought about through the activity of the natural forces of inanimate matter in accordance with the laws of nature. *If* the Author of nature has endowed matter with forces that can naturally lead to the emergence of living bodies, it would seem unreasonable to suppose that He positively intervened in the process of natural development by suspending the activity of these forces and directly organizing inanimate matter. We say *if*, for it remains to be seen whether or not living bodies can have originated from inanimate matter acting in accordance with the laws of nature. [15]

Of course, it is a scientific question whether inanimate matter actually has an intrinsic potency to life, but both St. Augustine and St. Thomas, going by the science of their day, thought that it did. This seems to be implied in the words of Scripture, "Let the *earth*," - the earth seems to have played some role in the origin of life. The creationists, on the other hand, seem to maintain that matter has no intrinsic potency to life, and that God had to intervene directly by way of miracle in suspending the deterministic laws of inanimate matter. I suspect that they are afraid of taking the phrase "Let the earth," too literally, because they think it would open the door to chemical evolution and thus to evolution in general. So while the creationist position is not unreasonable, Fr. Korin thinks it less probable than the two following positions.

2) *Life produced by God acting through causes intrinsic to matter.* This is the position of St. Augustine, and here are St. Thomas' comments:

Concerning the production of plants, Augustine's opinion differs from that of others. For other commentators, in accordance with the surface meaning of the text, consider that the plants were produced in act in their various species on this third day, whereas Augustine...says that the earth is said to have then produced plants and trees in their causes, that is, it received then the power to produce them. He supports this view by the authority of Scripture, for it is said (Gen 2:4,5): "These are the generations of the heaven and the earth, and every plant of the field before it sprung up in the earth, and every herb of the ground before it grew." Therefore, the production of plants in their causes, within the earth, took place before they sprang up from the earth's surface. And this is confirmed by reason, as follows: In these first days God created all things in their origin or causes, and from this work He subsequently rested. Yet afterwards, by governing His creatures in the work of propagation, "He worketh until now." Now the production of plants from out of the earth is a work of propagation, and therefore they were not produced in act on the third day, but in their causes only. [16]

One of the wonderful things about St. Thomas is that he always gives St. Augustine's interpretation as well as his own. St. Augustine does not take the third day in its strictly literal sense. He is assigning the production of plants, not to the work of creation, but to God's work in governing the universe. St. Augustine seems to want to give matter a certain dignity, a potency to life, perhaps because his main opponents, the Manicheans, claimed that matter itself was evil.

3) *Life originated under the influence of secondary causes extraneous to matter.* This is the opinion of St. Thomas which differs somewhat from that of St. Augustine:

Whether the Lights of Heaven are Living Beings?...

Obj. 3. Further, a cause is nobler than its effect, but the sun, moon, and stars are a cause of life, as is especially evidenced in the case of animals, generated from putrefaction, which receives life from the power of the sun, moon, and stars. Much more therefore, have the heavenly bodies a soul...

Reply Obj. 3. Since the heavenly body is a mover moved, it is of the nature of an instrument, which acts in virtue of the agent; and therefore, since the agent is a living substance, the heavenly body can impart life in virtue of that agent. [17]

St. Thomas thought that the sun, moon, and stars, were moved by angels, and ultimately by God, who used these creatures as secondary causes in the production of life. St. Thomas seems to be concerned about the reasonableness of St. Augustine's position, that the earth was apparently the *only* secondary cause in the origin of life. This could give the impression that the effect was greater than the cause, since the effect, life, was obviously greater than the secondary cause, earth. So St. Thomas, following the science of his day, introduces an additional secondary cause, the sun, moon, and stars, which were also thought to be instrumental in the origin of life. The sun, moon, and stars, were considered superior to lower forms of life, such as insects, so this eliminates the problem of the effect being greater than the cause. St. Thomas' opinion is true to a certain extent even today, since the sun is still considered an instrumental cause in the origin of life. Of course it is not necessary to say that St. Thomas would have considered *abiogenesis*, the chance origin of life, absurd.

But if the sun and other heavenly bodies were instrumental in the origin of life, which takes place on the third day, why were they not mentioned until the fourth day? St. Thomas replies:

In the words of Basil (*Hom v in Hexam*), plants were recorded as produced before the sun and moon to prevent idolatry, since those who believe the heavenly bodies to be gods hold that plants originate primarily from these bodies; although, as Chrysostom remarks (*Hom vi in Gen*), the sun, moon, and stars cooperate in the work of production by their movements as the husbandman cooperates by his labor. [18]

We have seen that St. Thomas Aquinas does not interpret the Hexameron in the strictly literal sense, but in what is called the broad literal sense. Where were the sun, moon, and stars if they assisted in the generation of plants on the third day? St. Thomas thinks that they were indeed there, by in a somewhat formless state. They did not receive their final definitive forms until the fourth day.

4) *Life produced from matter without influence of extraneous causes.* This is the position of the secular humanists who would like the Hexameron to read something like: "And the earth put forth vegetation," because matter, they say, brought forth life all by itself. Here are Fr. Korin's comments:

> If the material causes operating in a living body, which the soul combines into a single unit, are able to cause the necessary dispositions for life and thus produce a new living body, why should it be *impossible* for those forces to be united "by chance" into an operational unit and thus give rise to a living body? If such a thing did happen, a living body would have been produced from inanimate matter. Thus it would not be impossible for a combination of inanimate forces to give rise to a living body.
>
> Granted that such a combination is a possibility, does it provide an *adequate* explanation for the origin of life? An adequate explanation is one which takes into consideration *all* the causes that are at work in the production of an effect. No one admits that in the present state of science it is possible to indicate even all the *physical* forces that are necessary for the production of the dispositions of matter required for actuation by a soul. But supposing that a time will come when man will know all the material causes the combination of which would result in the production of living bodies? The answer is in the negative, because he has failed to indicate the cause which led to the combination of these causes by unifying their activity. But could not this unification be brought about *by chance*, as was suggested above? We must answer that an appeal to chance is not an explanation, but a

confession of ignorance of the adequate explanation. Chance refers to the unpredictability of an effect produced by causes whose combined action cannot be forseen, because the cause of their combination is not known. To deny that their combination has a cause is tantamount to a denial of the principle of causality. Therefore, an appeal to chance is an admission that the known physical forces of inanimate matter cannot explain the origin of life. [19]

Matter, according to both St. Augustine and St. Thomas, has an intrinsic potency to life. But we have seen that if life arose by chance alone, it would have appeared in racemic or symmetrical form, that is, half left-handed and half right-handed molecules. The fact that life appears only in a left-handed or dissymetrical form, indicates that there was an Intelligence, not chance, directing that potency of matter. So George Salet's science and Fr. Korin's philosophy concur. The position of St. Augustine and St. Thomas makes good sense both from the philosophic and the scientific point of view. To claim that life arose by chance alone is bad philosophy and worse science.

5) *Life has always existed.* This is the position of the pantheists and implicitly of Fr. Teilhard de Chardin. We have heard that Teilhard thought there was no such thing as "brute matter," that the more complex matter became, the more consciousness it possessed. Fr. Korin rejects this position as both unreasonable and unscientific.

6) *Life came from other planets.* This is the position of Sir Fred Hoyle who after abandoning an unreasonable theory of the origin of the universe, the Steady State Theory, has now produced an unreasonable theory of the origin of life. He claims that life arose when organic molecules fell to earth from a comet. So how did the organic molecules arise on the comet?
I frankly believe that the creationists made a tactical blunder during the 1982 trial in Arkansas, when a state law allowing equal time for teaching creationism in the public schools was declared unconstitutional. The creationists called to the stand Hoyle's

partner, N.C. Wickramsinghe, and although he did ridicule the evolutionist position on the origin of life, he then presented his own position which is just as ridiculous.

Rev. De Verne Swezey

I think by now I have sufficiently made my point that we creationists are not plotting to teach the Bible in the public schools. So from now on when I read from Dr. Morris' *Scientific Creationism* about science you will know without my specifying, that it is from the public school section of the book, and when I read about the Bible, it is from the edition intended to be used only in Christian schools.

We have heard Dr. Bronowski claim that life arose by chance alone in the primordial seas. Now, chance is the realm of a branch of mathematics called probability math. So, let us take a look at what mathematics can tell us about the probability of the most simple self-replicating chemical structure that can be conceived arising by chance alone. An argument from math is always a little difficult to follow, but Dr. Morris does it about as well as I have ever seen it done:

> The evolutionary model attributes all the systems and structures of the universe to the operation of natural processes operating under the impetus of the innate properties of matter and the laws of nature. It assumes that no external supernatural agent plans and directs these processes; the universe is self-contained and self-evolving by random action of its components. On the other hand, the creation model attributes the system and structures of the cosmos to a planned, purposive creation of all things in the beginning by an omniscient Creator. The creationist maintains that the degree of complexity and order which science has discovered in the universe could never be generated by chance or accident.
>
> This issue actually can be attacked quantitatively, using the simple principles of mathematical probability. The problem is simply whether a complex system, in which many compo-

nents function unitedly together, and in which each component is uniquely necessary to the efficient functioning of the
whole, could ever arise by random processes. The question is
especially incisive when we deal with living systems.
Although inorganic relationships are often quite complex,
living organisms are immensely more so. The evolution
model nevertheless assumes all these have arisen by chance
and naturalism. [20]

Dr. Morris, for the sake of argument, grants the possibility of
Oparin's "primordial soup." The basic chemicals of life are the
proteins and DNA, but Dr. Morris lets the DNA go and concentrates
just on the protein. Proteins are composed of long chains of
twenty different amino acids, and can function only if the chain is
in one particular sequence. Now, as long as there are only a few
components, the odds of the probability of the correct sequence
arising by chance alone in the "primordial soup" are not too great.
    For example, suppose we have two components A and B that
function only in the sequence A-B. The only other possible
combination B-A does not work. So we have a one-in-two chance
of success, just like tossing a coin - heads or tails.
    Let us add a third component C, and assume that only the
sequence A-B-C works. There are six possible ways these three
components can combine: A-B-C, A-C-B, B-A-C, B-C-A, C-A-B, and
C-B-A. So now the odds of getting the correct system by chance
have risen to one in six. As we continue to add components, the
odds rise sharply. For five components A-B-C-D-E, the probability is
one in one-hundred-and-twenty.
    Let us jump to a protein chain composed of one hundred units.
Remember this system will work only if it appears in one
particular sequence. Believe it or not, there are 10^{158} possible
sequences in a system composed of one hundred units. 10^{158} is a
one followed by 158 zeros. So the odds are now one in 10^{158}.
    Now suppose in the "primordial soup" these 100 components
keep trying to hit the proper sequence, getting together, breaking
up, and trying again. The humanists tell us that the universe is less
than thirty billion years old. Suppose we let one hundred
components combine a billion times a second for thirty billion

years. We will have reached 10^{105} of the possible sequences. Remember we need 10^{158} chances to be sure of success. So the evolutionists are hoist on their own petard. Thirty billion years is just not enough time. And this is just for the protein. We haven't even considered the other necessary chemical for life, DNA.

And yet an organism composed of only 100 parts is impossibly simple. Research sponsored by NASA (for the purpose of enabling astronauts to recognize even the most rudimentary forms of life on other planets) has shown that the simplest type of protein molecule that could be said to be "living" is composed of a chain of at least 400 linked amino acids, and each amino acid is a specific combination of four or five basic chemical elements, and each chemical element is a unique assemblage of protons, electrons, and neutrons. It is thus inconceivable (to anyone but a doctrinaire evolutionist) that a living system could ever be formed by chance. Yet, if a Creator is excluded from the problem, there is no other way that at least the *first* living system could ever have been formed. [21]

Let me go on now to the biblical account of the third day. If you remember from my presentation of the second day of creation, the creationists take the phrase "upper waters" in the strictly literal sense, and think that the earth must have been covered by a vast water canopy which screened out harmful radiations coming in from outer space, thus drastically reducing the mutation rate in living cells. This vast canopy is thought to have fallen down in the days of Noah causing the great Flood.

In addition to all this, there was in the beginning no death! Death only came into the world when sin came into the world (Rom 5:12; 8:22). Man would have lived forever had he not sinned, and so apparently would the animals (at least all those possessing the *nepesh*, the "soul"). Plant life, of course, is not conscious life, but only very complex replicating chemicals. The eating of fruits and herbs was not to considered "death" of the plant materials since they had no created "life" (in the sense of consciousness) anyhow.

All this has changed now. Decay and death came with the Curse, and the antedilivian environment changed to the present environmental economy at the time of the great Flood. [22]

The third day of creation deals only with the origin of plants, and Dr. Morris has a footnote explaining why the origin of plants cannot properly be understood as the origin of life, at least in the biblical sense:

> The exact boundary line between unconscious replicating chemical systems and creatures that have life in the biblical sense (that is, creatures possessing *nepesh*) is not yet clear from either science or Scripture. It may be possible that some of the simpler invertebrate animals are in the former category. In the case of plants, at least, the fact that they were designed by God to used as food by men and animals means that they did not really possess life and therefore they could not "die." Death came into the world only as the result of man's sin (Rom 5:12). [23]

Dean Smalley

We scheduled only one meeting for the third day of creation which deals with the origin of life.

To summarize: Dr. Schonfield claimed that the basic chemicals of life, the twenty amino acids and the four bases of DNA, had evolved by chance alone in the "primordial soup." He claimed that this thesis had been demonstrated in two quite simple laboratory experiments by Stanley Miller and Lesley Orgel.

Fr. Staatz maintained that it was impossible to harmonize the biblical and the scientific accounts of the origin of life. He then described Teilhard de Chardin's "law of complexity-consciousness" (the more complex the arrangement of matter the more the consciousness), which he says, makes the origin of life less of a problem to theologians than formerly. This notion, he said, while similar to scientific proposals concerning the origin of life, has the advantage of knowing where emerging life is ultimately tending - to Omega or God.

Mrs Stepan said that the chemicals in non-living matter are always half left-handed and half right-handed, while those in living matter are only left-handed. She claimed that this phenomenon, which she referred to as the "thumbprint of the Creator," precluded the possiblity of life having arisen by chance alone, but pointed to a directing Intelligence. Mrs. Stepan then, Fr. Staatz notwithstanding, proposed a harmony between contemporary science and the biblical account of the third day. She said that the phrase "let the dry land appear," could easily be harmonized with the Continental Drift Theory, which postulates that all the land masses of the earth were once gathered together into one place called *Pangea*. She also claimed that the phrase "And *God* said, 'Let the earth bring forth the (left-handed) vegetation,'" could easily be harmonized with contemporary science. Matter, she claimed, the "earth," has an intrinsic potency to life, but that tendency has to be directed, not by chance, but by God.

Rev. Swezey by a simple demonstration in probability math, proposed that the most rudimentary form of life, a simple protein composed of a chain of 400 amino acids, could not possibly have arisen by chance even in 30 billion years, let alone the 4.5 billion years currently claimed as the age of the earth. He then offered a strictly literal interpretation of the biblical statement that death did not enter the world until after the Fall of our first parents. This implies, he said, that both men and animals would have been immortal, and since they would have lived on plants, and there could be no death before the Fall, plants should not be considered living, but rather complex replicating chemicals.

This concludes our discussion on the third day of creation.

REFERENCES

1 Jacob Bronowski, *The Ascent of Man,*
   Little, Brown and Co., Boston, 1973, pp.309,310.
2 Bronowski, *Op. cit.*, P.313.
3 Francis Darwin, editor of: *The Life and Letters of Charles Darwin,*
   John Murray, London, 1887, p.18.
4 *Idem*, pp.314,316.

5 *Idem*, p.316.
6 Ignatius Hunt, o.s.b., *Understanding the Bible,*
   Sheed and Ward, New York, 1962, pp.46,47.
7 Owen Garrigan, *Man's Intervention in Nature,*
   Hawthorne Books, New York, 1967, pp.76-78.
8 Robert Faricy, s.j., *Teilhard de Chardin's Theology of the Christian
   in the World,* Sheed and Ward, New York, 1967, pp.44,45.
9 George Salet, *Hasard et Certitude,*
   Editions Scientifiques, Paris, pp.288,289.
10 Salet, *Op. cit.*, p.290.
11 *Idem*, p.290.
12 J. Tuzo, *Land Masses in Motion,*
   The Book of Popular Science, Vol. 2,
   Grolier, New York, 1972, pp.164,165.
13 George Alexander, *How Life on Earth Began,*
   Reader's Digest, November, 1982, p.120,
   Pleasantville, N.Y.
14 Henry Korin, c.s.sp., *An Introduction to the Philosophy of Animate Nature,*
   Herder Book Co., St. Louis, 1955, p.286.
15 Korin, *Op. cit.* pp.287,289.
16 St. Thomas Aquinas, *Summa Theologica*, (I, Q69, a2),
   Benziger Brothers, New York, 1947, pp.344,345.
17 St. Thomas Aquinas, *Op. cit.*, (I, Q70, a3, ad3), pp.348,349.
18 *Idem*, (I, Q70, a1, ad4), p.347.
19 *Idem*, pp.290,291.
20 Henry Morris, *Scientific Creationism,*
   Creation-Life Publishers, San Diego, Cal., 1974, p.59.
21 Morris, *Op. cit.*, pp.61,62.
22 *Idem*, p.211.
23 *Idem*, p.208.

THE FOURTH DAY

The Origin of the Sun, Moon, and Stars

Creation of the Sun and Moon and the Plants

"In this fresco Michaelangelo takes up and renews in a completely different manner, the medieval custom of representing various phases of the same story against a single background, as the fifteenth century artists had already done in various occasions in the Sistine Chapel itself. On the right the Creator breaks forward with open arms, and all the superhuman force of his body is re-echoed in the austere concentrated expression of the features. On the right emerges the gilded globe of the sun, on the left the silvery moon, and the angels gaze wondering at these new bodies risen out of the void. In the same panel, on the left, God having made the earth brings forth plants (represented by one green bush), moves away into space - shown from behind, in very bold foreshortening - to continue the Six Days' work. The figure which was almost diaphanous in the first panel of the *Creation of Light*, takes on here a plastic compactness which will increase as the frescos proceed, as if revealing Himself ever more clearly, to show Himself at last in man in His own likeness, as a father."

D. Redig de Campos, *Cappella Sistina*

THE SIXTH MEETING
The Galileo Case

Dean Smalley

Good evening. Tonight we come to the fourth day of creation, which deals with the origin of the sun, moon and stars. At our preliminary discussions we considered devoting this meeting to the origin of the solar system, but finally decided since we had quite thoroughly studied the origin of the universe on the second day, it would be more appropriate, considering the aims of our dialogue, to devote this meeting to the Galileo Case. We also plan a second meeting for this day dealing with the topic of Extraterrestrial Intelligence. Let me begin tonight's meeting with a reading of the Scriptural account of the fourth day of creation:

> And God said, "Let there be lights in the firmament of the heavens to separate the day from the night; and let them be for signs and for seasons and for days and years, and let them be lights in the firmament of the heavens to give light upon the earth." And it was so. And God made the two great lights, the greater light to rule the day, and the lesser light to rule the night; he made the stars also. And God set them in the firmament of the heavens to give light upon the earth, to rule over the day and over the night, and to separate the light from the darkness. And God saw that it was good. And there was evening and there was morning a fourth day (Gen 1:14-19).

Dr. Arthur Schonfield

Jacob Bronowski devoted one entire program in his TV series *The Ascent of Man* to the famous case of Galileo Galilei, which gives us some idea of its importance in the eyes of the humanists. Dr. Bronowski began with a description of the geocentric or earth-

161

centered system, of the ancient Greek astronomer, Ptolemy. This system lasted until the time of the Renaissance when Nicholas Copernicus proposed his heliocentric or sun-centered system, which was vigorously championed by Galileo. Today, of course, the sun has been demoted from the center of the universe to the center of the solar system, while our solar system itself has been tucked away in a somewhat obscure corner of the Milky Way Galaxy. So, while the astronomy of the Galileo Case, a geocentric versus a heliocentric universe, is now *passé*, the real issue involved in the case, the attempt of the Church to dominate science, is still very much with us, as is evident from the recent trials concerning the teaching of evolution in the public schools.

So let me turn now to Dr. Bronowski, who explains that the Galileo Case can only be understood against the background of the great wars of religion which were raging at the time:

> The successes of the Protestant Reformation in the sixteenth century had caused the Catholic Church to mount a fierce Counter-Reformation. The reaction against Luther was in full cry: the struggle in Europe was for authority. In 1618 the Thirty Years War began. In 1622 Rome created the institution for the propagation of the faith from which we derive the word *propaganda*. Catholics and Protestants were embattled in what we should now call a cold war, in which, if Galileo had only known it, no quarter was given to a great man or small. The judgment was very simple on both sides: whoever is not for us is - a heretic. Even so unworldly an interpreter of faith as Cardinal Bellarmine had found the astronomical speculations of Giordano Bruno intolerable, and sent him to the stake. The Church was a great temporal power, and in that bitter time it was fighting a political crusade in which all means were justified by the end - the ethics of the police state.
>
> Galileo seems to me to have been strangely innocent about the world of politics, and most innocent in thinking that he could outwit it because he was clever. For twenty years and more, he moved along a path that led inevitably to his condemnation. It took a long time to undermine him but there was never any doubt that Galileo would be silenced, because

the division between him and those in authority was absolute. They believed that faith should dominate; and Galileo believed that truth should persuade. [1]

In the television presentation of the Galileo Case, we saw Dr. Bronowski in the "Secret Vatican Archives," where he opened a small safe and took out several documents:

...Every political trial has a long hidden history of what went on behind the scenes. And the underground history of what came before the trial lies in the locked Secret Archives of the Vatican. Among all these corridors of documents, there is one modest safe in which the Vatican keeps what it regards as the crucial documents. Here, for example, is the application of Henry VIII for divorce - the refusal of which brought the Reformation to England, and ended the tie to Rome. The trial of Giordano Bruno has not left many documents, for the bulk were destroyed; but what exists is here.

And there is the famous Codex 1181, *Proceedings Against Galileo Galilei.* The trial was in 1633. And the first remarkable thing is that the documents begin - when? In 1611, at the moment of Galileo's triumph in Venice, in Florence, and here in Rome, secret information was being laid against Galileo before the Holy Office of the Inquisition. The evidence of the earliest document, not in this file, is that Cardinal Bellarmine instigated inquiries against him. Reports are filed in 1613, 1614, and 1615. By then Galileo himself becomes alarmed. Unbidden, he goes to Rome in order to persuade his friends among the Cardinals not to prohibit the Copernican world system.

But it is too late. In February 1616, here are the formal words as they stand in the draft in the Codex, freely translated:

"Propositions to be forbidden: that the sun in immovable at the center of the heaven; that the earth is not at the center of the heaven, and is not immovable, but moves by a double motion."

Galileo seems to have escaped any severe censure himself. At any rate, he is called before the great Cardinal Bellarmine and he is convinced, and has a letter to say that he must not hold or defend the Copernican World System - but here the document stops. Unhappily there is a document here in the record which goes further, and on which the trial is going to turn. But that is all seventeen years in the future. [2]

Galileo went back to Florence in 1616 determined to wait for a more propitious moment to introduce the Copernican system. Cardinal Bellarmine died in 1621 and in 1628 Galileo thought his time had come. One of his admirers, Cardinal Nicholas Baberini, was elected Pope taking the name of Urban VIII. Galileo hurried down to Rome hoping to persuade the new Pope to lift the prohibition of 1616 against the Copernican system. He had six long private interviews with Urban but was not completely successful.

Galileo finally proposed that he write a dialogue in which one speaker presented the Ptolemaic system and another the Copernican. The Pope, somewhat reluctantly, agreed provided that Galileo not come down too hard for either system, but allow the dialogue to end in a draw. He also insisted that he bring out that neither system could be considered absolutely true, since it would limit the power of God to run the universe by miracle if He so chose.

The *Dialogue on the Great World Systems* appeared in 1632 and was a complete disaster for Galileo. The Ptolemaic spokesman, who had been made to look like a fool throughout, set forth at the end the proviso which was so dear to the Pope. Urban was outraged, thinking that the Ptolemaic spokesman, who was named Simplicius, was a caricature of himself, and that Galileo was mocking him. Galileo was summoned to Rome to stand trial. In the TV production Bronowski was seated in the room where the trial actually took place.

So, on 12 April 1633, Galileo was brought into this room, sat at this table, and answered questions from the Inquisitor. The questions were addressed to him courteously in the intellectual atmosphere which reigned in the Inquisition - in Latin, in the third person. How was he brought to Rome? Is this his book? How did he come to write it? What is in his book? All these questions Galileo expected; he expected to defend the book. But then came a question which he did not expect...

Galileo has a signed document which says that he was forbidden only to hold or defend the theory of Copernicus as though it were a proven matter of fact. That was a prohibition laid on every Catholic at the time. The Inquisition claims that there is a document which prohibits Galileo, and Galileo alone, to teach it *in any way whatsoever* - that is, even by way of discussion or speculation or as a hypothesis. The Inquisition does not have to produce this document. That is not part of the rules of procedure. But we have the document; it is in the Secret Archives, and it is manifestly a forgery - or, at the most charitable, a draft for some suggested meeting which was rejected. It is not signed by Cardinal Bellarmine. It is not signed by the witnesses. It is not signed by the notary. It is not signed by Galileo to show that he received it.

Did the Inquisition really have to stoop to the use of legal quibbles between "hold and defend," or "teach in any way whatsoever," in the face of documents which could not have stood up in any court of law? Yes, it did. There was nothing else to do. The book had been published; it had been passed by several censors. The Pope could rage at the censors now - he ruined his own Secretary because he had been helpful to Galileo. But some remarkable public display had to be made to show that the book was to be condemned (it was on the Index for two hundred years) *because of some deceit practiced by Galileo.* This was why the trial avoided any matters of substance, either in the book or in Copernicus, and was bent on juggling with formulae and documents. Galileo was to appear deliberately to have tricked the censors, and to have acted not only defiantly but dishonestly. [3]

I think the most powerful scene in the TV production was a closeup of the creaking wheels of a rack, and in the background the agonized voice of a man describing his torture on that infernal machine:

> ...Galileo was to retract; and he was to be shown the instruments of torture as though they were to be used. What that threat meant to a man who had started life as a doctor we can judge from the testimony of a contemporary who had actually suffered the rack and survived it. That was William Lithgow, an Englishman who had been racked in 1620 by the Spanish Inquisition:

> "I was brought to the rack, then mounted on top of it. My legs were drawn down through the two sides of the three-planked rack. A chord was tied about my ankles. As the levers bent forward, the main force of my knees against the two planks burst asunder the sinews of my hams, and the lids of my knees were crushed. My eyes began to startle, my mouth to foam and froth, and my teeth to chatter like the doubling of a drummer's sticks. My lips were shivering, my groans were vehement, and the blood sprang from my arms, broken sinews, hands, and knees. Being loosed from these pinacles of pain, I was hand-fast set on the floor, with this incessant imploration: 'Confess! Confess!'"

> Galileo was not tortured. He was only threatened with torture twice. His imagination could do the rest. This was the object of the trial, to show men of imagination that they were not immune from the process of primitive animal fear that was irreversible. [4]

Dr. Bronowski concluded with a summary of the inevitable results of the condemnation of Galileo - the end, for all practical purposes, of the tradition of science in the Catholic countries of Europe.

> Galileo was confined for the rest of his life in his villa in Arcetri at some distance from Florence, under strict house arrest. The Pope was implacable. Nothing was to be

published. The forbidden doctrine was not to be discussed. Galileo was not even to talk to Protestants. The result was silence among Catholic scientists everywhere from then on. Galileo's greatest contemporary, René Descartes, stopped publishing in France and finally went to Sweden.

Galileo made up his mind to do one thing. He was going to write the book that the trial had interrupted: the *New Sciences*, by which he meant physics, not in the stars, but concerning matter here on earth. He finished it in 1636, that is, three years after the trial, an old man of seventy-two. Of course he could not get it published, until finally some Protestants in Leyden in the Netherlands printed it two years later. By that time Galileo was totally blind. He writes of himself:

"Alas...Galileo, your devoted friend and servant, has been for a month totally and incurably blind; so that this heaven, this earth, this universe, which by my remarkable observations and clear demonstrations I have enlarged a hundred, nay a thousand fold beyond the limits universally accepted by the learned men of all previous ages, are now shrivelled up for me into such a narrow compass as is filled by my own bodily sensations."

Among those who came to see Galileo at Arcetri was the young poet John Milton from England preparing for his life's work, an epic poem that he planned. It is ironic that by the time Milton came to write the great poem, thirty years later, he also was dependent on his children to help him finish it.

Milton at the end of his life idenitified himself with Samson Agonistes, Samson among the Philistines

"Eyeless in Gaza at the Mill with slaves,"

who destroyed the Philistine empire at the moment of his death. And that is what Galileo did, against his own will. The effect of the trial and of the imprisonment was to put a total stop to the scientific tradition in the Mediterranean. From now on, the Scientific Revolution moved to Northern Europe. Galileo died, still a prisoner in his house, in 1642. On Christmas Day of the same year, in England, Isaac Newton was born. [5]

It was the great synthesis of Newton built on the works of Copernicus and Galileo which would finally convince the world of the truth of the heliocentric system. And so concluded the most famous of the attempts by religion to dominate science, which had it been successful would have ended the scientific revolution at its very inception. But the recent court cases in Arkansas and elsewhere on creationism versus evolutionism in the public schools indicate that the battle is not yet completely won.

Fr. Robert A. Staatz

The Galileo Case was very much on the minds of the Council Fathers during the Second Vatican Council. Let me read a few excerpts from *Man's Intervention in Nature* one of the volumes in *The Twentieth Century Encyclopedia of Catholicism* by Fr. Owen Garrigan, a professor of chemistry at Seton Hall University. These excerpts, however, are from the Preface which was written by Fr. Francis Nead, the Chairman of the Department of Theology at Seton Hall:

> With the words "One Galileo trial is enough for the Church," Cardinal Suenens took formal notice at Vatican II of the death of an age...The adolescence of religious man is finished. He is on the threshold of maturity. His childhood was marked by extensive ignorance of the real nature both of his world and of God. So in his fear he confused the two. His adolescent period saw the growth of his awareness that the world has its own immanent laws...
> Those who thought they knew God well turned upon the rash discoverers of the world's immanent forces in righteous indignation. They condemned Galileo and announced a state of war between science and religion. They cited God's holy word in support of their fulminations. Galileo was perplexed.

He could not see, he said, why there was religious opposition
to his theories. What difference does it make for man's
eternal salvation whether the sun turns around the earth or
vice versa? He was right. His judges had made a mistake. As
they studied God's word they learned more about its real
meaning...

The Pastoral Constitution "On the Church in the Modern
World" of Vatican II rings with repeated assertions of the solidarity of the Church with developments in today's world. She
does not chide, bemoan the "death of religion," seek to call
men back to former times, lament the disappearance of her
influence. In her new consciousness of self and in fuller
freedom she ratifies the transition from a sacral to a secular
world. She declares her union with secular man struggling to
subject the world to himself...

The Constitution sounds a belated (but necessary) warning
to Christians about a warlike attitude evidenced even now.
"We cannot but deplore certain habits of mind, which are
sometimes found, too, among Christians, which do not sufficiently attend to the rightful independence of science and
which, from the arguments and controversies they spark, lead
many minds to conclude that faith and science are mutually
opposed."

Led by Scripture scholars, theology has entered into a new
freedom, which is to say, a fuller maturity. It is ready to enter
into an open and genuine dialogue with man's natural aware-
ness of himself and the world. Freed by its realizing that there
are sources of religious knowledge outside of historical revelation, theology is ready to listen as the sciences speak of
themselves. [6]

One of the discoveries by Scripture scholars mentioned by Fr.
Nead which has led theology to a new maturity is that of "literary
forms." We have seen that the Hexameron is a purified form of the
Enuma elish myth, which means that it does not contain historical,
but rather religious truth. Now, while we are on the subject of
literary forms, we had better take a look at the famous so-called
"miracle of the sun," which is in the background of the whole

Galileo Case. Here is the story as it is told in the Book of Joshua:

> Then spoke Joshua to the Lord in the day when the Lord gave the Amorites over to the men of Israel; in the sight of Israel:
> "Sun, stand thou still at Gibeon,
> and thou Moon in the valley of Aijalon."
> And the sun stood still, and the moon stayed,
> until the nation took vengeance on their enemies.
> Is it not written in the book of Jashar? The sun stayed in the midst of heaven, and did not hasten to go down for about a whole day. There had been no day like it before or since, when the Lord hearkened to the voice of a man, for the Lord fought for Israel (Jos 10:12-14).

Let me turn now to the biography *Robert Bellarmine*, by the Jesuit historian James Broderick. Bellarmine, as we have heard from Dr. Bronowski, was very much involved in the Galileo Case. Here is Broderick on the so-called "miracle of the sun":

> The texts have been a difficulty to biblical exegetes all through the centuries. But since the publication by Pius XII in 1943 of *Divino Afflante Spiritu*, there has been a great and salutary revival in Catholic biblical criticism, due largely to the Pope's sanction of the conception of "literary forms" of various kinds, poetry, epic, history, legend, allegory, each with its own form of truth, in the construction of the Scriptures.
> Archaeology developed at an extraordinary rate since the Second World War and brought to light much new knowledge of the great pagan civilizations, in the midst of which the Hebrew people grew to political maturity and were in many ways effected by the cultures of the nations around them. The Book of Joshua is now seen to be peculiarly rich in "literary forms." The difficult chapter x is "epic history." The capture of Jericho, and the battle of Gabaon as described by the sacred writer, are not history in the modern Western sense of the word, but have the strictly religious design of exalting

the greatness of Yahweh.

[Footnote] "An ancient poem containing an incantation to the sun and the moon is first cited and then transferred into a story. The narrator thus adds to the victory of Gabaon a detail calculated to fill the hearers with admiration: The day of victory was the longest that men had ever seen." [7]

So for us there is no problem of whether the sun stood still or the earth stood still as was the case in Galileo's time. Here is Broderick's summary of his fellow Jesuit, Robert Bellarmine, and the unfortunate role he played in the Galileo Case:

It would obviously be anachronistic and unfair to judge Robert Bellarmine's views on Scripture and the Fathers of the Church by the standards of modern Catholic biblical criticism, especially as developed since the publication of Pope Pius xii's encyclical *Divino Afflante Spiritu* in 1943 - curiously the fourth centenary of the publication of *De Revolutionibus Orbium Caelestium* [Copernicus' book on the heliocentric system]. The development of Christian doctrine has been a continuous process since the Apostolic age, as the implications of divine Revelation became clearer to the Church under the guidance of the Holy Spirit; and much is obvious now to the instructed Catholic mind which was far from plain even to so great a man as Bellarmine. But, it might be asked, how does the Cardinal stand when judged by the standards of such highly intelligent Catholics of his own age as Galileo himself, Foscarini, the Jesuit Pereira, and others? The answer must surely be not too well. For instance, when he [Bellarmine] says that "the Council of Trent forbids the interpretation of the Scriptures in a way contrary to the common opinion of the Fathers," Galileo was able to reply with the very words of the conciliar Fathers at the fourth session, held on April 9, 1546: "So far as I can find," he wrote in the *Letter to the Grand Duchess Christina*, "all that is prohibited is the 'perverting into senses contrary to that of holy mother Church, or that of the unanimous agreement of the Fathers, matters of faith and morals pertaining to the upbuilding...of Christian doctrine.' But the mobility or stability of the earth or sun is neither a matter of faith nor contrary to morals." As for "the common opinion of the Fathers" in the matter of the earth's stability, Galileo again scores heavily against St. Robert whose principles of patristic interpretation were very superficial and not accepted by some good theologians of his own time, e.g. the Spanish Augustinian Didacus à Stunica, in his *Commentary on the Book of Job*, published at Toledo in 1584, or the Jesuit Pereira *On Genesis*, or the Carmelite Foscarini...

Bellarmine's rather "fundamentalist" views were not special to him. They were widespread at the time and, in a sense inevitable, owing to the cautionary and defensive attitude with regard to the Scriptures forced on the Church by the Protestant revolution. [8]

Finally, I would like to read Broderick's comments on the infamous document, mentioned by Dr. Bronowski, that was used to bring about Galileo's condemnation in 1633:

What then is to be made of the document dated February 26 in the Vatican files and produced by the prosecution in 1633 in proof that Galileo had been given a absolute injunction by the Commissary of the Holy Office, in 1616?...The dark truth of the matter...is that the document...is not an original text but somebody's concoction, probably that same year, to embroil Galileo with the Inquisition should he at any time seek to maintain Copernicanism as a physical reality.

The bogus injunction is in the same handwriting as that of neighboring and certainly genuine documents, so the man responsible must have been some unscrupulous curial offical hostile to Galileo, now impossible to identify. He succeeded beyond his wildest hopes seventeen years later, when his imaginary injunction was produced as a trump card against the unfortunate astronomer during his trial in Rome. He was taken completely by surprise, and maintained that he had never been given such an injunction. In proof, he produced

Cardinal Bellarmine's certificate in 1616; and it is incomprehensible if the Dominican Commissary Firenzuola in 1633 was really trying to discover the truth and not predetermined on a verdict of guilty, that he should not have seen the complete incompatibility between the false injunction and St. Robert's certificate. [9]

Let me conclude with the somewhat similar case of Teilhard de Chardin. The spirit of the Inquisition which persecuted Galileo is very much alive in the Church today, as is evident from the troubles of Fathers Kung and Schillebeeckx over their progressive theology. But it is even more in evidence in what amounted to a lifetime persecution of Teilhard on the part of the Roman authorities.

Teilhard's troubles first began in 1924 when he was teaching at the *Institut Catholique* in Paris over a paper he had written on the subject of original sin. We will see later when we come to the sixth day of creation, which deals with the origin of man, that Teilhard did not believe in the historicity of the biblical story of Adam and Eve, since it is incompatible with the scientific fact of the evolution of man. This means that the doctrine of original sin will have to be reformulated. His paper on original sin somehow found its way to Rome, and Teilhard was compelled by his superiors to sign a retraction against his will, and was eventually exiled to China - in other words, an almost exact replay of the Galileo Case.

Teilhard spent twenty years in China, yet his exile backfired because, when he returned to France after the Communist takeover in China, he found that he had become a sort of folk hero to both the scientific community and the progressive element in the Church, which saw him as a modern day Galileo. He was showered with honors including an offer of a professorship at the prestigious *College de France*, France's highest academic honor. The Roman authorities, however, would not allow him to accept the post and once again he was ordered to leave the country. Here is Teilhard's biographer, Robert Speaight:

The Roman theologians, Teilhard thought, were less important in themselves than for what they represented; and he met their intransigience with serenity. "I am prepared to go on to the end," he said, "and with a smile if possible." What put him out of patience, and momentarily out of temper, was the invitation of an ex-religious to join a small dissident community of freethinkers. If the people said to him, as they sometimes did: "Your religion is admirable, but it is not the Catholic religion," he would answer severely: "Do you think me mad enough to want to found a new religion, or to imagine myself a second Jesus Christ?" There are still Catholics who doubt whether Teilhard's religion was the religion of the Church which he claimed to serve; but if the authorities of that Church are alarmed by the expansion of his ideas, they have only themselves to thank. The *consensus fidelium* - and *infidelium* - does not, in the case of Pierre de Chardin, amount to unanimity, but it has given a pretty reverberating answer to tribunals who pronounce, in secret, sentences against which there is no appeal. [10]

Teilhard did not have to wait 200 years, the way Galileo did, to have his books taken off the Index. Immediately after his death his humanist friends got together and published his works which had been forbidden by Rome. These have met with astonishing success among humanists and Christians alike. Finally the Church herself, not more than ten years after his death, has made many of his teachings her own in the decrees of the Second Vatican Council, especially the famous *Gaudium et Spes*, the Pastoral Constitution on the Church in the Modern World.

To the new and acrid secularism of the West, the Church in which Teilhard never ceased to believe has replied with a dramatic *aggiornamento*. Nothing that Teilhard said in public or in private - and much that he did not say - was left unsaid at the Second Vatican Council. Much that he clamored for was implied or incorporated in its decrees. When he wrote of inspiration that "it is not limited to the composition of a text, but it envelopes that text and *lives* in it to the extent that the Church very slowly understands it," he was stating what is now a theological commonplace. If Teilhard were alive today, he would accept his *reclame* with such equanimity as his modesty allowed; but he would find his optimism vindicated in the popularity and progress of his ideas. [11]

Not to be outdone by the final triumph of Teilhard de Chardin, I would like to conclude on a hopeful note concerning Teilhard's prototype, Galileo. There is underway in Rome today, at long last, a movement to reopen the Galileo Case, and thus bring about the complete exoneration of that unfortunate scientist. Let me conclude with a few excerpts from an address given in November of 1979 by Pope John Paul II to the Pontifical Academy of Science:

> [Galileo] had to suffer a great deal - we cannot conceal the fact - at the hands of men and organisms of the Church. The Vatican Council recognized and deplored certain unwarranted interventions: "We cannot but deplore - it is written in number 36 of the conciliar constitution *Gaudium et Spes* - certain attitudes (not unknown among Christians) deriving from a shortsighted view of the rightful autonomy of science; they have occasioned conflict and controversy and misled many into thinking that faith and science are opposed." The reference to Galileo is clearly expressed in the note to this text, which cites the volume *Vita e opere di Galileo Galilei* by Msgr. Pio Paschini, published by the Pontifical Academy of Science.
>
> To go beyond this stand taken by the Council, I hope that theologians, scholars and historians, animated by a spirit of sincere collaboration, will study the Galileo Case more deeply and, in loyal recognition of wrongs from whatever side they come, will dispel the mistrust that still opposes, in many minds, a fruitful concord between science and faith, between the Church and the world. I give all my support to this task, which will be able to honor the truth of faith and of science and open the door to future collaboration. [12]

True to his word the Pope has set up a mixed commission of theologians, scientists, and historians, who are currently re-examining the Case.

Mrs. Maria Stepan

Before I approach the fourth day I would like to comment on
Dr. Morris' biblical interpretation of the third day of creation. If
you remember, I had originally given from the philosopher Fr.
Korin, what I thought would have been the fundamentalist
interpretation of the third day, namely that God would have
intervened directly by way of miracle without the benefit of
secondary causes in the production of life. I commented at the
time that while this position was reasonable, I did not think it
probable. But the position actually brought forward by Dr.
Morris I think is not only improbable but also unreasonable. Dr.
Morris said that death did not enter the world until after the fall of
our first parents. Men would have been immortal and, apparently,
he said, the animals as well. Therefore the plants could not have
been alive, since they would have died when eaten by men and
animals. So plants, according to Dr. Morris, do not possess life, at
least in the biblical sense. Now this interpretation, that plants are
not alive, puts the creationists in some very strange company. So
let me turn to a standard text entitled *Psychology: A Class Manual
in the Philosophy of Organic and Rational Life* by Msgr. Paul
Glenn:

> There have been in times past, and indeed there are today,
> physicists (from the atomists of ancient Greece to the
> Cartesians of the past three centuries and the materialists of
> the present) who maintain that plants are not alive at all. But
> this contention stands fully confuted by the fact that plants
> have life-activity, and hence a life-principle, and therefore life
> itself. Plants are alive. The plant has its own fixed and
> determinate mode of action, and its action is really its own: it
> is immanent action, performed by, in, and for the plant itself;
> it is action originated by the plant, directed by the plant, and
> finished by the plant. Thus, for example, a plant takes food or
> nourishment, and shows a nice discrimination in selecting and
> assimilating what suits its nature. It transforms the food into
> its own substance, building and maintaining the various parts
> of a highly complex and delicately interbalanced whole. Now

no operation of lifeless bodies or of lifeless forces (physical, chemical, mechanical) is thus self-originating and self-directive and self-perfective. Chemical affinites, physical union, gravitation, cohesion, inertia, electrical vibration or impulse, local movements, - all these and all other lifeless forces or energies are, in non-living bodies, exercised by the wholly *extrinsic* influence of one bodily thing upon another, even when this influence ends in the substantial union or fusion of the bodies in question. There is nothing *self*-directive in lifeless activities considered in themselves. There is in them no inner drive or tendency to keep on functioning for the benefit of the bodies in which they are found; there is rather the tendency excited externally or extrinsically, to exercise their mutual function *and have done with it*; there is a tendency to equilibrium, and rest and inertia. Thus lifeless forces are always *transient* and extrinsic in their manifested activity; they show no tendency towards development, preservation, and propagation in themselves or in the bodies which they affect. Living bodies, on the contrary, tend, not to equilibrium and rest, but to continuous, unremmiting, self-perfective action; and the plant is, on this score, a truly living body. [13]

The idea that in the state of innocence carnivorous animals, such as lions, ate plants rather than flesh, would have to have been miraculous, since these animals can't now assimilate grass. They don't chew their cud or have the three-chambered stomachs of cows and other herbivores. St. Thomas Aquinas would consider this opinion improbable, though not of course, impossible:

> In the opinion of some, those animals which are now fierce and kill others, would in that state, have been tame, not only in regard to man, but also in regard to other animals. But this is quite unreasonable. For the nature of animals was not changed by man's sin, as if those whose nature it is to devour the flesh of others, would have then lived on herbs. [14]

I should also point out that St. Thomas would not agree with

Dr. Morris' overly literal rendering of the effects of the Curse on Adam and on the earth. "Cursed is the earth in thy work...thorns and thistles shall it bring forth to thee"(Gen 3:17,18). St. Thomas did not think that thorns and thistles appeared on the earth by a special creation after the fall of our first parents. He thought that noxious plants were created at the same time as beneficial plants, but by God's Providence, they would not have harmed Adam and Eve in the state of innocence:

> Even before the earth was accursed, the thorns and thistles had been produced, either virtually or actually. But they were not produced in punishment of man; as though the earth, which he tilled to gain his food, produced unfruitful and noxious plants. Hence it was said: "Shall it bring forth to thee." [15]

Let me go on to our subject for this evening, the Galileo Case. The liberal Protestant biblical scholar, Rudolf Bultman, began a campaign against the historicity of the Gospels which he called "demythologizing." This campaign has, unfortunately, been taken over by liberal Catholics, and a good example of it is their attitude toward Joshua's "miracle of the sun." We heard Fr. Broderick, in the face of all Catholic Tradition, assign this miracle to the literary genre of "epic history," a euphemism for myth. But what really needs to be demythologized is the humanist account of the relations between the Church and Science, a good example of which is the humanist myth regarding the Galileo Case.

Now all it should take, theoretically at least, to refute a mythological account of an historical event, is a simple recitation of the historical facts. So I thought I would depart tonight from my usual format of commenting first on Dr. Schonfield's presentation and then on Fr. Staatz's, and offer a simple presentation of the historical facts in the Galileo Case. But we need to have at least a minimum background in astronomy in order to be able to follow the Case, so let's begin with the Greek astronomer Ptolemy, who lived in Alexandria around 150 A.D. Ptolemy's geocentric or earth-centered system made possible for the first time accurate predictions of eclipses, conjunctions of the planets, and so forth. His system lasted for about 1200 years, which is quite a tribute to his genius.

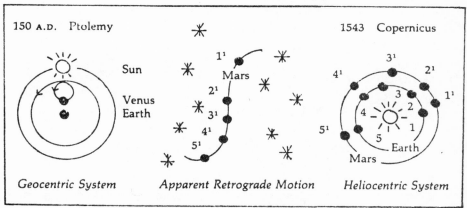

Plate VIII   *Geocentric and Heliocentric Systems*

In the illustration on the blackboard, I have indicated in the middle what is called the "apparent retrograde motion" of the planets. As we observe the planets, they appear to move back and forth against the background of the fixed stars. This is why they are called "planets," from the Greek word for "wanderer." To explain this motion, Ptolemy proposed that the planets were moving in "epicycles," another Greek word meaning "a circle upon a circle." In other words, the planets, as they were circling the earth, were looping the loop. I have indicated the planet Venus executing one of these loops. These epicycles explained the apparent retrograde motion of the planets. As the planet moved forward, and at the same time down on one of its loops, it appeared to be going backward; but as it came to the top of its loop, it appeared to be going forward. This was an ingenious mathematical explanation, but the physics of it just wouldn't work. Imagine if a baseball pitcher could throw a ball in such a way that just as it got to the plate it looped the loop. Every game would be a no-hitter!

In 1543 Nicholas Copernicus, a Polish priest, proposed his heliocentric or sun-centered system. This system offers a much simpler explanation of the apparent retrograde motion of the planets than the Ptolemaic system. In the diagram on the board, the sun is the center of the universe (it wasn't until much later that it was reduced to being just the center of the solar system) with the earth plus the planet Mars in orbit around it. From Position 1 on earth, we observe Mars at Position 1^1. At the next Position $2/2^1$, Mars appears to have gone ahead of earth; then at Position $3/3^1$, Mars appears to have fallen behind. It is like two racing cars on concentric tracks. From the point of view of the car on the inner track (earth), the car on the outer track (Mars) appears at one time to have fallen behind, and at another time to be catching up.

This is obviously a much simpler explanation than the complex Ptolemaic system, but the Copernican system had one serious flaw; all the orbits were perfect circles. This made the system useless for predictions of eclipses, conjunctions of planets, and so on. So, to make the system useful, Copernicus had to add his own system of epicycles, just as Ptolemy did. In all, he had 34 epicycles, four for the moon, three for the earth (which was something new), seven for Mercury, and five each for the other planets. Again, the physics of it just wouldn't work; you can't throw a baseball in such a way that it loops the loop. Copernicus' epicycles were just a crutch to make his system useful for predictions.

The Danish astronomer Tycho Brahe (d. 1601), was a Lutheran, but eventually became the court astronomer of the Catholic Emperor at Prague. One of Brahe's great contributions to astronomy was his study of comets. You can see how comets would be a tremendous problem in a universe such as Ptolemy's which was filled with crystalline spheres. A comet has a huge elliptical orbit, sometimes coming very close to the sun and then going way out beyond the orbit of Pluto, often taking hundreds of years in the process. A comet then, would have to pierce the crystalline spheres. For this reason Aristotle thought that comets were just atmospheric phenomena, well below the sphere of the moon. It is interesting to note that Galileo, whose whole crusade was against the Aristotelian Establishment of his day, rejected Brahe's interpretation of comets, and continued to hold all his life with Aristotle that they were just atmospheric phenomena.

Tycho Brahe never accepted the Copernican system because he

could never get a parallax on the fixed stars. Brahe took the angle a fixed star makes with the earth, and then six months later when the earth supposedly was on the other side of its orbit, he took the angle again. It was the same. This meant that either the stars were much further from us than had ever been thought, or that the earth was not moving. Brahe decided that the latter was the case. (Stellar parallax cannot be detected with the naked eye, but only with a very good telescope. It was not until 1838 that the astronomer Friedrich Bessel detected an almost infinitesimal parallax in the star 61 Cygni.) So Brahe proposed his own unique model of the universe based on a stationary earth.

In the Tychonic system, the earth is the center of the universe and the sun is going around it, but the inner planets, Mercury and Venus, are going around the sun. The Jesuits, who were among the outstanding scientists of the day, expected to see the eventual confirmation of the heliocentric system, but felt at the time it lacked sufficient proof to warrant its complete acceptance, and so adopted the Tychonic system as a transitional model.

Johannes Kepler (d. 1630) was a German, also a Lutheran, and he succeeded Brahe as court astronomer at Prague. Kepler discovered that the orbits of the planets were not perfect circles as Ptolemy and Copernicus thought, but rather ellipses. Kepler arrived at the elliptical concept by careful observation, begun by Brahe, of the planet Mars, over a period of many years. Kepler deduced from this that the orbits of all the planets were elliptical. He saw immediately that if the elliptical orbits, rather than perfect circles, were placed on the Copernican model, eclipses, and so on, could be predicted without the crutch of epicycles. This made it possible for the first time to figure out the physics of the heavens, and Kepler, who was a much greater astronomer than Galileo, wrote to him about his new discoveries, but Galileo continuously spurned Kepler's offers of friendly collaboration. To the end of his life, Galileo held fast to Copernicus' cumbersome epicycles. Galileo actually wrote: "To me and to me alone, it has been given to make all the discoveries in astronomy." It was this terrific arrogance which was the source of all Galileo's troubles with the Church.

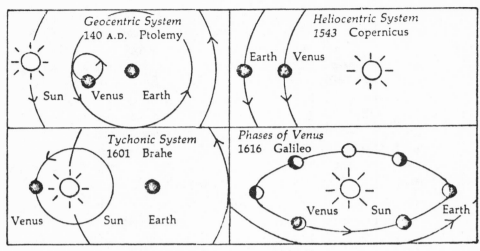

Plate IX   *Phases of Venus*

Galileo Galilei (d. 1642) was the first to study the heavens with a telescope, and the first to observe the phases of Venus, which he considered a convincing proof of the Copernican system. In the diagram on the board, on the lower right, we can see that when Venus is in front of the sun, it is in its crescent and gibbous phases. When it is to the left and right of the sun, it is in its half phase, and when directly behind the sun, in its full phase. As you can see in the Ptolemaic diagram (upper left), Venus is always in front of the sun, so it should always be in its crescent or gibbous phase. Thus Galileo's discovery finished the Ptolemaic system, but did it completely *prove* the heliocentric system? When Galileo appeared before St. Robert Bellarmine he claimed that he had convincingly proved the Copernican system by his discovery of the phases of Venus. St. Robert consulted the Jesuit astronomer Fr. Grienberger, who informed him that the phases of Venus could also be explained by the Tychonic system. You can see from the diagram on the board (lower left), that in the Tychonic system Venus also goes behind the sun. So St. Robert at the time (1616) allowed Galileo to hold the Copernican system as a working hypothesis but, because of Brahe's unresolved problem of stellar parallax, forbade him to claim it a proven fact, at least until he could produce something more convincing than the phases of Venus.

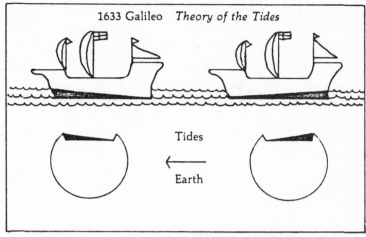

Plate x   *Galileo's Theory of the Tides*

Galileo soon came up with what he considered a final, conclusive proof of the Copernican system, his theory of the tides. Galileo was trying to show that the earth was moving through space, rather than stationary as in the Ptolemaic and Tychonic systems, so he compared the earth to a ship moving through the water. As a ship moved through the water, Galileo thought that the water in the bottom of the boat, the bilge, moved back and forth from one end of the boat to the other. So, as the earth moved through space, it caused the oceans to move back and forth in their basins in the action called tides. What is hard to believe is that Galileo apparently never tested this theory by experiment. He must have gotten the idea of the water in the boat by hearsay from sailors. Galileo, who was a genius at making experimental apparatus, could easily have rigged up something like a fishbowl on a hand cart, and then merely pushed the cart to see whether the water moved back and forth in the bowl. He would have found that, if he started the cart off slowly and had a smooth path, the water wouldn't have moved at all!

We have seen that Galileo's main opponents during his lifetime, what we would today call the Establishment, were the Aristotelians. Galileo despised Aristotelian science because it wasn't experimental but speculative, and often *a priori*. Now, here he is in what he would consider a typical Aristotelian type of argument, in complete violation of all his principles. What makes it worse is that Kepler had written him suggesting that the moon was the cause of the tides, the idea that Newton would later develop, but Galileo as usual spurned Kepler's proposal.

Armed with this new "proof," and with St. Robert Bellarmine now dead and a sympathetic Pope, Urban VIII, now reigning, Galileo hurried down to Rome to get permission to publish on the Copernican system. (He had been forbidden to publish by St. Robert.) He suggested to Urban that he present the problem in the form of a dialogue in which one speaker presented the Ptolemaic system and another the Copernican. Urban agreed, but told him not to endorse either system, but to let the dialogue end in a draw, since there was still the unresolved problem of stellar parallax. Galileo agreed, but unfortunately did not live up to his agreement. He had his Copernican spokesman utterly demolish the Ptolemaic speaker, his final climactic argument being his theory of the tides. Urban was understandably furious, and after learning from the Jesuit scientists at the University of Rome that Galileo's theory of the tides was just bad physics, he ordered Galileo to be tried by the Inquisition.

Galileo was condemned and sentenced to confinement at his estate near Florence for the rest of his life. It was here that he wrote his greatest book, which is not on astronomy, but on physics, entitled *Dialogue Concerning Two New Sciences*, in which he worked out for the first time some of the movements of earthly bodies. You will remember that Kepler had already worked out the physics of the heavenly bodies. It only remained for Isaac Newton to put these discoveries together. Using the new mathematical tool which he had invented, calculus, Newton for the first time developed a comprehensive physics that was the same for both the heavens and the earth. Of course, it is possible to speculate, that had Galileo not been so arrogant, and had he been able to collaborate with Kepler, the great Newtonian synthesis could have been reached years earlier.

So I am sure that after considering the facts in the Case, any fair-minded person would agree that Galileo should have been to called to task. Had he lived up to his agreement with Urban and treated each of the world systems in an equitable manner, there would have been no Galileo Case. Evidently he did not inform the censors of the substance of his agreement with the Pope, and thus was guilty of subterfuge in obtaining the *Imprimatur* ("Let it be printed"). Also possibly if he had been able to demonstrate the Copernican system convincingly, there would have been no Case, but his false theory of the tides was fatal.

The agreement that Galileo had made with Pope Urban was oral, and apparently there was no question of calling the Pope as a witness during the trial, but no Catholic will defend the questionable legal methods of the Inquisition, especially the use of the alleged absolute injunction of 1616. However this injunction was probably not a plot, as Fr. Broderick suggests, but the work of some officious secretary of Cardinal Bellarime, who drew it up and then placed it the Galileo file, despite its never having been issued. Galileo was a good Catholic despite his faults, and immediately submitted in 1616 to St. Robert's injunction to refrain from teaching the Copernican system as an established fact, and no further action was called for at that time.

Also any Catholic will admit that the heliocentric theory should not have been condemned, but will deny that the infallibility of the Church was involved in that condemnation. The decrees of a commission of Cardinals, even if approved by a Pope, are not infallible. Only the decrees of an ecumenical council - that is, a council representing all the bishops of the world, which are approved by a Pope are infallible, and then only in matters of faith and morals. The Pope is also personally infallible when he speaks *ex cathedra*: that is, when he solemnly announces that he is speaking infallibly, as for example in the definition of the Assumption of Our Blessed Lady, but again only in matters of faith and morals.

Although the Humanist Establishment has used the Galileo Case for years as a club to beat the Church, there have always been a few notable exceptions to this general rule. For instance, Thomas Henry Huxley, "Darwin's bulldog," went to Rome and examined the Case a little more thoroughly than the average humanist, probably intending to use it in his ongoing controversy with the Anglican bishop, Samuel Wilberforce. In a letter written to Mivart in 1885 he concluded, rather disappointedly, I presume - "I looked into the matter when I was in Italy and I arrived at the conclusion that the Pope and the College of Cardinals had rather the best of it. [21]

This opinion is much more common today among dissident humanists - Lewis Mumford, for example. But the best story I have come across about the Galileo Case is one which concerns the English journalist, Sherwood Taylor. Taylor was a member of the anti-Catholic Rationalist Society, one of the forerunners of today's Humanist Society in England, of which Dr. Bronowski was one of the Directors. (Incidentally, this same Humanist Society is currently engaged in yet another well-financed propaganda and political campaign against the Catholic school system in England - so much for their cry of "freedom of thought.") Sherwood Taylor was assigned by the Rationalist Society to write a book attacking the Church by means of the Galileo Case. After studying the Case, Taylor was converted and received into the Catholic Church - grace sometimes works in strange ways!

In conclusion, I agree with Fr. Staatz that it would probably be a good thing for the Church to review the facts in the Galileo Case, but the *facts*, not the myth. It is often claimed that science is autonomous, neutral, amoral, or whatever, but this is only in the abstract. In the real world, science is practiced by men possessed of a fallen nature like the rest of us. Scientific research should never become an end in itself, but always be subordinated to a higher good, the good of man, which is not always the good of science. This is no time for the Church to seem to abdicate its rightful duty to remind scientists of their moral responsibilities. Would that the Church still had the authority over scientists it possessed in the days of Galileo; we might not have the atomic bomb.

Rev. De Verne Swezey

Although Galileo is still considered a hero in establishment humanism, he is often considered a villain in counter-culture humanism. One of the favorite authors of many of the students with whom I work in my campus ministry is the philosopher and historian, the late Arthur Koestler. The students like him for the ease with which he deflates the dogmas of contemporary scientism. In 1959 Koestler brought out a wonderful book on the history of astronomy entitled *The Sleepwalkers*, which majors in the Galileo Case. We have just heard Mrs. Stepan's excellent attempt to "demythologize" the humanist version of the Case. Arthur Koestler begins in a similar fashion with a chapter entitled *A Digression on Mythography*:

> ...In rationalist mythography [Galileo appears] as the Maid of Orleans of Science, the St. George who slew the dragon of the Inquisition. It is therefore, hardly surprising that the fame of this outstanding genius rests mostly on discoveries he never made, and on feats which he never performed. Contrary to statements in even recent outlines of science, Galileo did not invent the telescope, nor the microscope, nor the thermometer, nor the pendulum clock. He did not discover the law of inertia, nor the parallelogram of forces or motions, nor the sun spots. He made no contribution to theoretical astronomy, he did not throw down weights from the leaning tower of Pisa, and did not prove the truth of the Copernican system. He was not tortured by the Inquisition, did not languish in its dungeons...and he was not a martyr of science. [17]

St. Robert Bellarmine is often presented by the humanists as one of the chief villains in the Galileo Case, usually with the concurrence of liberal Catholics such as Fr. Broderick who should know better. Here is Koestler, who is not a Christian, on Bellarmine:

> As an individual, Bellarmine was the opposite of what one would expect from a formidable theologian who defied popes and kings. He was a lover of music and the arts; he had lectured on astronomy in his youth. He had a simple manner and led a simple, ascetic life, in contrast to other princes of the Church; but above all he had a "childlike quality that was noted by all who came in contact with him." At the time of the Galileo controversy, he was writing a devotional book called *Lament of the Dove*, which his most ferocious

opponent, James I, in his later years constantly carried about his person, and described as a wonderful aid to spiritual comfort.

One of Bellarmine's official functions was that of a "Master of Controversial Questions" at the Roman College. Here he was in constant touch with the leading astronomers of the capital, Fathers Clavius and Grienberger, who had been among the first converts to Galileo's telescopic discoveries and had acclaimed him on his first visit to Rome. Thus it can hardly be said that Galileo's opposite number in the drama was an ignorant fanatic. Bellarmine's independence of mind is further illustrated by the fact that in 1590 his *magnus opus* the *Disputationes*, was temporarily put on the Index of Forbidden Books.

Sixteen years before he became involved with Galileo, Bellarmine had been one of the nine Cardinal Inquisitors who participated in the trial of Giordano Bruno, and some writers have tried to see a sinister connection between the two events. In fact, there is none. Bruno was burnt alive, on 16 February, 1600, under the most horrible circumstances on the Square of Flowers in Rome, as an impenitent apostate, who during seven years of imprisonment refused to abjure his theological heresies, and persisted in his refusal to the last moment. Giordano Bruno and Michael Servetus (burned in 1553, by the Calvinists in Geneva) seem to have been the only scholars of repute who became victims of religious intolerance in the sixteenth and seventeenth centuries - not of course, because of their scientific, but because of their religious, opinions. Coleridge's remark: "If ever a poor fanatic thrust himself into the fire, it was Michael Servetus," applies to the irascible and tempestuous Bruno as well. His teachings of the infinity of the universe and the plurality of inhabited worlds, his pantheism and universal ethics exerted considerable influence on subsequent generations; but he was a poet and a metaphysician, not a scientific writer, and thus does not enter into this narrative. [18]

If you remember Dr. Bronowski claimed that Cardinal

Bellarmine "had found the astronomical speculations of Giordano Bruno intolerable, and sent him to the stake." This is just not true. Let me go on with Koestler's summary of the trial:

> He was then told that, by the manner in which the subject was treated in the *Dialogue*, and the fact that he had written the said book, he was presumed to have held the Copernican opinion; and was asked a second time to state the truth freely. He answered that he had written the book to confer a common benefit by setting forth the arguments for both sides, and repeated again "I do not now hold the condemned opinion, and have not held it since the decision of the authorities" [Galileo is referring to Bellarmine's injunction of 1616]. He was admonished a third time that on the contents of the book he was presumed to hold with Copernicus, or at least to have done so at the time he wrote it, and that therefore "unless he made up his mind to confess the truth, recourse would be had against him to the appropriate remedies of the law." Galileo answered, "I do not hold, and have not held, this opinion of Copernicus since the command was intimated to me that I must abandon it; for the rest I am here in your hands - do with me what you please." When he was for the last time bidden to speak the truth, under the threat of torture, Galileo repeated, "I am here to obey and I have not held this opinion since the decision was pronounced, as I have stated."

If it had been the Inquisition's intention to break Galileo, this obviously was the moment to confront him with the copious extracts from his book - which were in the files in front of the judge - to quote him on what he had said about the sub-human morons and pygmies who were opposing Copernicus, and to convict him of perjury. Instead, immediately following Galileo's last answer, the minutes of the trial say: "And as nothing further could be done in execution of the decree, his signature was obtained to his disposition and he was sent back."

Both the judges and the defendant knew that he was lying; both the judges and he knew that the threat of torture (*territio verbalis* - as opposed to *territio realis* where the instruments of torture are shown to the accused) was merely a ritual formula which could not be carried out [old or sick people, and Galileo was both, could not be tortured]; and that the hearing was a pure formality. Galileo was led back to his five room apartment, and on the next day the sentence was read out to him. It was signed by only seven of the ten judges. Among the three who abstained was Cardinal Francesco Barberini, Urban's brother. The *Dialogue* was prohibited; Galileo was to abjure the Copernican opinion; was sentenced to "formal prison during the Holy Office's pleasure"; and for three years to come, was to repeat once a week the seven penitential psalms. He was then presented with the formula of abjuration, which he read out. And that was the end of it.

The "formal prison" took the form of a sojourn at the Grand Duke's villa at Trinita del Monte, followed by a sojourn in the palace of the Archbishop Piccolomini in Siena where according to a French visitor, Galileo worked "in an apartment covered in silk and most richly furnished." Then he returned to his farm at Arcetri, and later to his house in Florence, where he spent the remaining years of his life. The recital of the penitential psalms was delegated with ecclesiastical consent, to his daughter, Sister Marie Celeste, a Carmelite nun. [19]

Of course Koestler agrees with Mrs. Stepan that the trial considered from the strictly legal point of view was a miscarriage of justice, but like Mrs. Stepan (amazingly for a non-Christian) he denies that the verdict compromised the infallibility of the Church. But the whole point of the Galileo Case is that it was more than a mere legal trial.

From the purely legal point of view the sentence was certainly a miscarriage of justice. If one works through the maze of verbiage, it appears that he was found guilty on two counts: firstly, of having contravened both Bellarmine's admonition, and the alleged formal injunction of 1616, and having "artfully and cunningly exorted the license to print by not notifying the censor of the command imposed upon him"; and secondly, of having rendered himself "vehemently suspect of heresy, namely, of having believed and held the doctrine which is contrary to Sacred Scripture that the sun is the center of the world." Concerning the first count, no more need be said about the dubious character of the document referring to the alleged absolute injunction; so for the second, the sun-centered universe had never been officially declared a heresy, since...the decree of the Congregation of 1616 had not been confirmed by infallible pronouncement *ex cathedra* or by ecumenical council. Had not Urban himself said that the Copernican opinion "was not heretical but merely reckless."

On the other hand, the judgment hushes up the incriminating contents of the book stating that Galileo had represented the Copernican system as merely "probable" - which is a whale of an understatement. It also hushes up the fact that Galileo had been lying and perjuring himself before his judges by pretending that he had written the book in refutation of Copernicus, that he had "neither maintained nor defended the opinion that the earth moves," and so forth. The gist of the matter is that Galileo could not legally be convicted without completely destroying him - which was not the intention of the Pope or the Holy Office. Instead, they resorted to a legally shaky concoction. The intention was, clearly, to treat the famous scholar with consideration and leniency, but at the same time to hurt his pride, to prove that not even a Galileo was allowed to mock Jesuits, Dominicans, Pope, and Holy Office; and lastly to prove that, in spite of his pose as a fearless crusader, he was not the stuff of which martyrs are made. [20]

Arthur Koestler does not agree that the final result of the Galileo Case was that the tradition of science fled the Catholic countries of Europe - the Samson analogy of Dr. Bronowski:

The first open conflict between the Church and Science was the Galileo scandal. I have tried to show that unless one believes in the dogma of historic inevitability - this form of fatalism in reverse gear - one must regard it as a scandal which could have been avoided; and it is not difficult to imagine the Catholic Church adopting, after a Tychonic transition, the Copernican cosmology some two hundred years earlier than she eventually did. The Galileo affair was an isolated, and in fact quite untypical, episode in the history of the relations between science and theology...But its dramatic circumstances, magnified out of all proportion, created a popular belief that science stood for freedom, the Church for oppression of thought. That is true only in a limited sense for a limited period of transition. Some historians, for instance, wish to make us believe that the decline of science in Italy was due to the "terror" caused by the trial of Galileo. But the next generation saw the rise of Toricelli, Cavallieri, Borelli, whose contributions to science were more substantial than those of any generation before or during Galileo's lifetime; the shift of the center of scientific activity to England and France and the gradual decline of Italian science, as of Italian painting, was due to different historical causes. Never since the Thirty Years War has the Church oppressed freedom of thought and expression to an extent comparable to the terror based on the "scientific" ideologies of Nazi Germany or Soviet Russia. [21]

I have tried to point out that the so-called counter-culture movement (an unfortunate phrase), is basically a religious movement. I mentioned how I prefer the sacral humanism of the Koestler type, as opposed to the secular humanism of the Bronowski type. Accordingly Arthur Koestler sees the real tragedy of the Galileo Case in the resulting split between Science and Religion which he thinks has led to their mutual impovrishment:

As a result of their divorce, neither faith nor science is able to satisfy man's intellectual cravings. In the divided house, both inhabitants lead a thwarted existence. Post-Galilean science claimed to be a substitute for, or the legitimate successor of, religion; thus its failure to provide the basic answers produced not only intellectual frustration but spiritual starvation. A summary recapitulation of European men's view of the world before and after the scientific revolution may help to put the situation into sharper relief. Taking the year 1600 as our dividing line or watershed, we find indeed virtually all rivers of thought and currents of feeling flow into opposite directions. The "pre-scientific" European lived in a closed universe with firm boundaries in space and time of a few million miles in diameter and a few thousand years of duration...

In this safely bounded world of comfortable dimensions, a well-ordered drama was taking its pre-ordained course. The stage remained static from beginning to end: there was no change in the species of animals and plants, no change in the nature, social order, and mentality of man. There was neither progress nor decline within the natural and spiritual hierarchy. The total body of possible knowledge was as limited as the universe itself; everything that could be known about the Creator and his creation had been revealed in Holy Scripture and the writings of the ancient sages. There existed no sharp boundaries between the natural and the supernatural;...natural law was interpenetrated with divine purpose; there was no event without a final cause. Transcendental justice and moral values were inseparable from the natural order; no single event was ethically neutral; no plant or metal, no insect or angel, exempt from moral judgment; no phenomenon was outside the hierarchy of values. Every suffering had its reward, every disaster its meaning; the plot of the drama had a simple outline, a clear beginning and end.

This briefly, was our forebears view of the world less than fifteen generations ago. Then, roughly within the five generations from Canon Koppernigk [Copernicus] to Isaac Newton, *homo sapiens* underwent the most decisive change in his history...

The *uomo universale* of the Renaissance, who was artist and craftsman, philosopher and inventor, humanist and scientist, astronomer and monk, all in one, split into his component parts. Art lost its mythical, science its mystical inspiration; man became again deaf to the harmony of the spheres. The Philosophy of Nature became ethically neutral, and "blind" became the favorite adjective for the working of natural law. The space-spirit hierarchy was replaced by the space-time continuum.

As a result, man's destiny was no longer determined from "above" by a super-human wisdom and will, but from "below" by the sub-human agencies of glands, genes, atoms, or waves of probability. The shift of the locus of destiny was decisive. So long as destiny had operated from a level of the hierarchy higher than man's own, it had not only shaped his fate, but also guided his conscience and imbued his world with meaning and value. The new masters of destiny were placed lower in the scale than the being they controlled; they could determine his fate, but could provide him with no moral guidance, no values and meaning. A puppet of the gods is a tragic figure, a puppet suspended on his chromosomes is merely grotesque. [22]

In conclusion let me say that Arthur Koestler, who was not a Christian, appears to me in many ways closer to Christian values than many of today's liberal Christians who seem to be Christian in name only.

Dean Smalley

Our meeting tonight was on the fourth day of creation which deals with the origin of the sun, moon, and stars, and we thought it an appropriate place to discuss the famous Galileo Case.

Dr. Schonfield presented what might be called the establishment humanist version of the Case from Jacob Bronowski. Fr. Staatz concurred with this version, including Bronowski's somewhat dim view of Cardinal Bellarmine.

Mrs. Stepan on the other hand, made an attempt to "demythologize" the humanist version of the Galileo Case by what she called a "simple recitation of the historical facts." These were, she said, that Galileo, despite his claim to the contrary, lacked scientific proof for the heliocentric system, and indeed his main "proof," the theory of the tides, was simply bad physics.

Rev. Swezey joined in Mrs. Stepan's demythologizing efforts from the anti-Establishment critic Arthur Koestler. Koestler was not a Christian but suprisingly completely supported Mrs. Stepan's recitation of the historical facts in the Case and concluded that this tragedy, which has led to the separation of religion and science, has resulted in their mutual impoverishment.

REFERENCES

1   Jacob Bronowski, *The Ascent of Man*,
    Little, Brown and Co., Boston, 1973, p.205.
2   Bronowski, *Op. cit.*, pp.205,207.
3   *Idem*, p.213.
4   *Idem*, pp.214,215.
5   *Idem*, p.218.
6   Frances Nead, Preface to:
    Owen Garrigan, *Man's Intervention in Nature*,
    Hawthorne Books, New York, 1967, pp.7-9.
7   James Broderick, s.j., *Robert Bellarmine*,
    Newman Press, Westminster, Md., 1961, p.354.
8   Broderick, *Op. cit.*, pp.363-365.
9   *Idem*, pp.376,377.
10 Robert Speaight, *Teilhard de Chardin*,
    Collins, London, 1967, pp.323,324.
11 Speaight, *Op. cit.*, pp.14,15.
12 Pope John Paul II, *Adress to the Pontifical Academy of Science*,
    L'Osservatore Romano, Nov 26, 1979.
13 Msgr. Paul Glenn, *Psychology: A Class Manual in the Philosophy of Organic and Rational Life*, B. Herder, New York, 1947, p.486.
14 St. Thomas Aquinas, *Summa Theologica*, (I, Q96, a1, ad2),
    Benziger Brothers, New York, 1947, p.486.
15 St. Thomas Aquinas, *Op. cit.*, (I, Q69, a2, ad2), pp.344,345.
16 Quoted in: John McKee, *The Enemy Within the Gate*,
    Lumen Christi Press, Houston, 1974, p.111.
17 Arthur Koestler, *The Sleepwalkers*,
    MacMillan Company, New York, 1959, p.353.
18 Koestler, *Op. cit.*, pp.443,444.
19 *Idem*, pp.491-493.
20 *Idem*, p.493.
21 *Idem*, pp.522,523.
22 *Idem*, pp.537-539.

THE SEVENTH MEETING
Extraterrestrial Intelligence

Dean Smalley

Tonight we will conclude our discussion of the fourth day of creation, which deals with the origin of the sun, moon, and stars. Our topic for this evening is the possibility of extraterrestrial intelligence. We will begin as usual, by reading the Scriptural account of the fourth day of creation:

> And God said, "Let there be lights in the firmament of the heavens to separate the day from the night; and let them be for signs and seasons and for days and years, and let them be lights in the firmament of the heavens to give light upon the earth," and it was so. And God made two great lights, the greater light to rule the day, and the lesser light to rule the night; he made the stars also. And God set them in the firmament of the heavens to give light upon the earth, to rule over the day and over the night, and to separate the light from the darkness. And God saw that it was good. And there was evening and there was morning a fourth day (Gen 1:14-19).

Dr. Arthur Schonfield

One of the world's leading authorities on the topic of extraterrestrial intelligence is Carl Sagan; and although all his books deal with the subject, I prefer his treatment in *Broca's Brain*. Chapter twenty-two is entitled *The Quest for Extraterrestrial Intelligence*, and it significantly appears just before Part V, *Ultimate Questions*, which we have already seen:

197

Throughout all of our history we have pondered the stars and mused whether humanity is unique or if, somewhere else in the dark of the night sky, there are other beings who contemplate and wonder as we do, fellow thinkers in the cosmos. Such beings might view themselves and the universe differently. Somewhere else there might be very exotic biologies and technologies and societies. In a cosmic setting vast and old beyond ordinary human understanding, we are a little lonely; and we ponder the ultimate significance, if any, of our tiny but exquisite blue planet. The search for extraterrestrial intelligence is the search for a generally acceptable cosmic context for the human species. In the deepest sense the search for extraterrestrial intelligence is a search for ourselves. [1]

Carl Sagan is by profession a highly respected radio astronomer and only incidentally a popularizer of science lore. He estimates that there are about a million advanced civilizations, which he defines as civilizations capable of radio astronomy, in our Milky Way Galaxy. This number is arrived at first by estimating the number of stars in our galaxy, now thought to be about 250 billion; then the rate of formation of planetary systems; then the likelihood of the origin of life; and finally, the probability of the evolution of intelligence - all matters about which Sagan admits we know very little.

The only practical way for us to begin the search for extraterrestrial intelligence at this time is by radio astronomy, that is by listening for radio signals from outer space. As Philip Morrison of the Massachusetts Institute of Technology said: "God knows how to make light but He doesn't know how to make [radio] microwaves. They're made on earth by people." The search was begun by the American astronomer, Frank Drake, later a close collaborator with Sagan, in 1959 and 1960 at the National Radio Astronomy Observatory in Greensbank, West Virginia. He listened to two nearby stars, Epsilon Eriani and Tau Ceti, for several weeks with negative results. In 1983 a more ambitious program was launched by Harvard astronomer Paul Horowitz using an 84 foot radio telescope in Harvard, Massachusetts.

Sagan estimates that out of the 250 billion stars in our galaxy there could be a million advanced civilizations. This means that we have made only a tiny fraction of the required effort. The search continues, and it could take many, many years; or we could make a lucky hit at any time.

The most important aspect of the quest for extraterrestrial intelligence, Sagan says, is that eventually we will be able to give more satisfactory answers to the "ultimate questions" than are available at present:

The detection of intelligent radio signals from the depths of space would approach in an experimental and scientifically rigorous manner many of the most profound questions that have concerned scientists and philosophers since prehistoric times. Such a signal would indicate that the origin of life is not an extraordinary, difficult, or unlikely event. It would imply that, given billions of years for natural selection, simple forms of life evolve generally into complex and intelligent forms, as on earth; and that such intelligent forms commonly produce an advanced technology, as also has occurred here. But it is not likely that the transmission we receive will be from a society at our own level of technological advance. A society only a little more backward than ours will not have radio astronomy at all. The most likely case is that the message will be from a civilization far in our technological future. Thus, even before we decode such a message, we will have gained an invaluable piece of knowledge: that it is possible to avoid the dangers of the period through which we are now passing.

There are some who look on our global problems here on earth - at our vast national anatagonisms, our nuclear arsenals, our growing populations, the disparity between the poor and the affluent, shortages of food and resources, and our inadvertent alterations of the natural environment - and conclude that we live in a system that is destined soon to collapse. There are others who believe that our problems are soluble, that humanity is still in its childhood, that one day soon we will grow up. The receipt of a single message from space would show that it is possible to live through such technological adolescence: the transmitting civilization, after all, has survived. Such knowledge, it seems to me, might be worth a great price. [2]

Sagan feels that the search for extraterrestrial intelligence should be given the highest priority, because the first message we receive might well tell us how to avoid a nuclear holocaust:

> In particular, it is possible that among the first contents of such a message may be detailed prescriptions for the avoidance of technological disaster, for a passage through adolescence to maturity. Perhaps the transmissions from advanced civilizations will describe which pathways of cultural evolution are likely to lead to the stability and longevity of an intelligent species, and which other paths lead to stagnation or degeneration or disaster. There is, of course, no guarantee that such would be the contents of an interstellar message, but it would be foolhardy to overlook the possibility. Perhaps there are straightforward solutions, still undiscovered on earth, to problems of food shortages, population growth, energy supplies, dwindling resources, pollution, and war.
>
> While there surely will be differences among civilizations, there may well be laws of development of civilizations which cannot be glimpsed until information is available about the evolution of many civilizations. Because of our isolation from the rest of the cosmos; we have information on the evolution of only one civilization - our own. And the most important aspect of that evolution - the future - remains closed to us. Perhaps it is not likely, but it is certainly possible that the future of human civilization depends on the receipt and decoding of interstellar messages from extraterrestrial civilizations.
>
> And what if we make a long-term, dedicated search for extraterrestrial intelligence and fail?...Such a finding will stress, as nothing else can, our responsibilities to the dangers of our time: because the most likely explanation of negative results, after a comprehensive and resourceful search, is that societies commonly destroy themselves before they are

advanced enough to establish a high-power radio-transmitting service. [3]

But despite this sobering possibility, Sagan concludes on a characteristically optimistic exhortation:

> But we will not know the outcome of such a search, much less the contents of messages from interstellar civilizations, if we do not make a serious effort to listen for signals. It may be that civilizations are divided into two great classes: those who make such an effort, achieve contact, and become new members of a loosely tied federation of galactic communities; and those that cannot or choose not to make such an effort, or who lack the imagination to try, and who in consequence soon decay and vanish. It is difficult to think of another enterprise within our capability and at a relatively modest cost that holds as much promise for the future of humanity. [4]

Let me say in conclusion, that I think the most significant line in these few brief excerpts from Carl Sagan was: "the search for extraterrestrial intelligence is a search for ourselves." Whether or not we finally discover other intelligent beings besides ourselves, and the great likelihood is that we will, we will soon be able to answer in a more rigorous manner the "ultimate questions" concerning the meaning, or lack or meaning, of life.

Fr. Robert A. Staatz

As far as I know, no Catholic theologian or philosopher has made an extensive study of the possibility of extraterrestrial intelligence, but many short articles have appeared on the subject in various Catholic periodicals. For example, the Jesuit national weekly *America* has reprinted two such articles in a pamphlet entitled *Rational Life in Outer Space*. Let me read a few excerpts from one of the articles humorously entitled *Are There Others Out Yonder?* by the Jesuit, L.C. McHugh, a professor of theology at Georgetown University. Fr. McHugh first examines the possibility of extraterrestrial intelligence from the point of view of science:

...Serious astronomers are striving to find meaningful patterns amid all the random static that pours into the dish of a big radio telescope in West Virginia. Project Ozma's outlay of tax money is not a boondoggle. It stems from statistical implications and the intuitional thrust of modern cosmogony and biochemistry.

Increasingly, biochemistry favors the view that life will arise as a normal result of chemical evolution whenever conditions are right. If favorable circumstances prevail over sufficient eons of time, the evolutionary quality of life verges naturally toward higher and eventually rational forms. As for astronomy, current theories of cosmic development generally suggest that planet formation is a common event in the evolution of the quintillions of stars that lie within our view. It is exceedingly probable that billions of planets occupy the "golden zones" of distant suns where temperature and other energy factors favor the emergence of life. Perhaps then the highest forms of organic existence are a widespread climax of cosmic history, rather than an isolated discontinuity that has appeared just once as a sort of "contamination" of the earth's mantle. [5]

So much for the possibility of extraterrestrial intelligence from the view point of science; McHugh then examines the possibility philosophically:

...Where science talks of statistical probability that life may arise by chance and develop through random variations, the Catholic philosopher holds that there can be no real chance in a world created by God. There are only lines of causality unintelligible to us but unified in the divine Mind and somehow expressive of His purposes. On the other hand, since we increasingly regard the origin of life as an event of the natural order rather than as a metaphysical problem demanding the miraculous intervention of creative power, there is no insurmountable difficulty in granting that life may arise whenever the apt conditions are present.

Moreover, in life as we know it, there are remarkable

powers of adaptability, differentiation, and movement toward rational organization. Organic life on earth evolved toward a specialized animal form that in God's design was apt
material for the infusion of a spiritual soul, while at the same
time the lower forms were ordained to serve as a substratum
for rational existence and its needs. Why should these things
not be generally true in a physical universe characterized by
uniformity of law and process? Hence, where suitable
conditions exist on a planetary mantle we may expect life to
emerge, perhaps as a normal aspect of development. Where
the conditions persist for billions of years, may not we expect
that God is preparing for a divine incursion of the biosphere
that will manifest His glory in the phenomenon of man? [6]

These ideas of course, are similar to those of Teilhard de
Chardin. McHugh goes on from philosophy to theology:

In his *Contra Gentes*, while discussing the providence of
God, Thomas Aquinas notes "that the first thing aimed at in
creatures is their multiplication...and to the gaining and
securing of this end all things else seem to be subordinated."
Aquinas held this position within the narrow framework of
Aristotelian physics and astronomy. If he had considered the
hierarchy of being within the framework of an expanding
universe, how would he have expressed himself? Would he
perchance have suggested that the irrational creation, where
numbers proliferated, cannot meaningfully establish and con-
serve that to which it is ordained, unless rational life is also
common in the physical universe?
...If he had possessed our knowledge of the cosmos, would he
perhaps have held that a few billions of our human stock, in-
habiting an isolated corner of creation, inadaquately manifest
the goodness of God as it can be shown in rational animals?
"Multiplication and variety were needful in the creation, to
the end that the perfect likeness of God might be found in
creatures according to their measure."
Perhaps, then, there are races that were never elevated to
grace. We sons of Adam are a race elevated, fallen, and

redeemed - a testimony to His mercy. Who will say that there are no races elevated but not fallen, as testimony to His holiness? Who can say that there are no races elevated, fallen, but forever without redemption to show forth the mystery of His justice? [These notions were developed extensively by C.S. Lewis in his science fiction.]

I am not aware of any grave theological objections to the probabilities I have described. The purpose of revelation was to teach us what we needed for salvation, not to instruct us in science or philosophy.

I am not perturbed, for example, at the imagination of a second Mother of God, for I do not even find difficulty in conceiving even a thousand incarnations of each or all of the Persons of the Trinity. Aquinas discussed several such possibilities centuries ago and found none of them repugnant to sound theology, though of course he did not suggest that they were actually realized. [7]

So there seems to be no serious problem regarding the possibility of extraterrestrial intelligence from the point of view of science, philosophy, or even theology. If, then, extraterrestrial intelligence is actually discovered, what will this mean for the Church?

Why do we normally resist the thought that man may not be alone in the universe? I think that our perennial jealousy of our status largely springs from the erroneous science that long ago placed us at the center of the visible creation. It was inevitable that we regarded ourselves as unique, when all the obvious signs indicated that the heavens revolved about us night and day.

During the course of the years, as we know, the supposed center of the cosmos moved from the earth to the sun, from the sun to the galaxy, until today man resides he knows not where in a metagalaxy of undisclosed structure and extent. Yet now that we know that we have lost our physical centrality, we still cling to the prejudice that we are unique, solely on the grounds of our intellectual superiority.

Where does the evidence for that uniqueness lie? Man as

such has no centrality in the total creation. The hub of that complex lies in the angelic world, not in any aspect of material creation. We on earth cannot argue uniqueness from the fact that we are images of God in a material mold: for the dignity of being such an image is endlessly shareable. And neither does our worth give any ground for complacency; the redemptive love that the Father showed us in sending His Only-Begotten Son was a proof of His generosity in the face of our desparate need, not an indication that God found some vein of gold in the corruption of our fallen nature.

Despite our lowliness, I feel that even our race has a destiny in space. We may not be able to assign a farthest limit to our lordship over nature, but it will not be limited to the earth alone. Earthly man will go as far as his ambition and inventiveness can carry him. And since he will take the Mystical Body with him, wherever he goes, his colonization of space may be looked upon as a providential extension of the Incarnation in space and time. The Church, perhaps has a physical dimesion beyond our ken. [8]

Mrs. Maria Stepan

The idea that there are other inhabited worlds besides our own was taught by many of the ancient pagan philosophers of Greece and Rome, such as Democritus and Lucretius. With the revival of pagan learning at the time of the Renaissance, the idea was again proposed by the Greek Cardinal, Nicholas of Chusa. Later, Giordano Bruno incorporated the notion into his pantheistic world system. St. Robert Bellarmine allowed Bruno to speculate philosophically on the possibility of extraterrestrial intelligence - it is of course possible that God could have created other inhabited worlds besides our own. This is legitimate philosophic speculation, but it is an entirely different matter to claim it as a fact, which Bruno eventually did. Bruno, who in many ways reminds me of Teilhard de Chardin, was unfortunately burned at the stake, not for this notion, but for refusing to abjure his theological heresies.

Let us see what the Tradition and Magisterium of the Church

teach concerning the possibility of extraterrestrial intelligence. St. Thomas Aquinas aslo speculated philosophically on the possibility of other worlds, but rejected the idea as an actual fact.

Whether There Is Only One World?

Objection 1.   It would seem that there is not only one world, but many. St. Augustine says, that it is unfitting to say that God has created things without a reason. But for the same reason He created one, He could create many, since His power is not limited to the creation of one world; but rather it is infinite...therefore God has produced many worlds...

On the contrary.   It is said (John 1:10): "The world was made by Him," where the world is named as one; as though one existed.

I answer that, the very order of things created by God shows the unity of the world. For this world is called one by the unity of order, whereby some things are ordered to others. But whatever things come from God have a relation of order to each other, and to God Himself...Hence it must be that all things should belong to one world. Therefore, those only can assert many worlds who do not acknowledge any ordaining wisdom, but rather believe in chance, as Democritus, who said that this world, besides an infinite number of other worlds, was made from a casual concourse of atoms. [9]

So while St. Augustine did not object to speculating philosophically on the possibility of extraterrestrial intelligence, St. Thomas, who seldom disagreed with St. Augustine, in this case did not agree. St. Thomas thought that, while many worlds were certainly compatible with God's power, they were not compatible with His wisdom.

In 1459 Pope Pius ii in his encyclical *Cum sicut accepimus*, condemned the following proposition:

That God also created another world besides this one, and

that many other men and women existed at this time, and consequently, that Adam was not the first man. [10]

We heard Fr. McHugh say in the course of his theological speculations, "I am not perturbed...at the imagination of a second Mother of God." But I must say that I *am* perturbed at such an imagination, and in the light of what I have just read from Tradition and the Magisterium, I would also like to engage in a little theological speculation. Fr. McHugh stated, "the redemptive love that the Father showed in sending His Only-Begotten Son was a proof of His generosity in the face of our desperate need, not an indication that God found some vein of gold in the corruption of our fallen nature." But Our Lady is that solitary "vein of gold" that God found in the corruption of our fallen nature.

When Our Lady appeared at Lourdes in 1858, she said to St. Bernadette, not "I am the one who was immaculately conceived," but "I am the Immaculate Conception." Our Lady meant by this that she was the whole singular idea in God's mind. But let me read this point about the Immaculate Conception from someone who can make it much better than I, St. Maximillian Mary Kolbe:

> To Bernadette's repeated request, the Immaculata replied by revealing her true name when she said, "I am the Immaculate Conception." *To no one else does such a name properly belong.*
>
> When God revealed his name to Moses, he said: "I am the One who is" (Ex 3:14). For God exists from all eternity and to all eternity. His being is unlimited, transcending all time under whatsoever aspect. Whatever exists apart from God is not "being" itself, but receives its being from him. Thus the Immaculata also began to exist in time.
>
> Among the creatures which began to exist, the angels and our first parents came into being without having been conceived. Mary, on the contrary, like all ordinary humans, began to exist when she was conceived. Jesus Christ, the Man-God, also began his human life by an act of conception. But we should rather say of him that he was conceived, not that he is a "conception," because as the Son of God he exists

without a beginning, whereas Mary, since she began in a conception, is different from him, and like all other human beings. But from the first instant of her existence she was distinguished from all the rest of humankind by the fact that their conceptions are sullied by Original Sin, since they are conceived by descendants of our first parents who sinned; Mary's conception, on the contrary, is entirely exempt from this general law; her conception was immaculate.

She does therefore have a full right to the name "Immaculate Conception; this is indeed her true name. [11]

St. Maximillian Mary also said, "She was immaculate because she was to become the Mother of God; she became the Mother of God because she was immaculate." So as there is only one Immaculate Conception, there can be only one Mother of God, and therefore only one Incarnation. A single Incarnation would seem to preclude the likelihood of other inhabited worlds.

We heard Carl Sagan say that he hoped that the first message we receive from an extraterrestrial creature will tell us how to avoid a nuclear disaster. But we have already received such a message from an extraterrestrial creature - Our Lady of Fatima. The story of Our Lady of Fatima was the subject of a popular movie a few years ago entitled *The Miracle of Fatima* which was very well received by believers and non-believers alike - I'm sure that many of you remember it. Let me conclude with a brief summary of that message by Msgr. William McGrath from an article entitled *The Lady of the Rosary*:

It still rests with Mary's children to avert appalling disaster for the world...Her diagnosis of such disaster is as true today as when she first flashed out of the skies of Heaven in 1917. The cause is revolt against God, and today that revolt is fast assuming the proportions of universal apostasy. There are many who believe that the situation is now out of human hands; that we have passed the point of no return; that only direct Divine intervention can now resolve the terrible impasse. Such intervention may truly be apocalyptic, and it is in the Hands of God to permit - or to prevent - a nuclear war that could wipe out our civilization, or world Communism that would mean universal slavery and martyrdom. "The Hand of my Son in Heaven is now so heavy that I cannot hold it back any longer."...

Fidelity to the message of Fatima; daily recitation of the Rosary; a serious determined effort at personal sanctity; the devotion of the First Saturdays and consecration to her Immaculate Heart; this on the part of her children, may still lighten the Hand of God and strengthen the arm of Our Blessed Mother as she tries to save us from "suffering such as humankind has never known before." [12]

Rev. De Verne Swezey

Carl Sagan claimed that of the estimated 250 billion stars in the Milky Way Galaxy at least one million should have advanced civilizations. This conclusion, he says, is based on a statistical analysis of the number of stars, plus scientific speculation on the formation of planetary systems, the origin of life, and the evolution of intelligence. But statistics requires a large sample, and in this case we have a sample on only *one* - the earth - so statistics do not apply. Here again is Dr. Morris:

So far as we *know*, in fact, the solar system is quite unique in the universe. There is an almost innumerable quantity of stars, but that does not mean any of them necessarily have planets. Evolutionary astronomers assume that many do, but the only reason for thinking so is what might be called evolutionary statistics. That is, they reason if our sun somehow evolved a planetary system by natural processes, then surely those same processes must have evolved similar planetary systems around at least a certain number of stars.

This kind of logic, however, begs the whole question. The only solar system about which we have any information is our own, and one does not use statistical analysis when his data consist of only one of a kind. No astronomer has ever viewed any other planet outside the solar system in his telescope and has no real evidence that any exists. [13]

Not only has the search for extraterrestrial intelligence by means of radio astronomy proven negative to date, but also the search for life in any form on Mars and other planets in our solar system has also produced negative results. Dr. Morris says that these results were predicted by the creation model:

...Some of the definite predictions from the creation model are as follows:

1) Since the earth, moon, and planets were created for a specific purpose, each would have a distinctive structure. They would not all be essentially of the same composition and structure, as would be the case if they had all evolved together from a common source.

2) Only the earth would be found to have a hydrosphere capable of supporting life as we know it.

3) Only the earth would be found to have an atmosphere capable of supporting life as we know it.

4) No evidence of past or present life would be found anywhere in the solar system except on earth.

5) Evidence would be found of decay and catastrophism on other planets and moons, but not of evolutionary growth in order and complexity.

All these predictions have been clearly confirmed by the moon landings and by the probes to Mars, Mercury, and Venus. Although some evolutionary scientists still cling to the hope that some evidence might yet be found which could support the existence of life in the distant past or distant future on one of these planets, the fact is that no such evidence has been found. [14]

I was a little disappointed that Dr. Schonfield didn't give any examples of just what he thought extraterrestrial life might be like, so let me read from just one typical example of humanist speculation on the subject. This is from an article on the planet Jupiter by Hal Clement, who is both a scientist (a chemist), and a science fiction writer. It appeared in *Closeup: New Worlds*, an anthology edited by Ben Bova:

Jovian life won't be much like ours...Mechanically, I would expect ocean-type life, floating or swimming (flying?) free in an environment something like ocean and something like air, with no sharp distinction between the two at the greater depths; Arthur C. Clarke, in his classic *A Meeting with Medusa*, probably called the shot pretty close here.

I am offering this as a serious prediction, not a casual speculation, I hope to live long enough to see it checked. I recognize the present negative attitude toward research in general and space research in particular; many people actually seem to believe that mankind already has enough knowledge to keep the present population alive indefinitely rather than the few decades we could actually manage. People complain about the "waste" of money spent on space.

I realize that such research is expensive; a single *Apollo* moon flight would keep the population of this country in cigarettes for fully fifteen days, and even in liquor for nearly six. I wonder what the Jovians, who well may not know what property lines are, would have for a social system? Maybe the dolphins would understand them and vice-versa better than we could.

John Campbell...spoke of Jovians looking wistfully and hopelessly out at other worlds, from which they were forever barred by an environment which keeps an intelligent species from exploring and discovering.

And, since I am still optimistic about human nature in spite of half a century's experience, I feel hopeful about living to see at least a photograph of a Jupiter life form. Intelligence applied to the real universe can do some wonderful things. [15]

"Maybe the dolphins would understand them and vice versa"!! How do these men get this way? I am sure that Hal Clement is a completely rational person, yet here he is talking utter nonsense.

Let me read one humorous explanation of this phenomena by Jack Catran from an article which appeared recently in the *Los Angeles Times*. Catran is a scientist who worked on the Apollo and other space shots, and is the author of *Is There Intelligent Life on Earth?*

At this moment, riding aboard the Voyager I and II space-craft, there are recordings of Bach, Beethoven, Louis Armstrong and Chuck Berry, just in case there may be someone out there hip to rock 'n' roll, all deposited aboard those spacecraft at the suggestion of Carl Sagan. Aboard Pioneer 10, which will take about 80,000 years just to reach our nearest star - which it will miss because it is not headed that way - there is that plaque featuring Earthman and Earthwoman waving greetings, another Sagan idea.

The Voyager recordings are based on a false premise. There are no space aliens out there waiting to listen to Chuck Berry. Neither are there E.T.s available to view those drawings aboard Pioneer 10. Yet it is understandable how such a comic strip view of the universe can arise; the study of any science always begins that way. Strange explanations precede the valid. Chemistry began as alchemy, astronomy as astrology and medicine as witchcraft. And the field of exobiology still has its astrologers and medicine men. [14]

In the 1976 Supplement *to the Encyclopedia Brittanica*, there is a very interesting article by Lawrence K. Lustig entitled *Science and Superstition: An Age of Unreason*. Lustig tries to examine the reasons for the current popularity of phenomena like UFOs, ESP, astrology, Uri Geller, the Bermuda Triangle, etc., etc. In this so-called scientific age, why are so many people turning back to mystery and superstition?

Any objective appraisal of the literature, reports, and events...leads inexorably to one basic question, namely: why? Why do large numbers of people in society deliberately choose mysteries, supernatural, and delusionary explanations in lieu of tried and tested rational patterns of causality? Some would answer, as did the eminent psychologist Carl Jung after an analysis of UFO sightings (*Flying Saucers*, 1959), that people do so simply because it suits them - because they *want* to believe in the mysterious...This suggestion is obviously unacceptable to supporters of the phenomena described here, and the question that remains is why people wish to believe that the unreal is real.

Elizabeth Janeway and others have said that the world of modern science and technology is too complex to be conveyed decently to the lay public by those who speak the language of science. Hence, the multitudes withdraw to the mysterious, for here, at least, they can feel as one - both with the author or performer in question, and with their own peers...The truth may well comprise elements of each of these explanations. But whatever the cause it is quite clear that we may awaken tomorrow to learn that some clever promoter has discovered a new and intriguing solution to the question of how light is transmitted. The dust jacket on a first edition of a million copies may ask: "Is there evidence that light is transmitted as an infinite series of invisible aardvarks whose tails glow when activated by a mysterious intelligence from outer space?" If we greet this absurd proposition with anything other than the ridicule it so richly deserves, then we will have moved one step further along a path of unreason that may well lead to one of darkness.

Those who doubt this is so might ponder the fact that the fall of Phom Penh, and thus of all Cambodia, was hastened by belief of the defenders in the existence of an invisible dragon beneath the city's outskirts. Obeying the portents of the stars, they severed their own supply road to relieve the pressure on this beast's tail. Obviously their astrologers failed them in this instance. [16]

Of course, Lustig didn't dare attack extraterrestrial intelligence; it is too much a part of the humanist Establishment. His article wouldn't have appeared in the *Brittanica* if he had. The basic explanation for this phenomenon is religious - get rid of the uniqueness of man in the universe, and God and His grace become unnecessary. Lustig's psychological and sociological explanations of the popularity of various phenomena like UFOs, TM, etc., are all valid, but any Christian could give a better explanation. All this turning back to mystery and superstition - and I would put extraterrestrial intelligence in the category of superstition - is a sort of backhanded compliment to the nature of man. Man is indeed a rational animal, but the whole man needs mystery as well as reason. Man was made for the mysteries of God, and if he won't look for mystery in God, he will look for it somewhere else.

Dean Smalley

Our topic for this evening was the possibility of extraterrestrial intelligence.

Dr. Schonfield presented the scientific case for extraterrestrial intelligence which was based on a statistical analysis of the number of stars, plus scientific speculation on the formation of planetary systems, the origin of life, and the evolution of intelligence, all matters about which he admitted, we know very little.

Fr. Staatz accepted the scientific case, such as it was, for extraterrestrial intelligence, and added that if chance is excluded, it offers no serious problems in either Christian philosophy or theology.

Mrs. Stepan admitted the philosophic possibility of extraterrestrial intelligence, but denied that it offered no serious problems in theology. She claimed that the dogma of the Immaculate Conception precluded the possibility of another Mother of God, and another Incarnation, and therefore the likelihood of other inhabited worlds.

Rev. Swezey rejected the statistical case for extraterrestrial intelligence, saying that statistics do not apply when the sample is one - the earth. He added that the creation model had actually predicted that Project Ozma and other similar ventures, would not detect intelligent radio signals from outer space, and that life in any form would not be discovered on Mars nor any other planet in the solar system.

REFERENCES

1   Carl Sagan, *Broca's Brain,*
    Random House, New York, 1979, p.268.
2   Sagan, *Op. cit.,* pp.274,275.
3   *Idem,* pp.276,277.
4   *Idem,* p.277.
5   L.C. McHugh, s.j., *Are There Others Out Yonder?*
    Rational Life in Outer Space,
    America Press, New York, 1966, pp.14,15.
6   McHugh, *Op. cit.,* pp.15,16.
7   *Idem,* pp.17-19.
8   *Idem,* pp.19,20.
9   St. Thomas Aquinas, *Summa Theologica,* (I, Q47, a3),
    Benziger Brothers, New York, pp.247,248.
10 Pope Pius ii, *Cum sicut accepimus,*
    Denziger, *Enchiridion Symbolorum,* (716c),
    Herder, Rome, 1958, p.344.
11 Fr. F.H.M. Manteau-Bonamy, o.p., *Immaculate Conception and the Holy Spirit,*
    Prow Books, Franciscan Marytown Press,
    Libertyville, Ill., 1977, p.132.
12 Msgr. William McGrath, *The Lady of the Rosary,* included in:
    John J. Delaney, *A Woman Clothed with the Sun,*
    Doubleday and Co., Image Books, Garden City, N.Y., 1961, pp.211,212.
12 Henry Morris, *Scientific Creationism,*
    Creation-Life Publishers, San Diego, Cal., 1974, p.29.
14 Morris, *Op. cit.,* p.30.
15 Hal Clement, *Jupiter: Eden with a Red Spot,* included in:
    Ben Bova, *Closeup: New Worlds,*
    St. Martin's Press, New York, 1971, pp.171-173.
16 Jack Catran, *Gee-Whiz Scientists Searching for Life,*
    Los Angeles Times, Mar 13, 1983.
17 Lawrence K. Lustig, *Science and Superstition: An Age of Unreason,*
    1976 Brittanica Book of the Year,
    Encyclopedia Brittanica, London, 1976, p.273.

THE FIFTH DAY

The Origin of Fish and Birds

THE EIGHTH MEETING
The Theory of Evolution

Dean Smalley

Tonight we come to the fifth day of creation which deals with the origin of fish and birds. We will devote only one meeting to this day; and we decided that this would be an appropriate place to discuss the theory of evolution, which maintains that birds have evolved from fish. However, the speakers will merely discuss the evolution of species in general, and reserve the evolution of man for the sixth day of creation which deals with the origin of man. Here is the Scriptural account of the fifth day:

> And God said, "Let the waters bring forth swarms of living creatures, and let birds fly above the earth across the firmament of the heavens." So God created the great sea monsters and every living creature that moves, and which swarm in the waters according to their kinds, and every winged bird according to its kind. And God saw that it was good. And God blessed them saying "Be fruitful and multiply and fill the waters in the seas, and let the birds multiply on the earth." And there was evening and there was morning, a fifth day (Gen 1:20-23).

Dr. Arthur Schonfield

Evolution is a big subject and there are many ways of presenting it, most familiarly from paleontology, the study of the fossil record. But I have chosen tonight to concentrate on molecular biology because this science stresses the most important mechanism of evolution, mutation, and also because of the current great interest in recombinant DNA research which we plan to examine in some detail during one of our meetings on the sixth day.

219

I would like to read tonight from the Nobel laureate, Jacques Monod's classic work *Chance and Necessity* which first appeared in 1970. Monod, unfortunately, does not have the easy popular style of Jacob Bronowski or Carl Sagan, so let me begin by giving a little background on a few of the things he takes for granted.

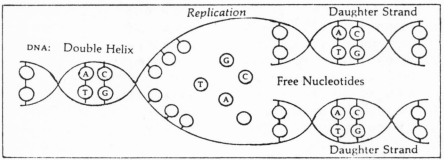

Plate xi   DNA *Replication*

This diagram shows the double helix structure of DNA (deoxy-ribose nucleic acid), which was discovered by Watson and Crick in 1953, and the phenomenon of "replication," which explains how a particular gene can be handed down from one generation to the next. The double helix is like a spiral staircase, the rungs being made up of four chemical bases called nucleotides: adenine, thymine, cytosine, and guanine - indicated by the letters A, T, C, G. During the process of meitosis, or cell division, the chromosomes in the nucleus split in half. At the same time, the genes on the chromosomes which are made up of DNA also split in half, and the half gene rebuilds itself into a whole gene. In the diagram, we are in the nucleus of the cell which is full of free nucleotides, the four bases indicated by the letters A, T, C, G. When the gene splits in half, the bases in the two half-strands pick up their opposite numbers from the free nucleotide pool. A can only pick up T, C only G, and vice versa. In this way, the two new daughter strands are formed from the single parent strands.

In 1961, Marshall Nirenberg cracked what is called the "genetic code." This code explains how the cell goes from RNA (ribose nucleic acid) to protein. The various proteins, the basic building blocks of life, are made up of long chains of twenty different amino acids. Using the metaphor of language, the nucleic acid RNA is considered one language, and is translated into a sentence in amino acids, which says: "Make this particular kind of protein."

Genetic Code					
II	U	C	A	G	III
	PHE	SER	TYR	CYS	U
I U	PHE	SER	Stop	TYR	U
	LEU	SER	Stop	TYR	G

Plate XII   *Genetic Code*

In the diagram I have included only a quarter of the code, just to give us a little idea of how it works. On the left is the Roman numeral I, meaning the first letter in the triplet code, which stands for the base uracil (U). Across the top is the Roman numeral II, meaning the second letter in the triplet code, which stands for the four bases in the nucleic acid RNA: uracil, cytosine, adenine, and guanine (U, C, A, G). The last column has the Roman numeral III, the third letter in the triplet code, and below it the four letters U, C, A, G. In the blocks are three letter abbreviations for the twenty amino acids. In the block in the upper left hand corner, the letters PHE stand for the amino acid phenylaline. When we read I-II-III, the three letters for the triplet code for the upper left hand corner, we find they are U, U, U. So uracil, uracil, uracil, translate into the amino acid phenylaline (U, U, U = PHE). In the next block to the right, we see the letters SER, which stand for the amino acid seryl, called for by I-II-III, U,C, U, uracil, cytosine, uracil (U, C, U = SER), and so on.

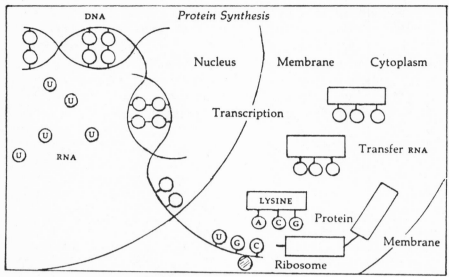

Plate xiii   *Protein Synthesis*

In this diagram we are again inside the cell, and on the left we see the process called *transcription*. It is similar to replication which we have just seen, only instead of making more DNA, as happens in meitosis, the cell now makes the other nucleic acid, RNA, ribose nucleic acid. The DNA again splits in half, but this time instead of picking up the base thymine from the free nucleotide pool, it picks up the base uracil, which joins only with the base adenine.

The molecular biologists speculate that the discriminating membrane of the nucleus won't let the DNA out, and in that way the cell protects its genetic inheritance. But the uracil of RNA is a chemical signal to the membrane saying: "Let me through into the cytoplasm." Also, RNA is more fragile than the very stable DNA, and after RNA has done its work, it breaks down and its components are re-used by the cell. The single strand of RNA that enters the cytoplasm, the messenger RNA, was discovered by our author Monod and his partner Jacob in 1960. This strand is drawn to a little organelle called a ribosome, the site of protein synthesis. This is where the *translation* takes place from the triplets of RNA into amino acids. The cytoplasm is also a chemical pool in which there are free amino acids. These amino acids are picked up by triplets of RNA, called transfer RNA, that are compared to little tugboats which pull their larger cargos of amino acids over to the ribosomes, where they are hooked together in long chains. In the diagram I have the messenger RNA, U, G, C, just coming up on the ribosome. These three bases call for their opposite numbers, A, C, G, which in turn call for the amino acid, lysine, and we see the transfer RNA, A, C, G with the amino acid lysine in tow, coming over to the ribosome. There the lysine is hooked on to the growing chain of amino acids. When the chain reaches the end specified by the strand of RNA, the protein that has been formed will bundle itself up into a particular shape. The particular sequence of amino acids determines whether it is, for example, the protein enzyme hemoglobin to oxygenate the blood, or the protein for muscle tissue, and so forth.

With that somewhat inadequate background in this admittedly difficult subject, let me now read from Jacques Monod's *Chance and Necessity*. Here is his humorous introduction to the subject of evolution:

> When one ponders the tremendous journey of evolution over the past three billion years or so, the prodigious wealth of structures it has engendered, and the extraordinarily effective teleonomic performances of living beings, from bacteria to man, one may well find oneself beginning to doubt again whether all this could conceivably be the product of an enormous lottery presided over by natural selection, blindly picking the rare winners from numbers drawn at utter random.
>
> While one's conviction may be restored by a detailed review of the accumulated modern evidence that this conception alone is compatible with the facts (notably the molecular mechanisms of replication, mutation, and translation), it affords no synthetic, intuitive, and immediate grasp of the vast sweep of evolution. the miracle stands "explained"; it does not strike us as any less miraculous. As François Mauriac wrote, "What this professor says is far more incredible than what we poor Christians believe." [1]

Monod briefly reviews abiogenesis, the origin of life from

non-life, which we discussed on the third day of creation. If you remember, before the apearance of the plants, the earth's atmosphere was composed mainly of methane, water vapor, and ammonia. Then in Oparin's "primordial soup," by sheer chance the basic chemicals of life were formed - the amino acids from which the proteins are made, and the bases which make up the DNA. This theory we saw, has been more or less substantiated by the experiments of Stanley Miller, Lesley Orgel, and others.

The two basic chemicals of life are protein and DNA. The building blocks of life are the proteins, and the particular proteins are determined by the particular sequence of DNA. This poses, admits Monod, "Herculean problems," similar to the old riddle "which came first, the chicken or the egg?" which in modern chemical terms would be rendered: "which came first, the protein or the DNA?"

> ...When and how did this circle become closed? It is exceedingly difficult to imagine...The riddle remains, and in doing so masks the answer to a question of profound interest. Life appeared on earth; what, *before the event*, were the chances that this would occur? The present structure of the biosphere far from excludes the possibility that the decisive event occurred *only once*. Which would mean that its *a priori* possibility was virtually zero.
>
> The idea is distasteful to most scientists. Science can neither say nor do anything about a unique occurrence. It can only consider occurrences that form a class, whose *a priori* probability, however faint, is yet definite...The universe was not pregnant with life, nor the biosphere with man. Our number came up in the Monte Carlo game. Is it any wonder, if like the person who has just made a million at the casino, we feel strange and a little unreal?[2]

Monod calls the cell a "chemical machine," a little automated factory for assembling proteins. The nucleus is the cybernetic or governing mechanism; the messenger RNA is like a program on perforated tape or punched cards, and the ribosomes like servomechanisms, tiny automated machine tools, which assemble the proteins.

Now Monod, of course, recognizes that this little "machine," the cell, as we know it today, is far too complicated to have arisen by chance in Oparin's soup. Today's cell must be the product of a long evolution. The fact that this "protein assembly machine" is universal, every living creature having the same genetic code and same translation mechanism, seems to imply that life arose only once. If life had arisen by chance more than once, it is hardly likely that by chance it would have evolved the same code; there would have been a variety of different chemical machines, each with different codes. In that case every living creature on earth is descended from a single proto-cell which arose by chance in the primordial soup. There are of course, none of these very simple cells around today.

...The fact that the code is now deciphered and known to be universal at least allows us to frame the problem in precise terms; simplifying just a little, in those of the following alternatives. Either

a) Chemical - or, to be more exact, stereo-chemical - reasons account for the structure of the code; if a certain codon [triplet of RNA] was "chosen" to represent a certain amino acid, it is because there existed a certain stereo-chemical affinity between them; or else

b) The code's structure is chemically arbitrary; the code as we know it today is the result of a series of random choices which gradually enriched it.

The first of these hypotheses seems by far the more appealing. To begin with, because it would explain the universality of the code. Next, because it permits us to imagine a primitive translation mechanism in which the sequential aligning of amino acids to form a polypeptide [protein] would be caused by direct interaction between the amino acids and the replicative structure itself. Finally and above all, because in principle this hypothesis would be verifiable. And numerous attempts to verify it have indeed been made: on the whole they have proven negative to date.

It may be that we have yet to hear the last word on this score. Pending the not-very-likely confirmation of this first hypothesis, we are reduced to the second, displeasing from the methodological viewpoint - which does not by any means signify that it is incorrect. Displeasing on other grounds also. It does not explain the code's universality. One is brought then to assume that, out of a multitude of efforts at elaboration, a single one survived. Which in itself makes sense, but leaves us unprovided with any model of primitive translation. Here speculation must take over. Much that is very ingenious has been put forward: the field is only too open. [3]

Monod suggests his own hypothetical model for the proto-cell that first evolved in the primordial soup. Perhaps, he says, the protein was synthesized right on the replicative structure, the DNA. As the double helix split in half, the chains of amino acid were hooked together right on the single strands of DNA. This would mean that the proto-cell would need no nucleus, just an outer membrane, and would have no need of messenger RNA, transfer RNA, or ribosomes.

Monod then explains the chemical accidents called "mutations," which enabled these first primitive cells to evolve into higher living forms. But let me once again give a little background for Monod's heavy-handed presentation. Unfortunately the Jacob Bronowski's and the Carl Sagan's are somewhat of a rarity among science writers, and the Jacques Monods are much more typical.

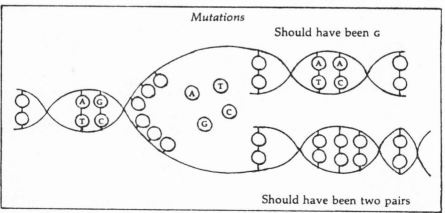

Plate xiv   *Mutations*

In the diagram we see the parent strand of DNA with the bases A, T, G, C. They are supposed to pair with their opposite numbers, A with T, G with C, and vice versa. When the DNA splits in half, these bases are picked up from the free nucleotide pool in the nucleus. Suppose something went wrong - for example: the C, which is supposed to pick up a G, picked up an A instead, as I have indicated on the top daughter strand, or when the helix started to spiral, one twist caught three pairs and the next, one, as I have indicated on the bottom daughter strand. Remember, we now think of the cell as an automated protein factory, so the kind of things that go wrong are similar to the accidents that happen on a factory assembly line.

> ...Various mutations have been identified as caused by:
> 1) The substitution of a single pair of nucleotides for another pair;
> 2) The deletion or addition of one or several pairs of nucleotides and
> 3) Various kinds of "scrambling" of the genetic text by inversion, duplication, displacement, or fusion of more or less extended segments.
> We call these events accidental; we say that they are random occurrences. And since they constitute the *only* possible source of modifications in the genetic text, itself the *sole* repository of the organism's hereditary structures, it necessarily follows that chance *alone* is at the source of every innovation, of all creation in the biosphere. Pure chance, absolutely free but blind, at the very root of the stupendous edifice of evolution: this central concept of modern biology is no longer one among other possible or even conceivable hypotheses. It is today the *sole* conceivable hypothesis, the only one that squares with observed and tested fact. And nothing warrants the supposition - or the hope - that on this score our position is ever likely to be revised. [4]

Let me conclude my presentation tonight with Monod's brief comment on our fifth day of creation, the origin of fish and birds. By the term "teleonomic," Monod does not intend any connotation of purpose or design. He defines teleonomy as "the transmission from generation to generation of the invariance content characteristic of the species."

It is the teleonomic apparatus, as it functions when a mutation first expresses itself, that lays down the essential *initial conditions* for the admission, temporary or permament, or rejection of the chance-bred innovative attempt. It is the teleonomic performance, the aggregate expression of the properties of the network of constructive and regulatory interactions, that is judged by selection; and that is why evolution itself seems to be fulfilling a design, seems to be carrying out a "project," that of perpetuating and amplifying some ancestral "dream"...As we all know, the great turning points in evolution have coincided with the invasion of ecological spaces. If terrestrial vertebrates appeared and were able to initiate that wonderful line from which amphibians, reptiles, birds, and mammals later developed, it was originally because a primitive fish "chose" to do some exploring on land, where it was however ill-provided with means for getting about. The same fish thereby created, as a consequence of a shift in behavior, the selective pressure which was to engender the powerful limbs of the quadrupeds. Among the descendants of this daring explorer, this Magellan of evolution, are some that can run at speeds of fifty miles an hour; others climb trees with astonishing agility, while yet others have conquered the air, in a fantastic manner fulfilling, extending, and amplifying the ancestral fish's hankering, its "dream." [5]

So in conclusion let me repeat the most important line I read from Jacques Monod tonight, which is the unanimous consensus of the scientific community. "Pure chance, absolutely free but blind, at the very root of the stupendous edifice of evolution..is today the *sole* conceivable hypothesis, the only one that squares with observed and tested fact. And nothing warrants the supposition - or the hope - that on this score our position is ever likely to be revised."

Fr. Robert A. Staatz

I would like to second Dr. Schonfield on the difficulty of our subject matter tonight, so a little repitition might be helpful - *repititio est mater studiorum;* "repitition is the mother of studies." But I will spare our students a rerun on the processes of DNA replition, translation and protein synthesis, and just repeat the conclusion of Dr. Schonfield's presentation - the actual mechanism of evolution, chance mutation. This is again from Fr. Owen Garrigan's *Man's Intervention in Nature:*

> It is not surprising then, that in such a long series of sequential operations, with so many "bits" of information to be processed, that there should be a certain more or less constant percentage of mistakes. The most efficient machine will make a finite number of errors. Perhaps one mistake in a million operations would seem near perfect, but even this relatively good record could result in an abnormally high mutation rate in a living organism. Biological processes are remarkably accurate in this regard. The incidence of a measurable mistake (mutation) in a given gene may be as low as only one in a billion offspring, but it is not zero.
>
> A single nucleotide out of place or miscopied can cause an error all along the line. If such an error, a "point mutation," prevents an essential activity in the offspring, there will be no living progeny: the mutation will be lethal. The nucleotide change may occur in a non-specific ("nonsense") part of DNA, if such parts exist; such a change would be ineffectual. If the mutation results in a change in a protein in part of the protein that does not remove an essential function, while at the same time it modifies that function, then the mutation can become a permanent part of the progeny and it may have an important effect on the genetic future of the race. It is this intermediate type of mutation, neither lethal nor ineffectual, that has most practical importance, especially with regard to evolution. Protein changes that produce functional changes, in an organism faced with a changing environment, will be sorted out in the offspring. That is to say, the principle of

natural selection will favor one protein form over another. A protein having one functional capability will confer a survival value...different from that of another, modified protein. The random, but statistically constant level of mistakes in information transfer brings to every living species a certain rate of mutation. Every gene in every living system, by reason of its complexity and the chance of error in making exact copies, has a built-in possibility, indeed a statistical necessity for change. Experimental evidence gathered along these lines has revealed the outlines of a chemical basis for the evolution of organisms. [6]

With that little repeat for an introduction let me go on now to the main part of my presentation for tonight, that is, the reaction of the Church to the theory of evolution. Garrigan contiunues:

Theories of evolution are not without serious implications for the Christian. In response to Darwin the Churchmen of the nineteenth century often reacted bitterly to the prospect of man's being equated with the animals, since this is what they thought evolution must imply. On their part, some evolutionists rejoiced over the "death of Adam." In an episode that typified the hostile relationship between religion and science, the Anglican Bishop Samuel Wilberforce confronted Thomas Henry Huxley in the famous Oxford debate of 1860. The exact details of the encounter and the nuances of the dialogue are not certain. It has been reported that the eloquent bishop, then fifty-four years old, spoke first. He referred to the high esteem in which Victorian England held womanhood and climaxed his oration with the *ad hominem* question, "Will the learned biologist tell me whether he is descended from the apes on his grandfather's side or on his grandmother's side?" During the guffaws that followed what seems to have been this breach of professional etiquette, Huxley, who had coined the word "agnostic" to describe his own attitude toward religion, whispered to his companion, "the Lord hath delivered him into my hands." The aroused biologist, then thirty-five, rose to reply: "If, then, the question is put to me would I rather have a miserable ape for a grandfather or a man highly endowed by nature and possessing great means and influence and yet who employs those faculties and that influence for the mere purpose of introducing ridicule into a grave scientific discussion - I unhesitatingly affirm my preference for the ape. [7]

The Catholic Church unfortunately, has also had its share of Bishop Wilberforces, but unlike Galileo, Darwin was never officially condemned by the Magisterium.

> Many individuals in the Church were undoubtedly defensive or even frightened in their posture toward evolution. On the question of man's origin, open-minded Christians seem to have been in the minority. The closer one comes to responsible authority in the Church, however, the less tendency one finds for narrow condemnations. The First Vatican Council in 1870 gave the commonsense advice that the same God is the author of reason and revelation. One truth cannot contradict another. Pope Leo XIII in 1893 applied the teaching of St. Augustine to cases of apparent conflict between science and the Bible: "Whatever...[scientists] can really demonstrate to be true of physical nature, let us show to be capable of reconciliation with our Scriptures," and, "The Holy Spirit [in the Scriptures]...did not intend to teach man these things in no way profitable unto salvation. [8]

St. Augustine's famous notion of *rationes seminales*, seminal causes, has often been considered a precursor of evolutionary thought. Augustine found no difficulty in showing that this notion was "capable of reconciliation with our Scriptures."

> St. Augustine speaks, in a famous passage, of *rationes seminales*, the seeds or germs present in the beginning of whatever would come to be in time. Some moderns have laid claim to Augustine as an early herald of the evolutionist gospel. His idea that God did not intervene in his creation once he had produced the original universe is quite consistent

with the evolutionary idea. He may indeed have intended that these seeds be understood as active powers in matter and not merely as passive potencies. [9]

Pope Leo xiii's *Providentissimus Deus* appeared in 1893 before the concept of the *Formsgeschichte*, the study of literary forms, was accepted by the Church. This did not take place, as I have pointed out, until fifty years later with the publication of *Divino Afflante Spiritu* by Pius xii. Since it is now generally conceded that the literary form of the Hexameron is the myth, it has become impossible "to show" that the theory of evolution is "capable of reconciliation with our Scriptures." Had Leo xiii lived today, he doubtless would have phrased it: "Whatever [scientists] can really demonstrate to be true of physical nature [the theory of evolution], let us show to be capable of reconciliation with our *theology*." Of course the one who has done the most to reconcile the theory of evolution with theology is Teilhard de Chardin.

...An increasing number of theologians have come to respect the well-documented majority opinion among scientists concerning evolutionary origins. The trend is to leave astronomy to the followers of Galileo, and biology to the followers of Darwin, and allow as an acceptable working hypothesis the notion of cosmic evolution, including mankind's. The Book of Genesis is seen as a religious account of man's total dependence on God, written perhaps a thousand centuries or more after the appearance of man on this planet, adapted to a people in a non-technological culture, with poetic intuition that celebrates in lyric fashion the glory of the Creator. Evolutionary insights are more and more applied to theology, especially since the posthumous publication of the works of Pierre Teilhard de Chardin. In fact, the view is beginning to emerge, inverting the common opinion of the last century, that revelation says less about evolution than evolution says about the theology of creation...

Religion supplies motives for wishing and believing that the evolution of man *is* true. Evolutionary theory can inspire enthusiasm for the unity and coherence, the simplicity and elegance of Divine Providence. The God of evolution seems ever so much wiser and more powerful than the watchmaker God who is forever returning to his masterpiece to readjust the mechanism so that it can function in a new way. In a famous passage in the *Origin of Species*, Darwin exclaimed: "There is a grandeur in this view of life, with its several powers, having been originally breathed by the Creator into a few forms or into one." (Today we would extend Darwin's remark to include the origin of life from inanimate nature. The grandeur is not lessened if the manner of God's "breathing" was actually a planned process of devolopment from a single element to complex molecules and from non-living molecules into cells.) There are many reasons to prompt Darwin and other Christians to welcome evolution and to celebrate its function as *the* method by which God accomplishes his creation. [10]

Let me conclude with the Jesuit Robert Faricy and his *Teilhard de Chardin's Theology of the Christian in the World*. Teilhard is just as emphatic in his own way about the *fact* of evolution as Jacques Monod is in his:

> ...Evolution is not just a hypothesis or a theory. "It is much more: it is a general condition to which all theories, all hypotheses, all systems must bow and which they must satisfy henceforward if they are to be thinkable and true." [11]

Mrs. Maria Stepan

Jacques Monod's book *Le Hasard et la Nécessité*, "Chance and Necessity," appeared in 1970 and was quickly translated into English. In 1972 there appeared a rebuttal of Monod by George Salet, a Catholic layman, who is a mathematician and a former pupil of Monod's partner and fellow Nobel laureate, François Jabob. Unfortunately Salet's excellent book entitled *Hasard et Certitude*, "Chance and Certitude," has not yet been translated into English. Salet, for the sake of argument, grants Monod's description of the cell as a "chemical machine":

The origin of the protein assembly machine

By "protein assembly machine" I understand the sum total of structural genes and regulatory genes which exists in every cell and which governs not only the linking of amino acids, according to given sequences, into proteins, but also the synthesis of all tools necessary for the assembly job, messenger RNA, ribosomes, transfer RNA, and a considerable amount of enzymes.

Can protein synthesis be effected by procedures other than those known to us or particularly by simpler procedures? It is quite possible. We can imagine, for example, a system without messenger RNA where the "reading" would be made directly on the DNA. We can even imagine (although the viability of the system seems doubtful) an assembly of amino acids by direct contact with the DNA. [This was the hypothetical model of the primitive cell suggested by Monod.] Ribosomes and transfer RNA would then be useless, but the enzymes which would function would be different than the present ones...

But assuming that the systems I have just envisaged are viable...it still remains that, simpler or not, they are different from the present one, in exactly the same way that a two-cycle engine is different from a four-cycle engine. [12]

A two-cycle engine is a simple engine used for example in model airplanes, while the more complicated four-cycle engine is used in automobiles. Monod is saying equivalently, that the chemical machine, the cell, began as a simple two-cycle engine and progressed gradually to a four-cycle engine. But there is no step in between a two and a four cycle engine; a third cycle would not only be useless but impossible!

Could the machine have "progressivley" passed from one system to another by a series of mutations? This is really impossible; for, inasmuch as every breakdown of the machine is lethal, every intermediary disposition must be viable. It is therefore just as impossible to pass "progressively" from a system without ribosomes and without transfer RNA (assuming such a system to be viable) to the present system, as it is to imagine a continual chain of *viable* intermediaries between a two-cycle and a four-cycle engine. [Salet's emphasis]

Passing from one system to another, therefore, cannot have taken place except by a *single mutation*, which means - either that the gene system which constitutes the protein assembly machine has been modified in one mutation only, a thing so inconceivable that no one would dare hold it [That is, that the two-cycle engine went to the four in one big jump.], or that a set of *supplementary genes* appeared which underwent *a long series of genetic mutations*, thereby acquiring the character to correspond to the fabrication of proteins by the new system. Let us notice that *the fabrication would have to continue by means of the old system during this whole series of mutations.* A sudden change would have taken place when the new set of genes acquired by chance the desired character. [13]

The two-cylce and the four-cycle engine are completely different designs. For example, in the two-cycle engine the intake and exhaust ports are on the sides of the cylinder, while in the four-cycle engine they are on top. So equivalently, while the two-cycle engine was still functioning, it would have to grow new ports and valves on the top of the cylinder. When these ports were completed, the new system would cut in. Imagine Monod trying to explain this theory to a group of mechanics!

It is a profound illusion to believe that certain mechanical functions can have been exercised by very simple mechanisms. Indeed, just as with our machines, a biological system *could not be simplified below a certain minimum*. The complexity of a machine does not result from a precise intention of its author, but from a necessity that *it be able to perform the function assigned to it*. Buy the cheapest radio set on the market. Look at its interior and you will understand that it would not be possible to listen to a broadcast with a very simple set. *There is a minimum of complexity below which it is impossible to descend and which results from the nature of things.*

Likewise a biological device able to put together amino acids in an order defined by a DNA sequence could not be a simple device any more than a machine able to fabricate pearl necklaces, with pearls of different types arranged in an order defined by punched cards, could be a simple machine.

It is certainly possible that the biological processes of protein assembly known to us are not the simplest processes possible. Still, it is true that this simpler system must be somewhat complex, *if it is to be capable of carrying on its function.* We may imagine because of unknown (in fact, unimaginable) reasons, that this simpler device came into existence *progressively.* What is impossible to admit is that it could have been able to work before it was completed. Let me repeat again, that a car does not work less well without a carburetor, or an ignition system, but rather not at all. [14]

So by reducing the living cell to a chemical machine and the theory of evolution to accidental mutations, Monod has unwittingly made that theory unworkable.

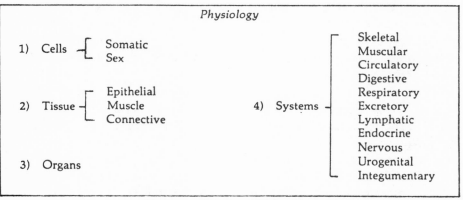

Plate xv   *Science of Physiology*

Louis Vialletion, a professor of physiology at the University of Montpelier in France, was one of the most articulate opponents of the theory of evolution. He maintained that the science of physiology proved that the theory of evolution, as proposed by Darwin and others, was completely untenable. On the blackboard I have an outline of the subject matter covered in physiology. First we have the cell, the basic unit of life, of which there are two kinds - the somatic or body cell, and the sex cell, which is really only a half cell. Secondly, the cells combine to form tissue of which there are four kinds - epithelial (e.g. skin), muscle, connective, and nerve tissue. Thirdly, the tissues combine to form organs, such as the eye. Fourthly, these organs are arranged into eleven systems, the skeletal, muscular, circulatory, digestive, respiratory, excretory, lymphatic, endocrine, nervous, urogenital, and integumentary.

The evolutionists seem to hold that evolution proceeds organ by organ. For example, Darwin said that the thought of the evolution of the eye made him sick, it seemed so impossible, yet contemporary evolutionists don't hesitate to claim that the eye evolved forty separate times. Vialleton maintained that you can't speak of the eye, or any organ for that matter, as having evolved by itself, because the eye is part of a whole interdependent system. If you want to speak of evolution, you have to speak in terms of the evolution of the whole system or not at all. The evolutionists do not attempt to respond to Vialleton's criticisms, but have simply ignored them. Salet has also been getting the silent treatment, and his book has been completely ignored by the whole secular humanist Establishment. Here is Salet's summary of Vialleton's argument:

Mutations happen by chance, and therefore we must see if chance, even if aided by natural selection, has been able to achieve any results...The desired result is that the new production not be an incoherent ensemble, but an "organ," i.e., something possessing different parts which *complement one another so that the whole may be able to exercise a definite function.* If we consider, e.g., the eye, it is necessary among other requirements that the crystalline be transparent and that its curvature, and therefore its focal distance, have a definite relation with its distance to the retina...Another result to be attained is that the *new organ form with its organism a coherent whole.* For example, an eye would have no use at all if it should develop inside the stomach.

Besides, an organ is not something you attach to an organism the same way you attach a rear view mirror to an automobile door. Its *coordination* with other already existing organs supposes a more or less profound revision of the whole living being; for example, the eye, even assuming that it appears on a suitable location and properly connected by nerves to the sensorial and motor centers of the brain and the cerbellum, would serve no purpose at all if these nervous centers had not at the same time become fit to use the stimuli received by the optic nerve in a manner useful to the individual...Vialleton showed how impossible it was for the new organs to form a coherent whole with what existed before, and therefore the need for a recasting of the whole individual. The reasons brought forward by...him have never been the object of serious discussion. I recall them briefly...in the hope that they will not fall into oblivion. [15]

Let me now go from Dr. Schonfield's presentation to that of Fr. Staatz. While it is true, as Fr. Staatz says, that some members of the scientific community were originally attracted to the evolutionary philosophy of Fr. Teilhard de Chardin, many were not, among whom was Jacques Monod. Let me also read a few excerpts from his *Chance and Necessity*:

The biological philosophy of Teilhard de Chardin would not merit attention but for the startling success it has encountered in scientific circles. A success which tells of the eagerness of the need, to revive the covenant. Teilhard revives it, and does so nakedly. His philosophy, like Bergson's, is based entirely upon an evolutionist postulate. But, unlike Bergson, he has the evolutionary force operating throughout the entire universe, from elementary particles to galaxies: there is no "inert" matter, and therefore no essential distinction between "matter" and "life." His wish to present this concept as "scientific" leads Teilhard to base it upon a new definition of energy. This is somehow distributed between two vectors, one of which would be (I presume) "ordinary" energy, whereas the other would correspond to the upward evolutionary surge. The biosphere and man are the latest products of this ascent along the spiritual vector of energy. This evolution is to continue until all energy has become concentrated along the spiritual vector: that will be the attaining of "point omega."

Although Teilhard's logic is hazy and his style laborious, some of those who do not entirely accept his ideology yet allow it a certain poetic grandeur. For my part, I am most of all struck by the intellectual spinelessness of this philosophy. In it I see more than anything else a systematic truckling, a willingness to conciliate at any price, to come to any compromise. Perhaps, after all, Teilhard was not for nothing a member of that order which, three centuries ago, Paschal assailed for its theological laxity. [16]

Jacques Monod, although he had a Calvinist father and a Jewish mother, was a militant atheist and actually said, "the only thing one can do is to die without calling the priest to one's bedside." But even he seems to be saying here that he would rather hear real Christianity from a Catholic priest, even though he doesn't believe it, rather than Christianity watered down by secular humanism.

Let me go on now from Dr. Schonfield and Fr. Staatz to Rev. Swezey. If you remember on the second day of creation, which deals with the origin of the universe, I mentioned that St. Thomas Aquinas teaches that creation out of nothing cannot be demonstrated by either science or philosophy but must be taken simply on faith. For this reason I suggested at the time that *Creationism versus Evolutionism* was not the best of dichotomies, and that the creationists were placing an unnecessary burden on themselves by maintaining that creationism is not a strictly religious but also a scientific idea. I suggested that a more proper dichotomy might be *Fixism versus Evolutionism*, since fixism is still a viable *scientific* alternative to evolutionism. Such a change in terminology might help in the ongoing legal battle against the exclusive teaching of evolutionism in the public schools.

Let me read a humorous presentation of fixism from the great Catholic controversialist, Hilaire Belloc:

> If Natural Selection be true, then what we call a pig is but a fleeting vision; and all the past he has been becoming a pig, and all the future he will spend evolving out of pigdom, and pig is but a moment's phase in the eternal flux, while all around us should be quarter-pigs, half-pigs, near-pigs, all-but-pigs, slightly-super-pigs, just beginning - and so on. But there aren't. There are just pigs. In other words, the evidence is all in favor of Fixed Types and all against a ceaseless process of change. [17]

Of course, Darwin replied that evolution is indeed proceeding all around us, but is so gradual that we don't notice it. But Darwin was actually a much better scientist than many of his disciples today. He said that if experimental proof for evolution was not forthcoming within a few years, he would abandon the theory. Darwin was a pigeon fancier and was confident that he could breed a new species of bird within ten years. Huxley thought too that by breeding sheep he would be able to produce a new species of animal within twenty years. Later generations of evolutionists, such as Morgan, Muller and Dobzhansky, have continued these experiments by tinkering with one of the most famous insects in science, the fruit fly *Drosophila melanogaster*. They drastically increased the mutation rate by bombarding these little creatures with x rays and by artificially selecting and isolating apparently favored individuals, they hoped to produce a new species within a few years.

Here is the Columban Father, Patrick O'Connell, from his wonderful *Science of Today and the Problems of Genesis* which I will be referring to frequently when we study the evolution of man:

> If a species be identified as a freely interbreeding commu-
> nity, no new animal species has yet been bred by any experi-

menter. This is very remarkable in view of the fact that breeding experiments lasting over some thirty years have been made with the fruit fly *Drosophila melanogaster*. This produces about twenty-five generations a year, hence some 900 successive generations of this species have been bred in the laboratory in the unsuccessful attempt to convert it into another type. This corresponds to about 30,000 years of human existence. [18]

Fr. O'Connell was writing in 1959 and these experiments on *Drosophila* have continued to this date, and still no new species.

Let me conclude with my own presentation from the Tradition and Magisterium of the Church. We heard Fr. Staatz claim that St. Augustine had no trouble showing that his own crude evolutionary ideas were "capable of reconciliation with our Scriptures." Cardinal Ernesto Ruffini in his excellent *The Theory of Evolution Judged by Reason and Faith*, has a long study of the thought of St. Augustine in this matter. Here are his summary and conclusions:

> The evolutionists maintain: 1) that the differentiation of the species is the product of successive generations; 2) that God's activity in regard to the world is restricted to the initial creative act. [Cardinal Ruffini is, of course, speaking of theistic not atheistic evolution.]
>
> St. Augustine's doctrine is diametrically opposed:
> 1) Corresponding to every species or different nature is a particular *ratio seminales* placed in the world by God the Creator as a scheme or invisible image, but capable of actuality in the course of time by His omnipotent word.
>
> 2) In the beginning God created all organisms together in a quasi-seminal state, but it is He, and He alone, who causes them to arise in the course of the centuries, that is, He causes them to pass from the seminal state into the actual state according to a fixed plan, by means of that providential government to which Jesus refers in the Gospel: *Pater usque nunc operatur et ego operor* ("the Father works even until now, and I work.")...This is the thought of the most wise bishop of Hippo. Therefore it is an outrage - and, worse, a

real calumny - to attribute to him in any way the opinion of the evolutionists, however moderate they may be. [19]

Let me go on now to the Magisterium of the Church. In 1907 Pope St. Pius x brought out his marvelous encyclical *Pascendi Gregis* condemning Modernism. The Holy Father says that the basis of all the Modernist errors in Scripture and theology is evolutionism. We have already commented briefly on the so-called *Religionsgeschichte*, the history or evolution or religions. The Pope is here speaking of the Modernist treatment of the Bible:

> The Modernists have no hesitation in affirming that these books, and especially the Pentateuch and the first three Gospels, have been gradually formed from a brief narration, by additions, by interpretations of theological or allegorical interpretations, or parts introduced only for the purpose of joining different passages together. This means to put it briefly and clearly, that in the Sacred Books we must admit a *vital evolution*, springing from and corresponding with the evolution of faith. The traces of this evolution, they tell us, are so visible in the books that one might almost write a history of it. Indeed, this history they actually do write, and with such an easy assurance that one might believe them to have seen with their own eyes the writers at work through the ages amplifying the Sacred Books. [20]

Then in 1950 Pope Pius xii issued his encyclical *Humani Generis* which was directed in large part against the works of Fr. Teilhard de Chardin then circulating privately throughout the Church:

> Looking around at those outside the fold of Christ, one can easily discern the principal trends not a few learned men follow. Some are imprudent and indiscreet enough to hold that the so-called theory of evolution, although not yet fully proved even in the domain of natural sciences, explains the origin of all things, and they go so far as to support the monistic and pantheistic notion that the whole world is subject to continual evolution. Communists eagerly seize

upon this theory in the hope of depriving souls of every idea of God and of defending and propagating the more effectively their dialectical materialism.

The fictitious tenets of evolution, which repudiate all that is absolute, firm and immutable, have paved the way for a new erroneous philosophy, a rival of idealism, immanentism, and pragmatism, which has come to be called existentialism, because, forgetful of the immutable essences of things, it concerns itself only with individual existence. [21]

This most important encyclical concentrates especially on the evolution of man, and I will return to it again when we come to the sixth day of creation, which deals with the origin of man.

Rev. De Verne Swezey

Evolution is much more than a scientific theory, it has become the central dogma of the religion of secular humanism, especially of establishment humanism. But the theory has been severely criticized even from within the ranks of humanism by what I have been calling the counter-culture. Accordingly, let me begin once again with one of the its leading spokesman, Theodore Roszak. This is from his review of Jacques Monod's *Chance and Necessity* which appeared in *Book World* for October of 1971:

...What is the message Monod finds for us in the molecules of life? Its spirit is captured by the two quotations that preface the book. One from Democritus ("Everything in the universe is the fruit of chance and necessity."); and the other from Albert Camus' *Myth of Sysiphus*, that classic existentialist hymn to heroic despair. What follows these bleak precepts is one of the most unrelenting exercises in philosophical tough-mindedness I have ever read.

For the science Monod serves is an unsparing mistress; she enforces an "ethic of knowledge" which is "austere, abstract, proud." Her single banner is "the postulate of objectivity" which insists that nature is neutral, purposeless, devoid of value. Only one world-view is compatible with scientific truth, Monod argues; a militant atheism that embraces the radical absurdity of human existence, yet defiantly asserts man's ethical project against the world. (The moral code Monod recommends is a compassionate, democratic social-ism; like most true-believing atheists, he is humane and highly principaled.) Any flinching from this cheerless reality - whether it leads to the ideological superstitions of Marxism or the "disgusting farrago of Judaeo-Christian religiosity" - is a plain "lie."...

The biology Monod reviews is marshalled stoically to the support of this dour vision. The details are often technologi-cal but the drift is clear. Molecular research proves that the living cell is but a "chemical machine." Its once mysterious activities - growth, metabolism, self-replication - can be reduced to routine chemical reactions. The chemistry is stupendously complex, but in no religious sense "miracu-lous." What once seemed to be purposiveness in the life process is fully explained by enzyme sequences and feedback mechanisms: "microscopic cybernetics"...

Admire the man. It takes stamina and no little blind faith to drive one's science to such a reductionist end. Atheism is, after all, a tenuous premise (not a conclusion), and chance the most dubious god of all. Could any dogma of the churches strain credulity more than to believe that the labrynthine chemistry of life emerges from a molecular lottery?...How sad to be Jacques Monod: to stare so expertly at miracles and meanings, but never see them. [22]

And here is another forceful critic of establishment humanism, Arthur Koestler from his excellent *The Ghost in the Machine*:

"I refuse to believe that God plays dice with the world.
                                              Albert Einstein

...The orthodox ("Neo-Darwinian" or "synthetic") theory attempts to explain all evolutionary changes by random mutations (and re-combinations) of genes; most mutations are harmful, but a very small proportion happen to be useful and is retained by natural selection..."Randomness" means in this context that the hereditary changes wrought by mutation are totally unrelated to the animal's adaptive needs - that they may alter its physique and behavior "in any and every direction." In this view, evolution appears as a game of blind man's bluff. Or, in the words of Professor Waddington - a quasi-Trotskyite member of the Establishment...: "To suppose that the evolution of the wonderfully adapted biological mechanisms has depended only on a selection out of a haphazard set of variations, each produced by blind chance, is like suggesting that if we went on throwing bricks together into heaps, we should eventually be able to choose ourselves the most desirable house." [23]

Arthur Koestler then goes on to discuss the hypothetical evolutionary step from amphibian to reptile. His criticism is based on the unanswered arguments of Louis Vialleton, which Mrs. Stepan reviewed briefly. Vialleton had said, if you remember, that you couldn't speak of evolution as having occurred organ by organ, such as the eye, but if it occurred at all, it would have had to have been from system to system. Here Koestler is just dealing with the reproductive systems of the amphibian and the reptile, but the same is true of all systems.

...The vertebrates' conquest of dry land started with the evolution of reptiles from some primitive amphibian form. The amphibians reproduced in the water, and their young were aquatic. The decisive novelty of the reptiles was that, unlike amphibians, they laid their eggs on dry land; they no longer depended on the water but were free to roam over the continents. But the unborn reptile inside the egg still needed an aquatic environment: it had to have water or else it would dry up long before it was born. It also needed a lot of food: amphibians hatch as larvae who fend for themselves, whereas reptiles hatch fully developed. So the reptilian egg had to be provided with a large mass of yolk for food, and also with albumen - the white of egg - to provide the water. Neither the yolk by itself, nor the egg-white itself, would have had any selective value. Moreover, the egg-white needed a vessel to contain it, otherwise its moisture would have evaporated. So there had to be a shell made of leathery or limey material, as part of the evolutionary package-deal. But that is not the end of the story. The reptilian embryo, because of this shell, could not get rid of its waste products. The soft-shelled amphibian embryo had the whole pond as a lavatory; the reptilian embryo had to be provided with a kind of bladder. It is called the allantois, and is in some respects the forerunner of the mammalian placenta. But this problem having been solved, the embryo would still remain trapped inside its tough shell; it needed a tool to get out. The embryos of some fish and amphibians, whose eggs are surrounded by a gelatinous membrane, have glands on their snouts: when the time is ripe, they secrete a chemical which dissolves the membrane. But embryos surrounded by a hard shell need a mechanical tool: thus snakes and lizards have a tooth transformed into a kind of tin-opener, while birds have a caruncle - a hard outgrowth near the tip of their beaks which serves the same purpose. In some birds - the honey guides - which lay their eggs like cuckoos in alien nests, the caruncle serves yet another purpose: it grows into a sharp hook with which the newly hatched invader kills off its foster-brethern, after which it amiably sheds its hook. [24]

The theory of evolution is a good example of what is called "reductionism. The evolutionists claim that the mutations which eventually led to a new species occurred one at a time. In Arthur Koestler's example, the first mutation to occur would be the egg shell, then the allantois, then the can opener, and so on. The anti-reductionist argument is called the "holist" argument, and maintains that you have to think in terms of the whole living organism, and not just in terms of the sum of its parts. The holists would say that if any of these parts, for example, the egg shell had mutated, it would have had to occur at the same time as the others to be beneficial to the whole organism.

All this refers to one aspect only of the evolution of reptiles;

needless to say, countless other essential transformations of structure and behavior were required to make the new creatures viable. The changes could have been gradual - but at each step, however small, *all* the factors involved in the story had to cooperate harmoniously. The liquid store in the egg makes no sense without the shell. The shell would be useless, in fact murderous, without the allantois and without the tin-opener. Each change, taken in isolation, would be harmful, and work *against* survival. You cannot have mutation A occurring alone, preserve it by natural selection, and then wait a few thousand or million years until mutation B joins it, and so on to C and D. Each mutation occurring alone would be wiped out before it could be combined with the others. They are all interdependent. The doctrine that their coming together was due to a series of blind coincidences is an affront not only to common-sense, but to the basic principles of scientific explanation. [25]

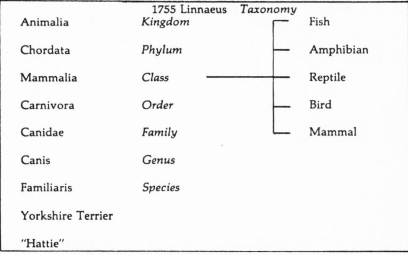

Plate XVI   *Taxonomy according to Linnaeus*

248 THE SIX DAYS OF CREATION

Let me go on now from the counter-culture movement to the creationist movement, but let me first try to clarify a few basic notions that Arthur Koestler was taking for granted. The Swedish naturalist Carolus Linnaeus is called the father of the science of taxonomy or classification. Linnaeus divided all of Nature into three great Kingdoms: the Mineral, the Vegetable, and the Animal. The Animal and Vegetable kingdoms he further subdivided into Phylum, Order, Family, Genus, and finally Species. On the blackboard I have followed a pet dog named "Hattie" through all these categories. We begin with the Kingdom, which in this case is the Animal; the Phylum is the Chordata, or creatures having a backbone; the Class, the Mammalia or creatures which nurse their young; the Order, the Carnivora or meat eaters; the Family, the Canidae or dog-like creatures; the Genus, Canis or dog; the Species, Familiaris or domestic dog, the Yorkshire Terrier; and finally the individual dog, "Hattie." So Hattie's full name is - Hattie, Yorkshire Terrier, Familiaris, Canis, Canidae, Carnivora, Mammalia, Chordata, Animalia. The fact that all the living creatures in the world can be so classified, shows that there is Design in the world put there by God. If evolution were true there would be no such order apparent but rather chaos.

Most biblical Christians who reject evolution, distinguish between micro and macro-evolution. Micro-evolution which should really not be called evolution but rather variation, they will admit, occurs in species, genera, and up to family, which many consider identical to the biblical "kind." "So God created the great sea monsters and every living creature that moves, and which swarm in the waters according to their *kinds*." For example, the horse and the donkey belong to the same family of horse-like creatures, but their offspring, the mule, is sterile. Thus the sterility of hybrids prevents macro-evolution or evolution between the great classes.

Ernst Haeckel, Darwin's German ally, was the first to propose a "genealogical tree" for the theory of evolution. On the right side of the "Hattie" chart, we see that Linnaeus has classified all the living creatures of the world into five great classes. (I have deliberately left out two classes of insects for purposes of simplification.) Haeckel merely took these five classes and arranged them into a genealogical tree. These five great classes are the Fish, Amphibian, Reptile, Bird, and Mammal.

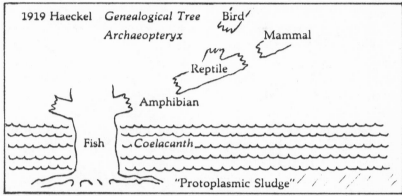

Plate XVII   *Genealogical Tree according to Haeckel*

We have seen that according to Haeckel, life evolved in the "protoplasmic sludge" at the bottom of the sea. These first life forms gradually evolved into fish, which then evolved into amphibians. A fish stays in the water and breathes through gills, while an amphibian goes back and forth between water and land, and breathes through lungs. The amphibians then evolved into reptiles which stay on land. Finally the reptiles split into two main branches, birds and mammals.

Haeckel also coined the phrase "missing link." He recognized that there were gaps between all the great classes, but prophesied that fossils of these missing links would soon be found, since scientists now knew just what to look for. We heard Monod speak of the "Magellan of evolution," the fish "that found its dream," which was evidently to become an amphibian. The fossil fish the evolutionists originally thought made the transition to amphibian was the coelacanth. This particular fish was chosen because its fins were thought to be in just the right places, where they could later develop into legs. Here again is the creationist Dr. Henry Morris:

The next major evolutionary advance must have been from fish to amphibian. Somehow the fin of the fish must have been transformed into the foot of the amphibian, not to mention the myriad of other necessary changes. To date, however, no fossil of a "fishbian," with fins partly converted into feet (or any other transitional characters) has ever been found.

The chief candidate for such a transitional form was long supposed to have been the coelacanth, a crossopterygian fish, which was supposed to have certain limb-like characters on its fins indicating initial advance toward amphibianhood. Ultimately it was destined, so it was believed, to become a primitive amphibian known as a labrynthodont. The coelacanth was believed to have finished this transition sometime in the Mesozoic, since no fossils have been found subsequent to that era.

Evolutionists were embarrassed when it was discovered in 1958 that these fish are still alive and well, living in the waters near Madagascar...It is hard to see how these fish could have become amphibians when they are still the same as they were a hundred million years ago when they began to make the transition. There seem, however, to be no other candidates. The lung-fish, the "walking catfish," and other fish that seem to have certain resemblances to land animals, have all been ruled out by the evolutionists for various other reasons. [26]

The so-called "missing link" between the reptile and the bird is thought to have been a fossil called *archaeopteryx*, which simply means in Greek "old bird," but doesn't it sound grand:

Evolutionists universally maintain that reptiles are the evolutionary ancestors of birds. Again, however, there is no fossil evidence of this, despite the famous fossil *archaeopteryx*. W.B. Swinton has admitted:

"The origin of birds is largely a matter of deduction. There is no fossil evidence of the stages through which the remarkable change from reptile to bird was achieved." [27]

The interesting fossil, *archaeopteryx*, however, had certain characteristics (e.g., teeth) which were deemed reptilian and others (e.g., wings and feathers) which were deemed avian. Consequently, this is always the most-emphasized example, in evolutionary textbooks, of evolution between two major classes of animals. If there is any transitional form at all, *archaeopteryx* is the one. As Dunbar says:

"It would be difficult to find a more perfect 'connecting link' between two great groups of animals, or even more cogent proof of the reptilian ancestry of the birds." [28]

Yet this same author, in the very same paragraph, recognizes that *archaeopteryx* is not part reptile at all, but 100 percent bird. He says it is:

"...because of its feathers distinctly to be classified as a bird. [29]

The fossilized impressions of the feathers on the wings of *archaeopteryx* have been found and this shows that it was warm-blooded, not a reptile with scales and cold blood. [30]

So embarrassed are the evolutionists by these gaps in the fossil record between the major classes that they are turning again to the old "saltation" theory, that is, that evolution proceeds by quantum jumps. In 1940 Dr. Richard Goldschmitt after twenty five years of unsucessful efforts to breed a new species of gypsy moth, proposed his "hopeful monster" theory. Occasionally monsters are born, a sheep with two heads, etc. which usually die very quickly. But suppose, Dr. Goldschmitt suggests, that occassionally these monsters don't die, but live to breed, and so pass on their odd genes to the next generation. These creatures could possibly bridge the gap between the great classes, and since they occurred so quickly they would leave no evidence in the fossil record.

At the time this theory was completely ridiculed by his fellow evolutionists, but in 1977 Stephen Jay Gould of Harvard suggested that Goldschmitt's "hopeful monster" theory would have to be embraced to some extent, because of the gaps in the fossil record.

Gould called his own version of the "hopeful monster" theory "punctuated equilibria." Species are usually in a state of equilibrium, he says, but at rare intervals they are punctuated by a quantum jump before settling back into a new equilibrium. Gould thinks a new species could evolve in this manner in 50 to 100 generations, or less than 100,000 years for some species. This is considered practically instantaneous by orthodox geological time standards and would explain why no transistional forms have been found in the fossil record.

Traditionally evolutionists have claimed that the reason they can't test the theory of evolution by breeding experiments, is because of the tremendous time periods involved. But this is no longer true if the punctuated equilibria theory is correct, and as Mrs. Stepan has pointed out, the fast breeding species, *Drosophila melanogaster*, is long overdue for a quantum jump!

In conclusion let me repeat that the atheist Ernst Haeckel who coined the term "missing link," to describe the absence of transitional forms in the fossil record between the great classes, prophesied that fossils of these forms would soon be found. The fossil record has proven this prophecy false.

Dean Smalley

The meeting tonight was on the fifth day of creation which deals with the origin of fish and birds. We thought this an appropriate place to begin our discussion of the theory of evolution.

Dr. Schonfield presented the case for evolution from the Nobel laureate Jacques Monod who maintains that the whole stupendous edifice of evolution was brought about by an accumulation of random accidents at the molecular level called "mutations" which have occurred regularly over the millenia.

Fr. Staatz accepted the theory of evolution on its scientific merits and claimed that Teilhard de Chardin had successfully reconciled the theory with Christian theology.

Mrs. Stepan offered a rebuttal of Jacques Monod by the French Catholic mathematician, George Salet, who compared the transition of Monod's hypothetical proto-cell to a more modern cell, to the impossible transition between a two cycle and four cycle engine.

Rev. Swezey claimed that the fossil record has shown that there are major gaps between all the great classes of Linnaeus, such as the gap between reptile and mammal, thus demonstrating that the theory of evolution is false.

REFERENCES

1 Jacques Monod, *Chance and Necessity*,
   (Translated from the French by Austryn Wainhouse),
   Vintage Books, Random House, New York, 1972, p.138.
2 Monod, *Op. cit.*, pp.143-146.
3 *Idem*, pp.143,144.
4 *Idem*, pp.112,113.
5 *Idem*, pp.119,120,126,127.
6 Owen Garrigan, *Man's Intervention in Nature*,
   Hawthorne Books, New York, 1967, pp.122,123.
7 Garrigan, *Op. cit.*, ppo83,84.
8 *Idem*, pp.85,86.
9 *Idem*, p.81.
10 *Idem*, pp.87,89.
11 Robert Faricy, s.j., *Teilhard de Chardin's Theology of the Christian in the World*, Sheed and Ward, New York, 1967, p.36.
12 George Salet, *Hasard et Certitude*,
   Editions Scientifique, Paris, 1972, pp.273,274.
13 Salet, *Op. cit.*, p.274.
14 *Idem*, pp.279,280.
15 *Idem*, pp.389-391.
16 Monod, *Op. cit.*, pp.31,32.
17 Hilaire Belloc, *A Companion to Mr. Wells's "Outline of History,"* Sheed and Ward, London, 1926, pp.54,55.

18 Fr. Patrick O'Connell, *Science of Today and the Problems of Genesis*,
    Christian Book Club of America, Hawthorne, Cal., 1959, p.52.
19 Cardinal Ernesto Ruffini, *The Theory of Evolution Judged by Reason and Faith*,
    (Translated from the Italian by Francis O'Hanlon),
    Joseph F. Wagner, New York, 1959, pp.196,197,190.
20 Pope St. Pius x, *Pascendi Gregis*,
    National Catholic Welfare Conference, Washington, 1963, p.24.
21 Pope Pius xii, *Humani Generis*,
    Weston College, Weston, 1951, p.7.
22 Review by Theodore Roszak of Jacques Monod's, *Chance and Necessity*,
    Book World, Oct 24, 1971, New York, pp.4,16.
23 Arthur Koestler, *The Ghost in the Machine*,
    MacMillan Company, New York, 1968, p.127.
24 Koestler, *Op. cit.*, pp.128,129.
25 *Idem*, p.129.
26 Henry Morris, *Scientific Creationism*,
    Creation-Life Publishers, San Diego, Cal., 1974, pp.82,83.
27 Morris, *Op. cit.*, footnote, p.84,
    W.E. Swinton, *Biology and Comparative Physiology of Birds*,
    New York Academic Press, 1960.
28 *Idem*, footnote, p.85,
    Carl O. Dunbar, *Historical Geology*,
    John Wiley and Sons, New York, 1961.
29 *Idem*, footnote, p.84, *Ibid*.
30 *Idem*, pp.84,85.

THE SIXTH DAY

The Origin of Man

The Creation of Adam

"The 'finger of God's right hand' (as the hymn puts it) is close to that of the first man without touching it, and the soul passes as a non-material spark into the body of Adam, as he rises out of the earth to contemplate his God with thankfulness and worship. The angels gathered around gaze with wonder on that new being that the Psalmist calls 'a little lower than the angels'; the artists of the Renaissance found in this figure their ideal of manly beauty and the mirror of 'divine proportion.'"

D. Redig de Campos, *Cappella Sistina*

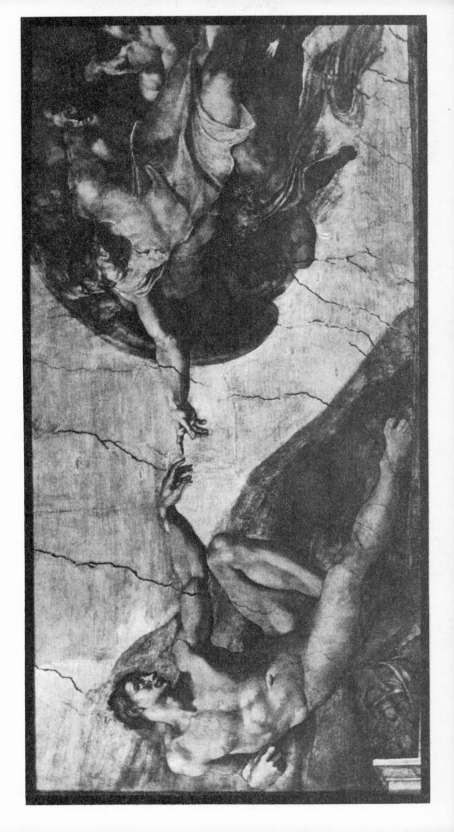

THE NINTH MEETING
The Evolution of Man

Dean Smalley

We come tonight to the sixth day of creation which deals with the origin of man. We have decided to devote three meetings to this most important day; the first to a discussion of the evolution of man, the second to the future evolution of man, during which we will examine the ethical problems associated with recombinant DNA research and genetic engineering or eugenics, and our final meeting to the existence of the soul. Let me begin as usual by reading the Scriptural account of the sixth day of creation:

> And God said, "Let the earth bring forth living creatures according to their kinds; cattle and creeping things and beasts of the earth according to their kinds." And it was so. And God made the beasts of the earth according to their kinds, and everything that creeps upon the ground according to its kind. And God saw that it was good. Then God said, "Let us make man in our image, and after our likeness; and let them have dominion over the fish of the sea, and over the birds of the air, and over the cattle, and over all the earth." So God created man in his image, in the image of God he created him; male and female he created them. And God blessed them, and God said to them, "Be fruitful and multiply, and fill the earth and subdue it; and have dominion over the fish of the sea and over the birds of the air and over every living thing that moves upon the earth." And God said, "Behold, I have given you every plant yielding seed which is upon the face of all the earth, and every tree with seed in its fruit; you shall have them for food. And to every beast of the earth, and to everything that he made, and behold, it was very good. And

there was evening and there was morning a sixth day (Gen 1:24-31).

Dr. Arthur Schonfield

	The Evolution of Man			
Age				*Brain Size*
30 Thousand	*Homo sapiens sapiens*	Cro-Magnon		1500 c.c.
100 Thousand	*Homo sapiens*	Neanderthal		1500 c.c.
1 Million	*Homo erectus*	Peking Man		1000 c.c.
5 Million	*Hominid*	*Australopithecus*		400 c.c.
14 Million		*Ramapithecus*		?
30 Million	*Ape*			
	Monkey			
50 Million	*Primate*	Lemur		
200 Million	*Mammal*			

Plate xviii *Ascent of Man according to Bronowski*

The diagram on the board is the big picture of the ascent of man according to Jacob Bronowski. Many scientists, however, would differ with him in a few details. Man belongs to the mammal class which is thought to have evolved from the reptile about 200 million years ago. Man also belongs to the order of primates, in which monkeys, apes, and men are classified as higher primates, while the lemur is classified as a lower primate. The lemur looks and acts very much like a monkey, but the reason it is not so classified is mainly because of its teeth. Monkeys, apes, and men have thirty-two teeth, while the lemur has many more.

In 1859 Charles Darwin published his *Origin of Species* in which he dealt only with evolution in general; but in 1871, in his *Descent of Man*, he asserted that man had evolved from the anthropoid or man-like apes. Most likely, he said, this had occurred in Africa, because two of the remaining species of anthropoid apes, the gorilla and the chimpanzee, were still found there; but also possibly in Asia, where the orangutan and the gibbon, the two other remaining species, were found. But in the 1950's Sir Julian Huxley and Louis Leakey decided that it was more proper to say that the apes, instead of being our parents, were rather our cousins, and that our common ancestor was one of the lower primates like the lemur.

The lower primates are thought to have appeared about 50 million years ago, and from that line the monkeys branched off about 20 million years later. The reason monkeys are considered more primitive than apes is again primarily because of their teeth. Although monkeys do have the thirty-two teeth of apes and men, their back teeth (the molars), have only four cusps (little bumps), while apes and men have five.

Next, the apes branched off from the main line and the hominids or near-men, appeared, but just when the apes and the hominids became distinct is not yet clear. Here is Dr. Bronowski:

> It is the change in the teeth that signals the separation of the line that leads to man when it comes. The first harbinger that we have is *Ramapithecus*, found in Kenya and in India. This creature is fourteen million years old, and we have only pieces of the jaw. But it is clear that the teeth are level and more human. The great canines of the anthropoid apes are gone, the face is much flatter and we are evidently near a branching of the evolutionary tree; some anthropologists would boldly put *Ramapithecus* among the hominids. [1]

The first generally accepted hominids, however, are the *Australopithecines*, southern apes, which were discovered by Raymond Dart and others, in southern Africa. Some scientists, however, think that the *Australopithecines* were not in the direct line to man, but rather a collateral branch which came to an end.

There are, of course, no hominids living today.

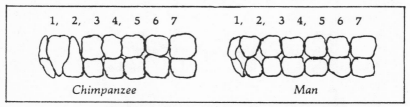

Plate xix   *Teeth of Chimpanzee and Man*

Again the main reason the *Australopithecines* are considered hominids, and not apes, is their teeth. This diagram is a side view of the thirty-two teeth of chimpanzees and men. We both have eight incissors 1, four canines 2, eight pre-molars 3 4, and twelve molars 5 6 7. Notice in the chimpanzee that the canines are huge, and that they lock together. Man has the same set of molars, pre-molars, canines, and incisors, but the canines are smaller and do not lock together. The canines of the *Australopithecus* are more like those of man than those of the chimpanzee.

In the television version of *The Ascent of Man*, Dr. Bronowski was seated before the display screen of a computer. He had programmed into the computer, drawings of about six fossil skulls representing the evolutionary steps from the lower primates to man. As he spoke, one drawing faded imperceptibly into another:

> ...He is the nearest thing we have to what used to be called the "missing link": *Australopithecus africanus,* one of a number of skulls found at Sterkfontein in the Transvaal and elsewhere in Africa, a fully grown female...fully erect, walking, and with a largish brain weighing between a pound and a pound-and-a-half. That is the size of the brain of a big ape now; but of course this was a small creature standing only four feet high. Indeed recent finds by Richard Leakey suggest that by two million years ago the brain was larger even than that.

...Two million years ago *Australopithecus* made rudimentary stone tools where a simple blow has put an edge on the pebble. And for the next million years, man in his further evolution did not change this type of tool. He made the fundamental invention, the purposeful act which prepares and stores a pebble for later use. By that lunge of skill and foresight, a symbolic act of discovery of the future, he had released the brake which the environment imposes on all other creatures. The steady use of the same tool for so long shows the strength of the invention. It was held in a power-grip. the ancestors of man had a short thumb, and therefore could not manipulate very delicately, but could use the power-grip.) And, of course, it is a meat-eater's tool almost certainly, to strike and cut. [2]

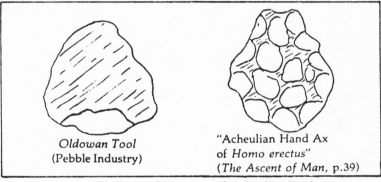

Oldowan Tool
(Pebble Industry)

"Acheulian Hand Ax
of *Homo erectus*"
(*The Ascent of Man*, p.39)

Plate xx   *Oldowan and Acheulian Tools*

The point at which the hominids, the near-men, became *homos*, or men, is a disputed one among scientists. Louis Leakey, for instance, defined man as a tool-using animal. He had discovered in the Oldowan Gorge the simple tools which Dr. Bronwski has described, called the "pebble industry" or Oldowan tools. He called the *Australopithecine* who used them, *Homo habilis*, handy man or tool man. Other scientists, however, Bronowski included, want to keep the hominid classification of *Australopithecus* and call *Homo erectus*, erect man, the first true man. *Homo erectus* used more sophisticated tools some of which are called Acheulian tools, named for the town of St. Acheuil in France, where they were first found. *Homo habilis* hunted only small game like rodents, while *Homo erectus* hunted much larger game. He must have hunted in small cooperative groups, which would have required some kind of rudimentary language. The group of scientists who want to make *Homo erectus* the first true man would define man as a language-using animal.

At what point can we say that the precursors of man became man himself? That is a delicate question, because such changes do not take place overnight. It would be foolish to try and make them seem more sudden than they really were - to fix the transition too sharply or to argue about names...Two million years ago we were not yet men. One million years ago we were, because by one million years ago a creature appears who can be called *Homo - Homo erectus*. He spreads far beyond Africa. The classical find of *Homo erectus* was in fact made in China. He is Peking Man, about four hundred thousand years old, and he is the first creature that certainly used fire.

The changes in *Homo erectus* that have led to us are substantial over a million years, but they seem gradual by comparison with those that went before. The successor that we know best was first found in Germany in the last century: another classic fossil skull; he is Neanderthal Man. He already has a three-pound brain, as large as modern man. Probably some lines of Neanderthal Man died out; but it seems likely that a line in the Middle East went on directly to us, *Homo sapiens*. [3]

Once again, some scientists would disagree with Dr. Bronowski here, maintaining that Neanderthal Man is not on the main line of evolution to modern man, but another collateral line that came to a dead end. Bronowski then concentrates on the most important step in our evolution, the emergence of language.

...A slow creature like man can stalk, pursue and corner a

large savannah animal that is adapted for flight only by cooperation. Hunting requires conscious planning and organization by means of language as well as special weapons. Indeed, language as we use it has something of the character of a hunting plan, in that (unlike the animals) we instruct one another in sentences which are put together from moveable units. The hunt is a communal undertaking of which the climax, but only the climax, is the kill. [4]

Dr. Bronowski concluded his presentation of the evolution of man with the discovery of agriculture. In the television version of *The Ascent of Man*, he was speaking from Jericho, one of the oldest cities in the world:

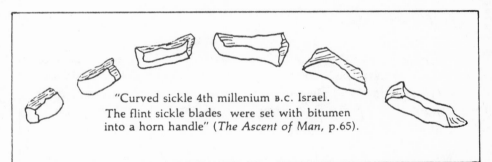

"Curved sickle 4th millenium B.C. Israel. The flint sickle blades were set with bitumen into a horn handle" (*The Ascent of Man*, p.65).

Plate xxi   *Natufian Sickle*

Jericho is older than agriculture. The first people who came here and settled by the spring in this otherwise desolate ground were people who harvested wheat, but did not yet know how to plant it. We know this because they made tools for the wild harvest, and that is an extraordinary piece of foresight. They made sickles out of flint which have survived; John Garstang found them when he was digging here in the 1930's. The ancient sickle would have been set in a piece of gazelle horn or bone...

Farming and husbandry seem simple pursuits, but the Natufian sickle is a signal to show us that they do not stand still. Every stage in the domestication of plant and animal life requires inventions, which begin as technical devices and from which flow scientific principles. The basic devices of the nimble-fingered mind lie about, unregarded, in any village anywhere in the world. Their cornucopia of small and subtle artifices is ingenious, and in a deep sense as important in the ascent of man as any apparatus of nuclear physics: the needle, the awl, the pot, the brazier, the spade, the nail, and the screw, the bellows, the string, the knot, the loom, the harness, the hook, the button, the shoe - one could name a hundred and not stop for breath. The richness comes from the interplay of inventions; a culture is a multiplier of ideas, in which each new device quickens and enlarges the power of the rest. [5]

Man's evolution then became cultural, rather than biological, and he could be considered truly civilized with the founding of the first agricultural villages, which eventually became cities.

Fr. Robert A. Staatz

I would like to read tonight from Fr. Owen Garrigan's analysis of the effects of the theory of evolution of man on both the biblical story of Adam and Eve, and on the Church's teaching concerning original sin. This is again from his excellent *Man's Intervention in Nature*:

The interpretation placed upon Adam and original sin in the conceptual framework of an evolving cosmos (a framework long unfamiliar to theologians) gives rise to some new departures in theological speculation. In Christian tradition, the Adam of Genesis has been understood as an individual, the progenitor of the entire human race. This monogenetic interpretation was reinforced from the earliest centuries by St. Paul's reference (Romans 5) to Christ as the "second Adam"...

This view was endorsed by Pope Pius xii as late as 1950. Since then, however, an attempt has been underway to disengage the basic religious message intended by the inspired writer from its manner of expression. The new approach tries to separate as far as possible the biological question of polygenism from the theological question of original sin. [Polygenism is a Greek word meaning many pairs of first parents, and it is opposed to monogenism, one pair of first parents.]

In some respects this new understanding of Scripture is difficult to reconcile with traditional teaching. But, at least for the present, these tentative proposals seem to fit more harmoniously into a world-view that takes evolution into account. (Polygenism seems to be biologically probable to provide a wide breeding base for the evolving human species. Moreover, the simultaneous occurrence of the critical "humanizing" mutation in both male and female individuals to produce the original pair seems highly improbable.) [6]

The "humanizing" mutation which Garrigan speaks of is usually thought of as an increase in brain size. But whether this occurred sometime in the transition from *Australopithecus* (500 c.c.) to *Homo erectus* (1000 c.c.), or from *Homo erectus* to Neanderthal Man (1500 c.c.), scientists frankly admit they don't know. But it is highly unlikely that such a mutation could have occurred simultaneously in both a male and a female.

Two lines of reinterpretation have issued from the vigorous biblical renaissance of our day:

1) Scripture scholars have suggested that "Adam" (literally, "the man") was used by the author of Genesis and other Old Testament writers to designate a corporate personality in the sense of the medieval "everyman." We can, indeed, see ourselves in the actions and reactions of Adam. The Adam encountered in the Hebrew Scriptures, therefore, was not a specific individual in the intention of the sacred writers. It is also quite conceivable that St. Paul was not pronouncing on the question of the biological unity of the human species when he spoke of the "second Adam." It seems, in fact, most probable that the question never occurred to him. Just as Christ's reference to the sign of Jonah in the belly of the whale, so St. Paul's reference to Christ as the second Adam does not guarantee physical monogenism.

2) Scriptural exegetes have recently given some prominence to the concept, quite general in biblical texts, of "sin of the

world." The sacred authors were so keenly aware of the universality of sin and of their own sinfulness that they formulated the story of everyman's fall. For them, the "sin of Adam" was a disordered will common to all those who share the human condition. It is the result of the free choice of man, but it is not restricted to one man's choice on a single occasion. In this view, the state of original sin in man depends on the condition of being human linking him to all mankind, rather than on the physical acts of generation linking him to a primal sinner. [7]

These ideas on original sin are those of Teilhard de Chardin which, we have seen, were unacceptable to the Church of the twenties, and were responsible for his exile to China; but they are much more acceptable to the more mature Church of today.

It seems unlikely (although possible) that these newer speculations will be found irreconcilable with traditional theology. Authoritative teaching has not definitely excluded this type of explanation. More profound than the question of monogenism, and fundamental to it, is the question of the unity of the human race and our solidarity with the incarnate Word of God. It may be asked whether this unity and solidarity are founded on consanguinity and monogenism. There are in reality two questions here. First, is monogenism whereby all men are related by blood and by a series of generative acts to each other and to Christ, of *a priori* necessity for the unity of mankind and for the solidarity of each man with the Redeemer? Second, is this monogenism in fact a basis chosen by God for human unity and solidarity in Christ? If this was his providential arrangement, then revelation may contain God's witness to the existence of *de facto* monogenism.

The answer to the first question seems to be "no." It was only before men understood our isolation together on this tiny island floating in uncharted oceans of space and time that they thought that blood would make us closer brothers. The unity of the human race does not require as a *sine qua non* condition physical descent from a single pair. Nor does our solidarity with Christ depend of necessity on our common blood descent. Although the origin of all men from Adam is a persuasive argument against racial prejudice in our day, there does not seem to be any compelling reason to conclude that polygenism is theoretically impossible, or that the human race would be less united if it descended from an evolving group, rather than from a single pair. [8]

Let me go on to Teilhard de Chardin and the important role he played in the development of the theory of the evolution of man. As many of you know, Teilhard was personally involved in two of the famous so-called "missing links": Piltdown Man, which later turned out to be a clever forgery, and Peking Man, now classified as a *Homo erectus*. Let me begin with Teilhard's involvement with Piltdown Man. Teilhard was only recently ordained when he became acquainted with the amateur English fossil hunter, Charles Dawson, the discoverer of the first Piltdown fossils. It was not until forty years later that it was found that the skull of a man and the jaw of an orangutan, cleverly doctored, had been planted at Piltdown by a forger or forgers, whose identity, in spite of many ingenious theories, is still a mystery. A few scientists have even suspected that Teilhard himself was somehow involved in the hoax.

Teilhard had discovered an elephant's molar (*Elephas planifrons*), and later a canine belonging to the jaw of Piltdown Man. The main reason he seems to be a suspect in the forgery is that the elephant's molar on examination turned out to be highly radioactive. The only place where such radioactive fossils are found is in Tunisia, which Teilhard had visited shortly before he came to Piltdown. Let me read a few excerpts from an excellent book on the Piltdown forgery which reads like a detective story - *The Piltdown Men*, by Ronald Millar:

> The other successful searcher at Piltdown was Pére Teilhard de Chardin. The evidence against the priest is as black, if not blacker, than that against Dawson. One has merely to recall the incredulity of Dawson and Woodward when Teilhard de Chardin discovered the missing canine

tooth in a stretch of gravel which had just been thoroughly searched. Oakley's discovery in connection with the *Elephas planifrons* is highly significant in this case. Before his arrival at Ore Place, Hastings, the student-priest had actually stayed near Ishkul, Tunisia...

Sir Wilfred Le Gros Clark told me that because of the Tunisian association he at one time strongly suspected Teilhard de Chardin. Oakley agreed, but like Le Gros Clark, he feels that not only the lack of the requisite anatomical knowledge but the whole nature of the man must exonerate him.

The discovery that Piltdown Man was a deception deeply hurt Teilhard de Chardin. According to Oakley he took the news harder than Sir Arthur Keith. He miserably told Oakley that throughout the viscissitudes of his life his main consolation was that he had helped to discover the Piltdown Man. Teilhard de Chardin might have been putting on an act but he did in fact arrive in England too late to have "planted" the original find in 1908. It is just possible however, that he might have added the *Elephas planifrons* molar to gain some kudos. That he likewise planted the controversial canine is highly doubtful. [9]

It has recently come to light that a nephew of Charles Dawson, who was in the British army, was stationed near Tunisia. This man was also an avid amateur fossil hunter and habitually sent his finds home to his uncle. Was this possibly the source of the radioactive *Elephas planifrons*? Here is Teilhard's own reaction to the exposure of the hoax as told by his biographer, Robert Speaight:

...This return from his last days in the field was crossed with an embarassing reminder of the first, when the forgery of Piltdown Man was finally attested. He was invited to give his views in an article, but he preferred to make no public statement. Dawson had died during the first World War, and Teilhard had too fond a memory of their excavations to believe in his bad faith. In answer to a letter from Kenneth

Oakley announcing the exposure, he replied:

"No one would think of suspecting Smith-Woodward. I knew pretty well Dawson - a methodical and enthusiastic character. When we were in the field I never noticed anything suspicious in his behavior. The only thing which puzzled me, one day, was when I saw him picking two large fragments of skull out of a sort of rubble in a corner of the pit (these fragments had probably been rejected by the workmen the year before). I was not in Piltdown when the jaw was found. But a year later when I found the canine, it was so inconspicuous among the gravels which had been spread on the ground for sifting that it seems to me quite unlikely that the tooth would have been planted. I can even remember Sir Arthur congratulating me on the sharpness of my eyesight.

"Don't forget: the pit at Piltdown was a perfect dumping place for the farm and cottages. It was flooded in winter, and water in the wealden clay can stain at a remarkable speed. In 1912, in a stream near Hastings, I was unpleasantly surprised to see a fresh-sawed bone (from the butcher's) stained almost as deep brown as the human remains from Piltdown. Had a collector possessing some ape bones thrown his discarded specimens into the pit? The idea sounds fantastic; but in my opinion, no more fantastic than to make Dawson the perpetrator of a hoax." [10]

The idea that a man like Teilhard could in any way be involved in a hoax, is too ridiculous to take seriously. Teilhard is also associated with the discovery of the famous Peking Man (*Sinanthropus*), now classified as a *Homo erectus*. Let me conclude by reading Robert Speaight's account of the tragic death of Davidson Black, the discoverer of Peking Man, who was Teilhard's very close friend:

...Teilhard broke the news in a letter to Breuil:

"His heart had been giving him trouble for some time, and five weeks ago we had a warning of what might happen. We were hoping that he was pulling round, but then the end came suddenly. Black was feeling better (or seemed to be); he had just been talking briskly with some friends and was full of plans, as usual. A moment later he was found dead, by this table, in this lab you know so well, between *Sinanthropus* and the skull from the Upper Cave."

The loss put Teilhard's faith to a severe trial; in the same letter he goes on:

"But what an absurd thing life is, looked at superficially; so absurd that you feel yourself forced back on a stubborn, desperate faith in the reality and survival of the spirit. Otherwise - were there no such thing as spirit, I mean - we should have to be idiots not to call off the whole human effort."

Some critics have gone so far as to assert that Teilhard had lost his faith in personal immortality. To such a calumny these lines are a sufficient answer. Nevertheless, the death of Davidson Black was "like a shadow continually overhanging me." Teilhard had "loved him almost more than a brother," and he was not comforted by "the stifling atmosphere of agnostic condolences." He concluded in a letter to the Bégouëns with a resolution wholly in keeping with his character:

"I swore to myself, on the body of my dead friend, to fight more vigorously than ever to give hope to man's work and inquiry." [11]

In conclusion, let me say again, that any interpretation of Holy Scripture with contradicts an established fact of science, cannot be a true interpretation. There is only one truth. The older monogenistic basis of the doctrine of original sin contradicts the established scientific fact of the evolution of man which, as we have seen, is based on polygenism. This demands a reformulation of the Church's teaching concerning original sin.

Mrs. Maria Stepan

Cultural Evolution		Industries
5000 B.C.	Agriculture	Neolithic Polished stone Friction
40,000	Higher Hunter Cro-Magnon	Paleolithic Aurignacian Burin
100,000	Neanderthal	Mousterian Flake tool Precision-grip
400,000	Hunter-Gatherer Homo erectus	Acheulian Pressure flaking
1,000,000	Homo habilis	Oldowan Percussion flaking Power-grip
2,000,000	Food-Gatherer Australopithecus	

Plate xxii   *Cultural Evolution*

I would like to begin my presentation tonight with a few comments on Dr. Bronowski's review of the theory of the evolution of man. On the board I have a simplified outline of what is called the "cultural evolution" of man, and the so-called "industries" associated with each stage in that evolution. We are supposed to have evolved from food-gatherers, to hunter-gatherers, to higher hunters, and finally to have reached the agricultural stage. You supposedly can identify the cultural stage by the industry that is found at a particular site.

It is said that it all began around 2,000,000 years ago or earlier with the *Australopithecines*, who were originally food-gatherers. They moved about continually foraging for food like fruit, just as monkeys and apes do today. The *Australopithecines* had only recently come down from the trees, and were beginning to venture out onto the open savannah, however, because they had small fighting canines, they returned to the forest at night.

Then around 1,000,000 B.C. came what Louis Leakey called *Homo habilis*, Tool Man. The *Australopithecines*, Leakey claimed, discovered how to make small tools which he named Oldowan tools, from the gorge where they were first found. Some scientists have actually attempted to make these tools themselves to see how our alleged ancestors did it. One explanation is that the Oldowan tools were made by a method called percussion flaking, that is, the stone was struck a couple of times by another stone, knocking off a few flakes and leaving a sharp ragged edge. These were all-purpose tools used for killing and butchering small game. They were held in a power-grip, that is, with the whole hand, as one holds a hammer, supposedly because *Homo habilis* had a short thumb and therefore limited manipulative ability. Let me add in passing - Louis Leakey claimed that in a gorge in California, similar to the Oldowan gorge, some of his disciples had discovered hundreds of Oldowan type tools. These "tools" were rejected almost unanimously by American evolutionists, who insisted that they were the accidental results of purely natural processes.

Next came *Homo erectus* around 400,000 B.C., and one industry called Acheulian. This kind of tool is thought to be made by a method called pressure flaking, in which a bone or a piece of wood is used as a chisel, giving a greater control of the flaking process so that a sharp edge could be made around the whole stone. The Acheulian tool was also held in the power-grip and used for killing and butchering animals. Both the Oldowan and Acheulian tools are said to belong to the Lower Paleolithic, or early Old Stone Age.

Next we come to the Upper Paleothic, the late Old Stone Age, to Neanderthal and Cro-Magnon Man. These men who lived during the Ice Ages are sometimes called Higher Hunters, which means that they could tackle wooly mammoths, sabre tooth cats, bears, etc. One of Neanderthal Man's industries is called Mousterian, again named for a town in France, and included a whole kit of tools for various specialized purposes. The particular tool in the diagram is called a backed knife and its significance is that it was held with a precision-grip, as one holds a pen with the thumb and fingers. Man's digital abilities had supposedly evloved from the simple power-grip. The backed knife is thought to have been used for making clothes out of skins.

Neanderthal Man is dated around 100,000 B.C., and was followed by Cro-Magnon Man who is supposed to have appeared around 40,000 B.C. One of Cro-Magnon's industries is called Aurignacian, and the tool in the diagram is called a burin. It was sharp on both sides and on both ends, which means that it could be used either as a knife or a chisel. The significance of the tool is that it could be used in engraving. Cro-Magnon was a great artist, and made beautiful engravings on the tusks of mammoths and on the antlers of reindeer. He also did the wonderful cave paintings at Altamira in Spain.

The next stage in cultural evolution is supposed to be the discovery of agriculture and the domestication of animals. This is called the Neolithic or New Stone Age, and Neolithic tools are said to be made by friction and are polished. From the Neolithic Age, man went on to the various Metal Ages, first the Copper, then the Bronze, and finally the Iron Age. Neolithic Man first began to live in small villages, and by the Iron Age he was living in large cities, and could finally be considered truly civilized.

With that little background, let me read from Fr. Patrick O'Connell, one of the very few Catholic writers to attack the evolution of man. This is from his *Science of Today and the*

Problems of Genesis which first came out in 1959, so it is a little dated, but let me first explain some of the terms Fr. O'Connell will be using.

Plate xxiii *Fontéchevade Cave*

We see from the illustration that the Magdalenian industry was late Cro-Magnon, and the Aurignacian early Cro-Magnon. The so-called *"Hiatus"* is a complete gap in the fossil record between early Cro-Magnon and late Neanderthal Man. In my first chart I gave the commonly supposed dates of 100,000 B.C. for Neanderthal Man, and around 40,000 B.C. for Cro-Magnon. This *Hiatus* has been completely unexplained by the evolutionists, but some Christian writers, Fr. O'Connell included, have suggested that it could have been caused by the Noachian Deluge. The Mousterian industry was late Neanderthal, and the Acheulian industry, according to Dr. Bronowski, was supposed to belong to *Homo erectus*.

The actual cave where the Fontéchevade fossils were found had been known for a long time. In it there was the routine stratified sequence of Magdalenian flints on top, Aurignacian (the period after the *Hiatus*) next, then the sterile layer of clay without fossils or artifacts that was deposited by the Flood and marked the abandonment of the settlement, and finally, the Mousterian flints beneath it. Underneath these four strata was what appeared to be a limestone floor.

In 1937 Mlle. Henri-Martin discovered that this was not a floor at all but a layer of limestone that had fallen from the roof of the cave before the Neanderthal Man occupied it. When this layer was removed, no less than twenty feet of debris were found beneath it which contained the fossil remains of animals of warm climates and stone instruments of the Lower Paleolithic Age and two human skulls. These latter were not found until 1947.

In *Les Hommes Fossiles*...Vallois says: "The fact that the stalagmite floor which covered these deposits was found to be intact, guarantees the absolute authenticity of what was found beneath them. The flourine test (which was applied in 1951) confirms the authenticity of the fossils...which have a brain capacity of about 1450 c.c....

The Fontéchevade cave is the best example of a stratified cave we have in Europe. It shows the fossils of artifacts of the various families or races in the order in which they came to Europe. The earliest (i.e. those of Fontéchevade Man) resembled modern man very closely; next came the Neanderthal Man, with his marked peculiarities; above him was the flood deposit of earth, probably laid down by the Deluge, containing neither fossils nor artifacts; above that was the post-*hiatus* Aurignacian stratum, and finally the stratum of the Magdalenian hunter who brought the Old Stone Age to a close. [12]

So below Neanderthal Man we find the tools of the Lower Paleolithic, in other words, Acheulian type tools supposedly used by *Homo erectus*, but modern type skulls of about 1450 c.c., exactly the average for man today. We have just seen a sketch of an Acheulian hand ax copied from a photograph in *The Ascent of Man*, and have heard Dr. Bronowski maintain that it was made by *Homo erectus* who had a brain capacity of around 1000 c.c. No wonder the evolutionists try to ignore Fontéchevade!

Fr. O'Connell is also very critical of the theory of cultural evolution - how we are supposed to have evolved from food-gatherers, to hunter-gatherers, to higher hunters, and finally to agriculture; and how each stage in this evolution can be determined by its associated "industries."

The fossils and artifacts of a race to which the name Natufian has been given were discovered in the vicinity of both Carmel and Bethlehem. Between 1928 and 1931, Miss Garrod of the American party unearthed the fossil remains of forty-five individuals in the cave of Shukbah, and eighty-seven in the cave of Mugharet-el-Wad in the vicinity of Carmel; and in 1931 M. Neuville of the French party found the fossils of six or seven individuals at Erq el Ahmar to the south of Bethlehem.

Instead of the stone instruments used by nomadic hunters...these had stone instruments suited to agriculture and domestic purposes. These stone instruments were not polished like the Neolithic instruments...The Natufians were rather small of stature; they cannot be identified with any living race, but in general they resembled the Fontéchevade Man. They practiced agriculture and kept domestic animals. Their stone instruments resembled those dug up in the lower strata of the city of Jericho...

When those writers who are evolutionists hear of agricultural instruments being found at any ancient site, they conclude immediately that they belong to the Neolithic Age. For instance, W.F. Albright in *From the Stone Age to Christianity* states: "The true Neolithic was first discovered by L. Garstang in his excavation of the lowest occupied levels of Jericho in 1935-36." Now, the Neolithic stone instruments are made by friction and are therefore polished. The stone instruments found in the lower strata of Jericho were made in the same manner as those of the Old Stone Age, i.e. by flaking and were not polished. Garstang, who was not an authority on the instruments of the Old Stone Age, refers to them as Neolithic, but in the photographs he gives of them in *The Story of Jericho*...they look like the instruments of the Old Stone Age. [13]

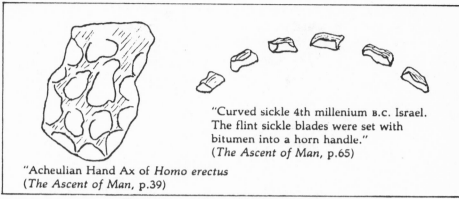

"Curved sickle 4th millenium B.C. Israel. The flint sickle blades were set with bitumen into a horn handle." (*The Ascent of Man*, p.65)

"Acheulian Hand Ax of *Homo erectus* (*The Ascent of Man*, p.39)

Plate xxiv   *Acheulian and Natufian Tools*

I have copied this Acheulian hand ax from a photograph in Dr. Bronowski's *The Ascent of Man*. He dates it at 400,000 B.C., and claims that it was made by *Homo erectus*, who is supposed to have had a brain capacity of around 1000 c.c. He dates the sickle which I have also copied from his book, at around 4000 B.C., and says that it was made by the Natufians, who had a brain capacity of about 1450 c.c. It seems obvious that both the sickle and the hand ax were made in the same way, by pressure flaking, yet the hand ax is considered Lower Paleolithic, early Old Stone Age, and the sickle Neolithic, New Stone Age, to fit the requirements of the theory of cultural evolution. Neolithic tools, unlike this sickle, are thought to be made by friction and to be polished. Fr. O'Connell thinks that it is not reasonable, based on the evidence available, to maintain that men slowly evolved from food-gatherers, to hunter-gatherers, to higher hunters, and finally to the agricultural stage. It seems much more reasonable to maintain that the man who made the hand ax, and the man who made the sickle were contemporaries. One man, or family or tribe, chose the nomadic life of the hunter, while the other chose the more settled life of the small agricultural village.

Let me go on now to Fr. Teilhard de Chardin and his close connection with the deveolpment of the theory of the evolution of man. I would like to make just a brief comment on the infamous Piltdown Man. This so-called fossil man was not exposed as a hoax until 1953 after having been accepted by the evolutionary establishment for over 40 years. Yet a simple reading of the facts presented in the journals of the time should have alerted any scientist of good will that there was something drastically wrong. Let me read just the conclusion of one such examination by Fr. George O'Toole, a professor of philosophy and biology at St. Vincent Archabbey and Seton Hall, from his excellent *The Case Against Evolution* which came out in 1925:

> To conclude, therefore, the *Eoanthropus Dawsoni* ["Dawn Man of Dawson"] is an invention, and not a discovery, an artistic creation, not a specimen. Anyone can combine a simian mandible with a human cranium, and, if the discovery of a connecting link entails no more than this, there is no reason why evidence of human evolution should not be turned out wholesale. [14]

But I would like to skip Fr. Teilhard's association with Piltdown Man, since the evolutionists themselves have finally admitted that this was a hoax, and concentrate instead on Peking Man, which the evolutionists still claim as a "missing link," but which Fr. Patrick O'Connell thinks is also, most probably, another case of fraud. Like Fr. O'Toole, Fr. O'Connell reaches this conclusion from a simple reading of the facts in the case availbale to any scientist who would care to peruse them. Fr. O'Connell spent over twenty years in China as a missionary, and had a great love for the Chinese people and a familiarity with their culture. For example, in rural areas the Chinese still burn limestone in kilns to make lime for use in building their homes. Fr. Teilhard, on the other hand, who also spent twenty years in China, never learned to speak Chinese (Fr. O'Connell seems especially indignant by the fact that he "could not even write his name in Chinese") and never made a single Chinese convert to the Church.

Fr. O'Connell's interpretation of Peking Man is based primarily on articles written on the subject by two famous authorities, Abbé Breuil, an expert on the industries of the Old Stone Age, and Marcellin Boule, an expert on fossil skulls, to the study of which he brings a special insight because of his long familiarity with the

Chinese people and their customs. Fr. Teilhard and his friends spent most of their time in a little European enclave in Peking, and seldom went to Chou-kou-tien. However, Fr. O'Connell's full treatment of Peking Man in *Science of Today and the Problems of Genesis* is much too long to give here, so I will read a brief summary from his excellent little pamphlet *Original Sin in the Light of Present-Day Science*:

...Dr. Davidson Black, an American surgeon, in 1926 obtained a yearly grant of $20,000 from the Rockfeller Institute for the purpose of carrying out excavations at a place called Chou-kou-tien, thirty seven miles from Peking...The excavations consisted in removing thousands of tons of limestone which had fallen down from a limestone hill in a landslide that occurred thousands of years ago. When a portion of the fallen limestone had been removed, beneath it were discovered; 1) an enormous heap of ashes, 2) thousands of dressed stones which had been brought from a distance, presumably for the purpose of constructing lime-kilns to burn limestone [this is the opinion of Abbé Breuil], and 3) a number of fossil skulls of monkeys, because fossil skulls of monkeys were found in abundance in the district [the opinion of Boule]. Dr. Black selected one of the skulls found in the ashes to represent the Peking Man. Fr. Teilhard de Chardin, in an article in the *Revues des Questions Scientifiques*, Paris, 1930, says that when the skull was found "the whole cerebral part was admirably preserved," but when Dr. Black exhibited the skull, the brain-case had been removed. Fr. Teilhard de Chardin invited his former professor, the famous Marcellin Boule, an evolutionist, but one of the world's greatest authorities on fossil skulls to come out to China. [He also invited Abbé Breuil.] Professor Boule came to China but when he saw that the only proof which was produced was a battered monkey's skull, he was very angry. He denounced Fr. De Chardin and poured ridicule on the claim that the creatures to which the battered skulls belonged could have carried on the large scale lime-burning industry which the excavations revealed. Professor Boule contended that the

industry was evidently the work of real men...One day Dr.
Pei brought in the fossil remains of ten real men, among
which were three complete skulls. Fr. Teilhard [in an article
published in the *Revues des Questions Scientifiques*]...at-
tempted to show that the real men whose fossils had been
found had nothing to do with the industry...

On the morning of the discovery of the fossils of real men,
Dr. Black went into the laboratory to examine them, but was
found later on, lying dead among them...Fr. Teilhard de
Chardin wrote a new article, which he published in *Études*. In
the article he denied what he had published in the *Revues des
Questions Scientifiques*, that the fossils of real men had been
found, and said that three more fossils of the Peking Man, like
the former had been found. After a lapse of five years Dr.
Weidenreich [who had been appointed by the Rockefeller
Institute to succeed Dr. Black] published the true account,
that fossils of real men had been found. [15]

So Fr. Teilhard seems to have changed his mind several times on
just what was and was not found at Chou-kou-tien. He also
completely ignores the opinions of Boule and Abbé Breuil in the
matter. After a very detailed examination of the documents
available, Fr. O'Connell concludes that Peking Man like Piltdown
Man is also a case of fraud. If this is true, however, it can never be
proved, because during the Japanese occupation of Peking all the
fossils conveniently (?) and mysterioulsy disappeared, and all that
remains of Peking Man are two imaginative plaster reconstruc-
tions made by Black and Weidenreich.

Let me go on now to my own presentation from the Tradition
and Magisterium of the Church. Here again is St. Thomas
Aquinas in his *Summa Theologica*:

*Whether the Human Body Was Immediately Produced by
God?*

...Obj. 4) Further Augustine says (*Gen ad Litt.*, 7:24) that
man's body was made during the work of the six days,
according to the causal virtues which God inserted in

corporeal creatures; and that afterwards it was actually produced. But what pre-exists in the corporeal creature by reason of causal virtues can be produced by some created power, and not immediately by God.

On the contrary, it is written (Ecclus 17:1): "God created man out of the earth."

I answer that, the first formation of the human body could not be by the instrumentality of any created power, but was immediately from God...Now God, though He is absolutely immaterial, can alone by His power produce matter, without the aid of any preceeding material form...Therefore as no pre-existing body had been formed whereby another body of the same species could be generated, the first human body was of necessity made immediately by God...

Reply Obj. 4) An effect may be said to pre-exist in the causal virtues of creatures in two ways. First, both in active and in passive potentiality, so that not only can it be produced out of pre-existing matter, but also that some pre-existing creature can produce it. Secondly in passive potentiality only; that is, that out of the pre-existing matter it can be produced by God. In this sense, according to Augustine, the human body pre-existed in the previous works in their causal virtues. [16]

St. Thomas says that the human body pre-existed in the slime of the earth in passive potency only. That is the slime of the earth could not have become a body by its own or any created power, but could only have been used by God in the production of a human body. Of course, St. Thomas is not speaking of evolution but, using this same reasoning, we can say that while the human body did exist in potency in the slime of the earth, no created power, such as evolution, could have produced a human body, but God alone. St. Thomas will allow a spiritual interpretation of the Hexameron, but insists on a strictly literal interpretation of Adam and Eve. This is also the position of the Magisterium of the Church. Let me read from a decision of the Biblical Commission given in 1909 during the reign of Pope St. Pius x:

On the Historical Character of the First Three Chapters of Genesis

...Whether, in particular we may call in question the literal and historical meaning where there is question of facts narrated in these chapters which touch the fundamental teachings of the Christian religion, as for example, the creation of all things which was accomplished by God at the beginning of time, the *special creation of man*, the formation of the first woman from man, *the unity of the human race*...

Answer: In the negative. [17]

In December of 1941 Pope Pius XII delivered an address to the Pontifical Academy of Science in the course of which he said:

On that day on which God formed man and crowned his brow with the diadem of His image and likeness, constituting him king of every living soul in the ocean, the sky, and the earth (Gen 1:26), on that day the Lord, the Omniscient God became his teacher. He taught him farming, the cultivation and care of the delightful garden in which He had placed him (Gen 2:15). He brought to him all the beasts of the fields and all the birds of the air that he might see how to name them, and he gave to each its proper and fitting name (Gen 2:19-20), but yet, in the midst of that multitude of beings placed below him, he felt sadly alone and sought in vain a face that resembled his, which would have a ray of that divine image which the eye of every son of Adam reflects. Only from man could there come another man that would call Him, Father and Progenitor; and the helper given by God to the first man comes really from him and is flesh of his flesh, made for a companion, and named from him because from him she was taken (Gen 2:23). Man endowed with a spiritual soul has been placed by God at the top of the ladder of living creatures, as the prince and sovereign of the animal kingdom.

The multiple researches of paleontology, biology, and morphology on various problems related to Man's origin, have not till now yielded any positively clear and certain results. Hence it remains to the future to determine whether one day science, enlightened and helped by revelation, will be able to give sure and positive results concerning such an important topic.

Do not wonder therefore if before you who have with such penetration studied, analyzed and compared the brain of man and the brains of irrational animals, We should exalt man who raises his brow enlightened with that intelligence which is the exclusive attribute of human-kind. True science will not lower nor debase man in his origins, but uplift and exalt him, because it sees, acknowledges, and admires, in every member of the human family, the more or less broad imprint left in him of the divine image and likeness. [18]

Let me also read a few excerpts from Pope Pius XII's encyclical *Humani Generis*, which was issued in 1950. This encyclical was directed, to a large extent against the works of Fr. Teilhard de Chardin which were then circulating privately:

Accordingly, the Magisterium of the Church does not forbid that the theory of evolution concerning the origin of the human body as coming from pre-existent and living matter (for the Catholic faith obliges us to hold that the human soul is immediately created by God) be investigated and discussed by experts as far as the present state of human sciences and sacred theology allows. However, this must be done so that reasons for both sides, that is those favorable and those unfavorable to evolution, be weighed and judged with the necessary gravity, moderation, and discretion; and let all be prepared to submit to the judgment of the Church to whom Christ has given the mission of interpreting authentically the Sacred Scriptures and of safeguarding the dogmas of faith. On the other hand, those go too far and transgress this liberty of discussion who act as though the living matter were already fully demonstrated by the facts discovered up to now and by reasoning on them, and as though there were nothing in the sources of divine revelation which demand the greatest reserve and caution in this controversy. [19]

Pope Pius is arguing from what is called the "analogy of faith," which means that one doctrine of the faith is in harmony with every other doctrine. The doctrine of the "special creation of man," as the Biblical Commission phrased it, is not yet a defined dogma of the faith, so on the related question of polygenism, Pope Pius argues from the doctrine of original sin, which *is* a defined doctrine of the faith. Here is one of the decrees of the Council of Trent to which he is referring:

> If anyone asserts that Adam's sin was injurious only to Adam and not to his descendents, and that it was for himself alone that he lost the holiness and justice which he had received from God, and not for us also; or that after his defilement by the sin of disobedience, he transmitted to the whole human race only death and punishment of the body but not sin itself which is the death of the soul: let him be anathema. For he contradicts the words of the Apostle: "As through *one man* sin entered into the world and through sin death, and thus death has passed into all men because all have sinned" (Rom 5:12). [20]

We see that Pope Pius rejects the notion that evolution is a proven fact, and would agree, at least in principle, with the creationist position that both the reasons for and the reasons against the theory should be openly discussed in our public schools. Pope Pius then goes on to the question of polygenism, many Adams and Eves:

> But as regards another conjecture, namely so-called polygenism, the children of the Church by no means enjoy the same liberty. No Catholic can hold that after Adam there existed on this earth true men who did not take their origin through natural generation from him as from the first parent of all, or that Adam is merely a symbol for a number of first parents. For it is unintelligible how such an opinion can be

reconciled with what the sources of revealed truth teach on original sin, which proceeds from sin actually committed by an individual Adam, and which, passed on to all by way of generation, is in everyone as his own. [21]

In 1966 Pope Paul VI held a symposium of scientists and theologians in Rome to deal with the challenge raised by polygenism to the doctrine of original sin. This challenge had been originally made by Fr. Teilhard de Chardin and carried on by his many disciples, the best known probably being Fr. Karl Rahner. In his address to the symposium Pope Paul repeated Pius XII's condemnation of polygenism:

> It is therefore evident that the explanations of original sin by some modern authors will seem to you irreconcilable with true Catholic doctrine. Starting from the undemonstrated premise of polygenism, they deny...that the sin from which so many cesspools of evil have come to mankind was...the disobedience of Adam, "first man"...committed at the beginning of history. Consequently these explanations do not even agree with the teaching of Scripture, of sacred tradition and the Church's Magisterium, according to which the sin of the first man is transmitted to all his descendants not through imitation but through propagation. [22]

So in conclusion we see that while the Church will permit Catholics to speculate philosophically on the origin of man's body (we are forbidden to speculate on the origin of his soul), we cannot insist that it is a proven fact. On the contrary the Holy Father has made it impossible for Catholics to hold the theory of the evolution of man, even so-called "theistic evolution," in its current "scientific" form. The current theory cannot possibly be true because it demands a wide breeding base in order that a so-called "humanizing" mutation might occur. This requires polygenism, many Adams and Eves, and necessarily rejects monogenism, one Adam and Eve, on which the defined doctrine of original sin depends. Many Catholic theologians such as Teilhard who feel they have to accept the theory of evolution, deny the historicity of

Adam and Eve and consequently the doctrine of original sin. If there is no Adam and Eve, there is no original sin, and if there is no original sin there is no Redemption, and our faith is in vain.

Rev. De Verne Swezey

One of the things that is very disconcerting about the theory of the evolution of man is that so many of the so-called "missing links" between man and ape, or now between man and lemur, have either been frauds or are, at the very least, highly suspicious. The term "missing link" was originally coined by Ernst Haeckel, Darwin's German champion, who himself seems to have been guilty of fraud. Haeckel is the author of the now discredited "recapitualation theory," which maintains that the human embryo in its development recapitulates or summarizes man's evolutionary history from fish to reptile, and so on. In one of his books, while trying to show the similarity between the embryos of different species, Haeckel in one instance gave the same picture of an embryo three different titles, and in another instance, doctored the picture of a dog and a human embryo to enhance their similarities. The fraud was immediately pointed out by two highly respected German embryologists, but Haeckel continued using the faked photographs for the rest of his career.

Then the Dutchman Eugene Dubois, a student of Haeckel, set off for Java determined to discover the first missing link. He found the top of a skull cap which he estimated to have a brain capacity of about 900 c.c. and, about fifty feet away, a straight thigh bone which appeared human, and two fossil teeth. At the same time and in the same strata he discovered two human skulls, now called the Wadjak skulls, of a brain capacity of around 1500 c.c. Returning to Holland he exhibited only the top of the skull cap, the straight thigh bone, and the teeth, which he claimed were the remains of a missing link which he named *Pithecanthropus erectus*, "the erect walking ape man." When a later expedition under Madame Selenka discovered a hearth at the same site, Dubois reluctantly produced the two Wadjak skulls, and announced that he was withdrawing his claim of having discovered a missing link, and now considered *Pithecanthropus* merely an extinct species of giant gibbon. If Dubois had displayed the two Wadjak skulls originally, no one would have taken his claim to have discovered a missing link seriously, but the evolutionists have refused to accept his tacit admission of duplicity, and Java Man, now classified as a *Homo erectus*, is still prominently featured in all books dealing with the evolution of man.

In 1953 Piltdown Man was finally exposed as a hoax after having faithfully served the evolutionary cause for forty years. Peking Man, which is also classified as a *Homo erectus*, has also been highly criticized, as Mrs. Stepan has pointed out, even by prominent evolutionists, such as Boule and Breuil.

Dr. Henry Morris is at his best in discussing the evolution of man, and my favorite chapter in *Scientific Creationism* is entitled *Apes or Men?* Dr. Morris proceeds step-by-step through our genealogy according to the evolutionists. Dr. Schonfield mentioned that there is some difference of opinion among evolutionary scientists regarding our genealogical tree. This is putting it mildly, to say the least, and it would be more correct to say that are no two scientists today who would propose the same tree. Let me begin with Dr. Morris' commentary of *Ramapithecus*. This fossil has become extremely important in recent years since so many scientists have eliminated his alleged successor *Australopithecus* from our genealogy:

Ramapithecus

The suffix "pithecus" means "ape," and a considerable number of fossils have been publicized of extinct "pithecine" animals, some of which have been considered as possible ancestors of man. These include *Dryopithecus, Oreopithecus, Limnopithecus, Kenyapithecus* and others, all dated roughly 14 million years ago.

Most evolutionary anthropologists consider *Ramapithecus* to be the most important of this group. This fossil was found in India in 1932 and consisted of several teeth and jaw fragments. Because the incissors and canine teeth of this creature, although apelike, are smaller than those or modern apes, some evolutionists consider this form a hominid. [23]

In 1983 Richard Leakey discovered in Kenya fossils of a *Ramapithecus* which he claims is 17,000,000 years old. I don't know how this date was arrived at, but most scientists will admit, at least privately, that this dating procedure is highly subjective. For example Skull 1470 (its museum file number) was dated by using the potassium-argon method of radiometric dating on adjoining rocks. According to the University of Cambridge laboratory, rock samples were 221 million, 19.5 million, 2.6 million, and 290,000 years old. The laboratory at the University of California in Berkely gave 1.8 million years. Leakey decided that the 2.6 million figure was correct. I should mention at this point, for whatever it might be worth, that another group of scientists, the "molecular anthropologists," disagree radically with the dating proposed by the paleontologists, the bone men. The molecular anthropologists study the similarities and differences in the proteins of living species and deduce how long ago they diverged from a common ancestor. These scientists claim that humans, chimpanzees, and gorillas diverged from a common ancestor "only" four to six million years ago, and completely reject the classification of *Ramapithecus* as a hominid. These conclusions have been completely ridiculed by the paleontologists.

Let me continue with Dr. Morris' comments on *Australopithecus*:

> The name (meaning "southern ape") has been assigned to a considerable number of different fossils, found mostly in East Africa by Louis Leakey and others. In addition to those of the *Australopithecine* name, others assigned to this group include *Zinjanthropus, Paranthropus, Plesianthropus, Telanthropus,* and *Homo habilis.*
>
> *Australopithecus* is considered to have lived from about two or three million years ago, to have walked erect, and to have used crude tools. However, he had a brain size of only about 500 c.c., the same as that of some apes. The teeth were similar to those of *Ramapithecus.* For many years, anthropologists have been confused and divided over the *Australopithecines,* some convinced that he was ancestral to man and others that he was an evolutionary dead end. [24]

After a detailed investigation of the conflicting claims of the evolutionists concerning these fossils, Dr. Morris concludes that they are not hominids, but simply extinct apes.

> ...He, the same as *Ramapithecus*, is no doubt simply an extinct ape. The reason for his peculiar teeth, the same as *Ramapithecus*, was probably because of his habitat and resulting diet. In that connection, there is living today in Ethiopia a species of high-altitude baboon, *Theropithecus galada*, which has teeth and jaw characteristics very much like those of both *Ramapithecus* and *Australopithecus*. The "human-like" characteristics of the teeth and jaws of this baboon are apparently related to his habitat and diet and are clearly *not* indicative of a near approach to humanhood! [25]

Dr. Morris continues his examination of our "genealogical tree" according to the evolutionists, with a discussion of *Homo erectus*:

> A number of fossil men are now grouped under the generic name *Homo erectus*, including the somewhat notorious Java Man, Peking Man, Heidleberg Man, and *Meganthropus*. These are believed to have lived about 500,000 years ago, to have walked upright, to have brains of about 1000 c.c., and to have developed a crude culture involving simple implements and weapons.
>
> The evidence for all this is equivocal, to say the least; Java Man was later repudiated by its discoverer, and the bones of Peking Man disappeared during World War II and are unavailable for examination. Heidleberg Man consisted of two lower jaw bones and four teeth and has been assigned by many to the *Australopithecines*.
>
> However, other fossils of this general type have apparently been found at various locations around the world. It may well be that *Homo erectus* was a true man, but somewhat degenerate in size and culture, possibly because of inbreeding and poor diet, and a hostile environment. In any case, the most recent discoveries of *Homo erectus* remains seem to rule him out as a possible evolutionary ancestor of modern man.

"Skulls that were buried a scant 10,000 years ago now suggest that, at a time, when elsewhere in the Old World the successor species *Homo sapiens* was turning from hunting and gathering to agriculture, some *Homo erectus* genes lingered in Australia. [26]

These *Homo erectus* skulls, found in Australia, show that modern man had already been in existence long before, ruling out *Homo erectus* as a possible ancestor; he is more likely a decadent descendant. Some may question the true humanness of *Homo erectus* on the basis of his small brain size (900-1000 c.c.). However, that is definitely within the range of brain size of modern man, though at the low end of the scale. Furthermore there is no necessary correlation between brain size with intelligence. [27]

So in summary Dr. Morris completely rejects the so-called "hominid" classification of *Ramapithecus* and *Australopithecus*, considering them simply extinct species of apes, yet will grant the possibility of the humanness of *Homo erectus* despite its somewhat shaky base of Java and Peking Man. He then goes on to discuss Neanderthal Man:

The most famous of all the so-called "missing links" is *Homo Neanderthalensis*, pictured for more than a hundred years as a stooped, brutish character with heavy brow ridges and the crudest of habits. Many skeletal remains of these people are available now, however, and there is no longer any doubt that Neanderthal Man was truly human, *Homo sapiens*, no more different from modern man than the various tribes of modern men are from each other. His brain capacity was certainly human...
As far as the stooped skeletal structure of Neanderthal is concerned, most anthropologists now believe that this was due to disease, possibly arthritis or rickets.

"Neanderthal Man may have looked like he did not because he was closely related to the great apes, but because he had rickets, an article in the British publication *Nature* suggests. The diet of Neanderthal Man was definitely lacking in Vitamin D during the 35,000 years he spent on earth." [28]

It is known that Neanderthal Man raised flowers, fashioned elegant tools, painted pictures, and practiced some kind of religion, burying his dead. There is now even some evidence that Neanderthal Man or some of his predecessors had a form of writing.

"Communications with inscribed symbols may go back as far as 135,000 years in Man's history, antedating the 50,000-year-old Neanderthal Man." Alexander Marshack of Harvard's Peabody Museum made this pronouncement recently after extensive microscopic analysis of a 135,000-year-old ox rib covered with symbolic engravings. The results of his findings are: that it is a sample of 'pre-writing,' that there is a distinct similarity in cognitive style between it and those 75,000 years later, and that...it establishes a tradition of carving that stretches over thousands of years." [29]

Both Neanderthal Man and Cro-Magnon Man have been assigned by the evolutionists to the Pleistocene or Ice Age, while *Homo erectus* is supposed to have lived during an earlier, warmer age, the Pliocene. Now, more and more modern type skulls are being discvovered in Pliocene deposits, of which the Fontéchevade Man, mentioned by Mrs. Stepan, is just one among many. These fossils have been consistently ignored by the evolutionists because they couldn't be fitted into their carefully constructed genealogical trees, but now since all these trees have fallen down, these modern type skulls, with all their implications, will have to be squarely faced by the evolutionists.

Contrary to common opinion there is much evidence that modern man existed contemporaneously with all these hypothetical and very doubtful ape-like ancestors.

"Last year Leakey and his co-workers found three jaw

bones, leg bones, and more than 400 man-made stone tools. The specimens were attributed to the genus *Homo* and were dated at 2.6 million years. Leakey further described the whole shape of the brain case as remarkably reminiscent of modern man, lacking the heavy protruding eyebrow ridges and thick bones characteristic of *Homo erectus*. In addition to the as-yet-unamed skull, [later named "Skull 1470," from its museum file number] the expedition turned up parts of the leg bones of two other individuals. These fossils surprisingly show that man's unique bipedal locomotion was developed at least 2.5 million years ago." [30]

Here is good evidence that modern man - modern anatomically at least - was living prior to Neanderthal, prior to *Homo erectus*, and even prior to *Australopithecus!* This would place man well back within the Pliocence Epoch, and for all practical purposes, completely eliminate his imagined evolutionary ancestry...[These were also the original conclusions of Richard Leakey, but apparently after he realized what he had done, he reclassified this skull as a *Homo habilis.*]

Now that man's origin is beginning to be recognized as being much earlier (geologically speaking, in terms of the orthodox geological time system) than previously thought, perhaps anthropologists will take a serious look at the many other fossils reported in earlier strata, but which had been ignored or explained away.

For example, there were the Castendolo and Olmo skulls, found in Italy in 1860 and 1863, respectively. Both were identified as modern skulls and yet were found in undisturbed Pliocene strata. The Calaveras skull found in California in 1886, also in Pliocene deposits, and it too was a fully developed modern skull. These were well-documented at the time, but later became more or less forgotten. Many others have been reported, but it has proved difficult to obtain convincing documentation. In any case, it seems the whole subject needs to be reopened. [31]

Dean Smalley

Tonight we began the first of three meetings on the sixth day of creation which deals with the origin of man. Our opening discussion was devoted to the theory of the evolution of man.

Dr. Schonfield presented the evolution of man according to Dr. Bronowski, but admitted that other scientists would differ with him in a few details. Bronowski claimed that the first hominid or near-man, was *Australopithecus* or possibly *Ramapithecus*, and the first true man was *Homo erectus*, who went on to become Neanderthal Man. Then in the Near East one line of Neanderthal Man went on to become modern man.

Fr. Staatz accepts the evolution of man as a proven scientific fact, and since the critical "humanizing" mutation demands a wide breeding base, it necessitates polygenism, many Adams and Eves. This fact, he said, demands a reformulation of the Church's teaching concerning original sin which has traditionally depended on monogenism, one Adam and Eve.

Mrs. Stepan said that while the Church has permitted philosophic speculation concerning the origin of the human body, it has forbidden Catholics to assume that it is a proven fact. On the contrary, she said, by its repeated condemnation of polygenism, the Church has implicitly declared the theory false, at least in its current scientific form. She said that the acceptance of this theory has led many Catholics, such as Teilhard de Chardin, to reject the historicity of the story of Adam and Eve, and consequently the doctrine of original sin. If there is no original sin, she said, then there is no Redemption, and the Christian faith is vain.

Rev. Swezey presented the creationist rebuttal of our genealogy according to the evolutionists. He rejected the hominid classification of *Ramapithecus* and *Australopithecus*, and asserted that these creatures were simply extinct apes. He granted however that *Australopithecus'* alleged descendant, *Homo erectus*, who is supposed to have had a brain capacity of about 1000 c.c., could well have been a true man, since this capacity is within the human range, though at the low end of the scale. The evolutionists now admit that Neanderthal Man, who lived during the Pleistocene or Ice Age, was a true man. Rev. Swezey concluded by claiming that more and more skulls of a modern type are being discovered in the preceeding Pliocene Age, which have been consistently ignored by the evolutionists, because they eliminate for all practical purposes our alleged evolutionary ancestry.

REFERENCES

1   Jacob Bronowski, *The Ascent of Man*,
    Little, Brown and Co., Boston, 1973, p.38.
2   Bronowski, *Op. cit.*, pp.38,40.
3   *Idem*, p.41.
4   *Idem*, p.45.
5   *Idem*, pp.64,65,73,74.
6   Owen Garrigan, *Man's Intervention in Nature*,
    Hawthorne Books, New York, 1967, pp.98,99.
7   Garrigan, *Op. cit.*, pp.99,100.
8   *Idem*, pp.100,101.
9   Ronald Millar, *The Piltdown Men*,
    Ballantine Books, New York, 1972, pp.243,244.
10 Robert Speaight, *Teilhard de Chardin*,
    Collins, London, 1967, pp.327,318.
11 Speaight, *Op. cit.*, pp.194,195.
12 Patrick O'Connell, *Science of Today and the Probelms of Genesis*,
    Christian Book Club of America, Hawthorne, Cal., 1968, pp.98,99.
13 O'Connell, *Op. cit.* pp.102,103.
14 George O'Toole, *The Case Against Evolution*,
    MacMillan Co., New York, 1925, p.323.
15 Patrick O'Connell, *Original Sin in the Light of Present-Day Science*,
    Lumen Christi Press, Houston, Tex., 1973, pp.24-26.
16 St. Thomas Aquinas, *Summa Theologica*, (*I, Q91, a2*),
    Benziger Brothers, New York, 1947, pp.462,463.

17 *Rome and the Study of Scripture,*
    Abbey Press, St. Meinrad, Ind., 1964, pp.122,123.
18 Pope Pius xii, *Adress to the Pontifical Academy of Science,*
    L'Osservatore Romano, December 1,2, 1941, p.1.
19 Pope Pius xii, *Humani Generis,*
    Weston College Press, Weston, Mass., 1951, p.41.
20 The Jesuit Fathers of St. Mary's College, *The Church Teaches,*
    Herder Book Co., St. Louis, 1955, p.159.
21 Pope Pius xii, *Op. cit.,* p.43.
22 Quoted in: John McKee, *The Enemy Within the Gate,*
    Lumen Christi Press, Houston, Tex., 1974, pp.286,287.
23 Henry Morris, *Scientific Creationism,*
    Creation-Life Publishers, San Diego, Cal., 1974, p.172.
    Footnote, p.173, *Science News,* Nov 27, 1971.
24 Morris, *Op. cit.,* p.173.
25 *Idem,* pp.173,174.
26 *Idem,* footnote, p.174,
    Scientific American, October, 1972.
27 *Idem,* pp.174,175.
28 *Idem,* footnote, p.175,
    Science Digest, February, 1971.
29 *Idem,* Footnote, p.176,
    Science Digest, March, 1973.
30 *Idem,* footnote, p.176,
    Science News, Nov 18, 1972.
31 *Idem,* pp.176,177.

THE TENTH MEETING
   The Future Evolution of Man
      A) Recombinant DNA Research
      B) Genetic Engineering

Dean Smalley

Tonight we come to our second meeting on the sixth day of creation and our discussion will be on the future evolution of man. Many scientists think that man will soon be able to take his future evolution into his own hands by means of genetic engineering or eugenics using the recently discovered technique of recombinant DNA. Let me begin our meeting as usual by reading the Scriptural account of the sixth day:

> And God said: "Let the earth bring forth living creatures according to their kinds; cattle and creeping things and beasts of the earth according to their kinds." And it so. And God made the beasts of the earth according to their kinds, and everything that creeps upon the ground according to its kind. And God saw that it was good. Then God said, "Let us make man in our image, and after our likeness: and let them have dominion over all the earth." So God created man in his own image, in the image of God he created him; male and female he created them. And God blessed them, and God said to them, "Be fruitful and multiply, and fill the earth and subdue it; and have dominion over the fish of the sea and over the birds of the air and over every living thing that moves upon the earth." And God said, "Behold, I have given you every plant yielding seed which is upon the face of all the earth, and every tree with its seed in its fruit: you shall have for food. And to every beast of the earth, and to everything that creeps

on the earth, everything that has the breath of life. I have given every green plant for food." And it was so. And God saw everything that he had made, and behold it was very good. And there was evening and there was morning a sixth day (Gen 1:24-31).

Dr. Arthur Schonfield

Evolutionists have recognized for many years that there is still much to learn about the subject, especially the mechanisms involved. Mutation, natural selection, and isolation, can't be the whole story. I think this is the underlying reason for the great excitement in the scientific community about recombinant DNA. I was quite surprised to hear during our discussion on the origin of species both Mrs. Stepan and Rev. Swezey defend the antiquated theory of fixism. If man can cross the so-called "species barrier" in the laboratory by recombining the DNA of different species, surely the same thing must also be occuring in nature, though of course there is much work yet to be done before we are clear just how this happens. But I am certain it is safe to say that the known mechanisms of evolution are now mutation, recombination, natural selection, and isolation.

But let me get on with the topic at hand, the future evolution of man. We no longer have to wait a million years or more for the future evolution of man to occur by *accidental* mutations. By means of new technique called recombinant DNA it will soon be possible by genetic engineering for men to achieve the equivalent of a million years of evolution in a few generations. Let me read from *The Ultimate Experiment: Man-Made Evolution*, by Nicholas Wade, a reporter for *Science*, the weekly journal of the American Association for the Advancement of Science. The first chapter is significantly entitled *The Keys of the Kingdom*:

> Some thirty-five years ago physicists learned how to manipulate the forces in the nucleus of the atom, and the world has been struggling to cope with the results of that discovery ever since. The ability to penetrate the nucleus of the living cell, to rearrange and transplant the nucleic acids

that constitute the genetic material of all forms of life, seems a more beneficent power but one that is likely to prove at least as profound in its consequences.

It could well prove comparable to that other biological revolution in man's history, the domestication of plants and animals. That achievement, by the people of the Neolithic Age, opened a doorway for man to pass from uncertain existence as a hunter and gatherer to life as a farmer, herder, and city dweller. From that beginning some seven thousand years of urban civilization have followed. Yet Neolithic man, like the animal and plant breeders ever since, did not create new species: he only selected, and reinforced by breeding, the characteristics he desired from among those already within the natural genetic potential of a species.

Scientists today cannot design entirely new genes any more than Neolithic man could (although that may eventually be possible). What the new gene-splicing technique does make possible is the transfer of genes from one species to another, regardless of the reproductive barriers that nature has built between them to isolate one species from another. It is now becoming technically possible (though practically fruitless) to intermingle the genes of man and fungus, ant and elephant, oak and cabbage. The whole gene pool of the planet, the product of three billion years of evolution, is at our disposal. The key to the living kingdom has been put into our hands.

There are occasional suggestions, made on scientific or moral grounds, that the key should be thrown away. Such abnegation of intellectual curiosity is not in man's nature, and in any case the question is moot: the door to the treasure-house is already ajar, and the only question remaining is what use will be made of the riches within. [1]

Let me give a little historical background for this new technology. Our story begins in 1865, when an Augustinian friar, Gregor Mendel, discovered the laws of heredity. Three years later in 1868, a German biologist, Friedrich Meischer, discovered an acid in the nucleus of the cell which he named deoxyribose nucleic acid (DNA). Meischer did not know what this acid did, and it was not until

1948 that an American medical doctor, Oswald Avery, put Mendel and Meischer together. Avery discovered that Mendel's hereditary units, which had later been called genes, were made of DNA. Finally, in 1972 Stanley Cohen and others at Stanford University developed the recombinant DNA technique.

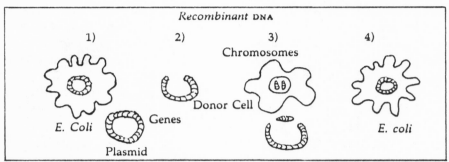

Plate xxv   *Recombinant* DNA

The favorite vehicle for recombinant DNA experiments is the bacterium *Escherchia coli* or *E. coli* for short. This little creature was discovered by a German biologist Theodor Escherich, in 1885, and named for him. In a single-cell creature as simple as *E. coli*, there is no proper nucleus, and extra chromosomes are floating around in the cytoplasm in little loops called plasmids. In Step 1) of the diagram on the board, one of the plasmids is removed, and in Step 2) the plasmid is broken open with an enzyme. Then from a different organism (it can be from a lower organism like a virus, or a higher organism like a fruit fly, or even from a man) a section of chromosome which contains the genes, the hereditary units, is removed, and 3) spliced into the open plasmid. Finally 4) the plasmid is reinserted into *E. coli*, and when it reproduces in the normal way by meitosis, the foreign DNA is also reproduced.

In 1971 Paul Berg, also of Stanford University and one of the first to develop the recombinant DNA technique, was about to combine the DNA of *E. coli* with the DNA of a virus called SV40 or Simian virus 40, which causes tumors in monkeys. Herbert Pollack, a cancer researcher at Cold Springs Harbor, Long Island, accidentally heard about the experiment and telephoned Berg to say he considered it extremely risky. *E. coli* is practically ubiquitous and very hardy. It lives in the intestines of every animal, including man, in sewers, in drinking water, and so on. If *E. coli* were combined with a dangerous virus and then infected a laboratory worker, it could spread to the community and theoretically cause a serious epidemic. Impressed, Berg called several of the most prominent researchers in the country, and in 1974 they met at the Massachusetts Institute of Technology, where they decided to call for a voluntary moratorium on recombinant DNA research until a conference of all the leading researchers in the world could be held to assess the possible risks of the new technology. In 1975 ninety American and fifty foreign scientists, the top men in the field, gathered at Asilomar in California. After long and at times heated discussion, the almost unanimous consensus was that the benefits of the research far outweighed the risks involved. They proposed to minimize, if not completely eliminate, the risks by a double system of containment which I have indicated on the board.

	Biological Containment			
Physical Containment	P1 K12			
	P2	K12		
	P3		K12	
	P4			Chi-1776

Plate xxvi *Double System of Containment*

In this graded system of physical containment, P1 is the ordinary laboratory with no particular safety features. Only an experiment that was considered completely harmless could be done in this type of facility. As the experiment was considered more risky, the safety features increased, until a P4 laboratory had to be entered by an air lock and the actual experiment performed in a glove box. Side by side with the physical containment, a method of biological containment was also proposed. *E. coli* in its natural state has been known to cause disease, but there is a strain developed in the laboratory called K12 which is considered completely harmless. K12 would be used in experiments in P1, P2, and even P3 laboratories. One of the researchers, Roy Curtiss of the University of Alabama, was assigned to develop an even more weakened strain of *E. coli*; and in 1976, our bicentenial year, he produced a strain that he named *Chi*-1776, which he says could not possibly survive outside the laboratory. It would be used in a P4 facility for experiments which were considered the most hazardous.

Then in 1976 the National Institutes of Health (NIH), which is the Federal Agency funding most of the research, adopted the Asilomar guidelines. The NIH funds the work done in the universities, but not the work in private industry. If, for instance, a researcher was found doing an experiment in a P2 facility that should have been done in a P3, his Federal funds could be withdrawn.

So far the discussion had been mostly within the scientific community, but in 1977 it spilled over into the public arena. The confrontation between the public and the scientific community came to a head in Cambridge, Massachusetts, the home of Harvard and MIT. When Harvard University announced plans to build a P3 facility, Mayor Alfred Vellucci called for public hearings to assess the possible risks to the people of Cambridge. A special citizen's review board was established by the Cambridge City Council to examine the facts in the case:

> The citizens chose their own ground for decision without falling captive to either side of the scientists' debate. The proponents had implied that restricting research would impede discovery of a cure for cancer and the like, but the review board decided that "the benefits to be derived from this research are uncertain at this time," although the possibility for advancement certainly existed.
>
> The opponents had said that since no containment system could be foolproof, the research should not take place in a city, if at all. The review board decided that absolute assurance of safety was an unreasonable expectation. The citizens did not define precisely what degree of risk was acceptable, but they at least grasped the metal that had hitherto been too hot for any other group to handle by

deciding that there was a risk but that they, on the public's behalf, were willing to accept it even without any immediate countervailing benefit.

"Knowledge, whether for its own sake or for its potential benefits to mankind, cannot serve as justification for introducing risks to the public unless an informed citizenry is willing to accept those risks," the review board wrote in its report. P3 research, it advised, should go ahead, although under certain additional safety conditions to those specified in the NIH guidelines, such as proper monitoring for the escape of the organisms used in the experiments.

The citizens' recommendations were accepted by the city council in February 1977, although with a few further restrictions, such as a ban on P4 research, which the universities have no known plans to perform. Biologists at Harvard and MIT now have to work under more stringent conditions than if the city had left them alone, but the extra conditions are tolerable and confer the advantage of enabling the research to proceed with the informed consent and approval of the public. [2]

So far we have dealt only with the health hazards of recombinant DNA research; let me proceed now to the more crucial issue of genetic engineering and eugenics:

The social acceptability of engineering the human gene set may prove a more formidable obstacle than the technical problems. George Wald, for example, has already proposed that the human genome [total genes] should be declared inviolable. But the precept, even if acceptable, is vulnerable to erosion. The advantages of genetic engineering are going to be demonstrated first in the skillful improvement of crop plants and domestic animals. Next will come a development opposed by only Luddites and religious obscurantists, the gene-splice treatment of some of the fifteen hundred human diseases known to be genetically determined. Means of genetic manipulation may then be discovered that enhance the natural process of development and enable each individual to realize his full genetic potential.

Each such advance would surely be as intensely debated as were the first uses of the gene-splicing technique, but the outcome of such debates is seldom in serious doubt: the forces of progress will generally prevail over unsubstantiated forebodings of theoretical hazards. Yet by the time that the human genome has been improved a little, for the best of reasons, there remains no clear barrier against improving it a lot. The dilemma then raised is more than purely taxonomic: a substantial improvement on the human gene set, once we know how to effect it, will produce a creature as different from man as is man from the apes - in other words, a new species. [3]

Nicholas Wade concludes his presentation of genetic engineering with a criticism of the negative attitude of counter-culture critics like Theodore Roszak, whom Rev. Swezey has quoted several times:

Social critics such as Theodore Roszak have made a major theme of science's corrosive effect on other systems of values. Science "has taken on the character of a nihilistic campaign against the legitimate mysteries of man and nature," says Roszak. The view of the scientist as a profaner of nature's mysteries is as old as the Romantic rebellion:

"Do not all charms fly
At the mere touch of cold philosophy?
There was an awful rainbow once in heaven:
We know her woof, her texture; she is given
In the dull catalogue of common things.
Philosophy will clip an Angel's wings,
conquer all mysteries by rule and line,
Empty the haunted air and gnom'ed mine -
Unweave a rainbow..." [Keats]

The price of listening to this particular lament would have been the industrial revolution; mankind would still be enjoying the buccolic simplicity that the Romantics idolized. Nevertheless, the discoveries flowing from the gene-splicing technique will eventually touch on the roots of human existence and can hardly fail to have an emotional and intellectual impact of some kind. To read a print-out of the complete sequence of one's own DNA would probably be a curious experience: no one likes to think of himself or herself as being based on a blueprint that is embodied in a purely chemical system and differs by only a few percent of an admittedly complex formula from some four billion other systems.

It would be a reductionist fallacy to equate a person with his DNA sequence: environmental as well as genetic influences weigh strongly in determining character. All the same, complete understanding of the human gene set, its developmental program, and its differences from the gene sets of other animals, could well affect, and perhaps degrade, humankind's view of itself and importance in the universal scheme of things. That is no argument for declaring the human gene set off bounds to gene splicers, but it is one of the factors to be considered in the technique's long-term balance sheet, possibly though not necessarily on the debit side.

The ability to manipulate the stuff of life is the ultimate technology. Other techniques are merely extensions of man's hands or mind or senses, serving to amplify or project the capabilities of the user. The further improvement and refinement of these technologies will doubtless continue to be a preoccupation for long into the future. But the impending ability to turn the tools inward for the reshaping of man himself would be an event quite out of the ordinary march of technological progress. Hitherto evolution has seemed an inexorable and irreversible a process as time or entropy; now at last there lies almost within man's grasp a tool for manipulating the force that shaped him, for controlling his own creator. [4]

Let me conclude my presentation tonight with a very appropriate quote from Carl Sagan's *The Dragons of Eden*:

...Societies will, of course, wish to exercise prudence in deciding which technologies - that is, which applications of science - are to be pursued and which not. But without funding basic research, without supporting the acquisition of knowledge for its own sake, our options become dangerously limited. Only one physicist in a thousand need stumble upon something like the displacement current to make the support of all thousand a superb investment for society. [James Clerk Maxwell's discovery of the displacement current, made both radio and television possible.] Without vigorous, farsighted, and continuing encouragement of fundamental scientific research, we are in the position of eating our seed corn: we may fend off starvation for one more winter, but we have removed the last hope of surviving the following winter.

In a time in some respects similar to our own, St. Augustine of Hippo, after a lusty and intellectually inventive young manhood, withdrew from the world of sense and intellect and advised others to do likewise: "There is another form of temptation, even more fraught with danger. This is the disease of curiosity...It is this which drives us on to try to discover the secrets of nature, those secrets which are beyond our understanding, which will avail us nothing and which men should not wish to learn...In this immense forest, full of pitfalls and perils, I have drawn myself back, and pulled myself away from these thorns. In the midst of all these things which float unceasingly around me in everyday life, I am never surprised at any of them, and never captivated by my genuine desire to study them...I no longer dream of the stars." The time of Augustine's death, 430 A.D., marks the beginning of the Dark Ages in Europe. [5]

Finally let me say that the apprehension felt by many people concerning recombinant DNA research has greatly diminished, especially among concerned scientists. In spite of intense activity in the field over the past few years, not one serious accident has been reported.

Fr. Robert A. Staatz

For my presentation tonight on the future evolution of man, I would like to turn again to Fr. Owen Garrigan, a professor of chemistry at Seton Hall University, and the author of the excellent *Man's Intervention in Nature*:

> Somewhere in the utopian future, mankind will build upon his legacy from his ancestors, taking advantage of his expanded mental capacity to guide the development of the biological foundation of human nature. Even now a new era is being opened as man begins consciously to be an agent of evolutionary change in his own species. The time is not far off when a man, by taking thought will indeed add a cubit to his own stature. Men will speak about the transition from *Homo sapiens* to *Homo hominefactus* (man-made man). And there will be an element of truth in their words. "Man-made man!" The term has a somewhat inflated and sensational ring in our day. But can we exclude the very real possibility of this phenomenon tomorrow. It has only begun to be apparent that *Homo sapiens*, as we know him, is only one stage in a long process of becoming. He is the product of many stages of development in the past. And it is not yet apparent what he will be. As evolution continues, our contemporary man seems destined to be used as raw material for the manufacture of the more advanced human product of the future. Man's commision to "build the universe" may allow, and even require, his building a new nature for himself. The methods are already being assembled to make the transition a reality. [6]

The phrase "build the universe" is from Teilhard de Chardin, a man, you will all agree, was way ahead of his time. Let me now give two of Garrigan's speculations concerning what form this man-directed evolution might take:

> If man learns how to separate the mechanisms of evolution, it may be possible for him in some ways to by-pass the actual intermediates that have determined his present status. In effect, he will be able to return to the earlier indeterminate stages and impose choices other than those historically

taken...

For example, man today derives his energy from the food he eats. Plants, on the other hand, derive their energy from the sun by means of photosynthesis. One of the choices on the route to man removed the indeterminancy regarding photosynthesis. The living species from which man sprang were not photosynthetic. With sufficient knowledge of biological mechanisms, however, it may be possible to give the option of photosynthetic capability to man. One might imagine a man with a patch of photosynthetic skin. He could then acquire energy like a solar battery from a light source. A few minutes outdoors or under a sunlamp would be the equivalent of a banquet. It would be a neat and efficient cycle if man could "fix" or assimilate the same carbon dioxide (CO_2) via photosynthesis that he exhales as the product of the digestion of food. The humans of the future, once they arrived at a more thorough knowledge of the molecular mechanisms of their own biology, may indeed have the option of being green. [7]

This example and one following may seem a little on the bizarre side today, but may perhaps be taken for granted tomorrow.

...At the present time man's mental capacity is remarkable, but quite limited compared with computer possibilities. Man can handle fewer than fifty bits of information each second. An attempt might be made to produce mental supermen by modifying the organ of thought so as to realize its maximum potential. Even if man were capable of only a few minutes of super-thought per day, who knows what good might result? It takes thirty-three normal cell divisions to account for the ten billion pyramidal cells already present in the young embryo brain. These cells will condition the mental activity of the brain during its whole life. Just one more division, the thirty-fourth, would double the number of these cells in the brain. The increase in size which doubling would entail would be formidable in the normal process of birth. It would no longer be formidable if birth were a process of decantation, as in

Huxley's *Brave New World*. Perhaps the blood supply to the fetus could be improved so that vitamins, hormones, enzymes, or other nutrients would make for maximal brain growth. Over twenty years ago it was found that rats treated with the anterior-pituitary-growth hormone had larger brains and eighty-six per cent more neurons when born. For the artificial stimulation of brain growth an embryo might be taken from the womb for culturing in a bottle at about two or three months. This would be no radical departure in itself, but merely an extension of our present competence in the viability of infants premature by many weeks. (The application of sex hormones at these early stages would almost certainly enable the parents to choose the sex of their child. [8]

After discussing the various genetic engineering techniques that are being proposed, and the results they may achieve, Garrigan goes on to discuss the moral implications of this new technology. As is usually the case, there are two extreme views. An absolute "yes" is given by men like B.F. Skinner of Harvard University, the behavioral psychologist and author of *Walden* II, who feels that men must actively manipulate their genetic endowment to achieve Utopia, and an absolute "no" by the Nobel laureate George Wald, who has proposed that the human genome be declared inviolable. Fr. Garrigan favors a middle road between these two extremes:

A Middle Course. Genetic intervention is accepted in principle, but each case is to be decided on its own merits. One must be reasonably certain that the proposed genetic change is good. Risk to the species must be entirely excluded. Risk to the individual must be minimal, that is of the same order of magnitude as ordinary acceptable risks. The history of evolution records certain mistakes, evolutionary trials that were not sucessful, the exploration of an avenue that became a dead end. Now that man is entering the field of directing evolution, it is unfair to expect him to avoid *all* mistakes. However, he must take due precautions. Trials on animals, for example, must have advanced to the stage where the experimenter can predict from solid scientific evidence what the outcome will be when applied to man.

In the matter of man's stewardship over human evolution, the present generation is well advised to remain open-minded. A closed mind would be unwise, because all the facts are not yet in. Detailed and definitive judgments would still be premature. Facile answers today may not survive the deeper insights of a future age. Just as we stand on the shoulders of our predecessors, so our descendants will stand on ours. If there is to be a "hyperethics" growing out of the controlled biology of the future, the men who meet the future problems will have future talents and abilities. The Church itself develops not only in its doctrine but also in its moral insight. The Church of the future, with its more intensely human understanding of revelation, will be in a better position to judge some of the issues of current speculation. In short, we must be slow to accept anything so momentous as genetic control, but open to future developments. [9]

Let me conclude by turning again to Teilhard de Chardin. His biographer, Robert Speaight, after briefly examining some of the techniques of man-directed evolution, concludes with Teilhard's own assessment of the morality of eugenics and of genetic engineering:

Such experiments would be delicate, to be sure, but they should be "healthily, respectfully, and religiously undertaken" - no longer merely in the sense of one man experimenting on another, but in the sense of "humanity as a whole feeling its way forward to a new acquisition of vitality." Writers like Wells and Aldous Huxley had painted their satirical pictures of what such a brave new world might be. Nevertheless the idea behind it was a noble one and need not, in practice, coarsen into caricature. Eugenics was not only a matter of selective reproduction:

"What attitude should the advancing sector of humanity adopt towards static and decidely unprogressive ethnic groups?...Up to what point should the development of the stronger - always supposing that this can be clearly defined - take precedence over the conservation of the weak? How shall we reconcile with a maximum of efficiency the care we expend on the wounded with the superior necessities of the attack? In what does true charity consist?"

These were dangerous questions, but Teilhard had gone some way to answer them by his own conduct in the trenches, where he served as a stretcher-bearer, not as a combatant. Indeed, now that he looked back on that time, he was bound to admit that most people could still understand the meaning of force - and force was the "symbol and key of greater being" - only in the shape of war. But in the world of the future Teilhard prophesied a "collective act of perception...a fusion of races leading directly to the establishment not only of a common language, but of a common morality and common ideals...a community of effort and struggle for the same objectives, accompanied *ipso facto* by fighting comradeship." In this way, and under the stress of these affinities, the organization of human energies was leading to the emergence of a "common human soul."[10]

Mrs. Maria Stepan

I was not surprised to hear Dr. Schonfield's criticism of fixism and his debunking of the so-called "species barrier." I once heard a debate on the radio between two scientists on the merits of recombinant DNA research. One of them was what Rev. Swezey has been calling an establishment type and the other a counter-type. The establishment type said: "There is no such thing as a species barrier." The counter-culture type asked: "Have you ever heard of a mule?"

We heard Rev. Swezey admit what is called micro-evolution, but assert that this is really not evolution at all, but merely variation. This variation occurs, he said, through species and even up through genera, but stops at family, (which he considers the equivalent of the biblical "kind"), because of the sterility of hybrids. The horse and the ass belong to the same family of horse-like creatures, but their offspring, the mule, is sterile. The sterility of hybrids renders macro-evolution, or evolution between the great classes, for example between reptile and mammal, manifestly impossible.

However, with the development of the new recombinant DNA technique it should be at long last possible to test experimentally the possibility of macro-evolution. The evolutionists have long maintained that the reason they can't demonstrate the theory by breeding experiments, as Darwin and Huxley originally hoped to do, is because of the tremendous lengths of time involved, but with the advent of recombinant DNA technology that excuse is no longer valid.

Why not try to reproduce these transitional types, the missing links between the great classes, in the laboratory by recombining the DNA of, say an amphibian and a reptile. This could be done at the single cell stage between two species that the evolutionists consider closely related. I presume, good scientists that they are, the evolutionists would abandon the theory if such experiments proved unsuccessful.

During the height of the controversy between Harvard University and Mayor Vellucci, Bishop Thomas Riley, one of the Auxiliary Bishops of Boston, made an excellent statement on the position of the Church with regard to the ethical problems raised by recombinant DNA research. The statement appeared in *The Pilot*, the official diocesan newspaper, and was entitled, *Will* DNA *Research Evoke Moral Concern?*

> The problems raised by this type of biological research have been compared to those presented in the field of physics by the development of nuclear energy. In each field, scientists seem to have penetrated to the very depth of the universe, to the sources of energy and life itself. Armed with such power, men have reason to ask themselves how long they can continue to rely on the apparent physical strength of the world in which they live, and on their own social institutions, to protect them from the indifference of people toward one another. In other words, one may ask, has human ingenuity at last created the power which, if irresponsibly employed,

may lead to the destruction of the universe and of humanity itself...

Two points seem to be suggested. First, the difficulty of restraining, even by self-discipline among the scientists themselves, the urge to follow up the possibilities of further research which collective investigation has opened up; and secondly, the danger that techniques developed honestly in view of beneficial results may become available to people who will use them unscrupously and ruthlessly for purposes inconsistent with the moral development of humanity. One of the inherent dangers of government is its tendency to usurp supreme and totalitarian power. This tendency is particularly strong when governmental policy issues from an atheistic philosophy and is directed toward perpetuation of narrowly conceived objectives.

For this reason it is important that the voices of religious leaders be loud and clear in protesting the attempts of government to constrain their freedom of expression, or to subordinate their spiritual influence to the achievement of merely material and ephemeral advantages...

There is great reason, however, for fearing the twofold danger of unscrupulous and irresponsible scientists and the misuse by government and industry of legitimately developed scientific techniques. The problems presented by DNA research and the related probelm of nuclear fission bring forcefully to our attention the disastrous possibilities of the power over nature and life which human ingenuity has generated. At the dawn of human history there was indication of what is likely to happen when those who do not fear God gain power over God's creation which enables them to destroy it. [11]

Bishop Riley is speaking of Adam and Eve who, in disobedience to God, ate of the "tree of knowledge of good and evil" and; although they did indeed become like gods, they did so at the price of expulsion from the garden of Eden.

Pope John Paul II has also repeatedly voiced his concern over the recent developments in scientific research in the field of genetic engineering and related areas. Let me read a few paragraphs from an allocution he delivered in 1980 to the Italian Society of Internal Medicine:

> The truth is that technological development characteristic of our time is suffering from a fundamental ambiance. While on the one hand it enables man to take in hand his own destiny, it exposes him on the other hand, to the temptation of going beyond the limits of a reasonable dominion over nature, jeopardizing the very survival and integrity of the human person.
>
> Just consider, to remain in the sphere of biology and medicine, the implicit danger to man's right to life represented by the discoveries in the field of artificial insemination, the control of births and fertility, hibernation and "retarded death," genetic engineering, psychic drugs, organ transplants, etc. Certainly scientific knowledge has its own laws by which it must abide. It must also recognize, however, especially in medicine, an impassible limit in respect for the person and in protection of his right to live in a way worthy of a human being.
>
> If a new method of investigation, for example, harms or threatens to harm this right, it is not to be considered lawful simply because it increases our knowledge. Science, in fact, is not the highest value to which all others must be subordinated. Higher up in the scale of values is precisely the individual's personal right to physical and spiritual life, to his psychic and functional integrity. The person, in fact, is the measure and criterion of good or evil in all human manifestations. Scientific progress, therefore cannot claim to lie in a kind of neutral ground. The ethical norm, based on respect for the dignity of the person, must illuminate and discipline both the research phase and the phase of the application of the results reached in it. [12]

Let me go on now to the topic of eugenics. The American geneticist, Herman Muller, was the first to propose a practical eugenics program, which he called Voluntary Control of Germ Plasm (vcogp). This plan, unlike some of the tentative proposals being put forward for genetic engineering, is already in use on a small scale and could be greatly expanded. The plan is based on artifical insemination (AI), and is similar to a program dairy farmers call Dairy Herd Improvement (DHI) in which the farmer selects the sperm of prize bulls from a catalogue. It is possible by this method to raise the milk production of a herd of cows in just a few years. This is the positive aspect of the plan; the negative side is that any cow which does not respond by increased productivity is immediately shipped off to the butcher. Muller first proposed his eugenics plan in 1927 and it is still in vogue. The Nobel laureate, William Shockley, the inventor of the transistor, recently got into the news by donating his sperm to such a plan.

Eugenics is basically an attack on Christian marriage; and, in 1930, Pope Pius XI brought out his wonderful encyclical on Christian marriage, *Casti Connubii*, in which he attacked sterilization, a form of negative eugenics, and always a basic part of any eugenics plan.

That pernicious practice must be condemned which closely touches upon the natural right of man to enter matrimony, but effects also in a real way the welfare of the offspring. For there are some who, oversolicitous for the cause of eugenics, not only give salutary counsel for more certainly procuring the strength and health of the future child - which indeed, is not contrary to right reason - but also put eugenics before the aims of a higher order, and by public authority wish to prevent from marrying all those who, according to the norms and conjectures of their investigations, would through hereditary transmission bring forth defective offspring. And more, they wish to legislate to deprive these of that natural faculty by medical action despite their unwillingness...and arrogate to itself a power over a faculty which it never had and can never legitimately possess.

Those who act in this way are at fault in losing sight of the fact that the family is more sacred than the State, and that men are begotten not for the earth and for time, but for heaven and eternity...Public magistrates have no direct power over the bodies of their subjects...Furthermore,

Christian doctrine establishes, and the light of human reason makes it most clear, that private individuals have no other power over members of their bodies than that which pertains to their natural ends; and they are not free to destroy or mutilate their members, or in any other way render themselves unfit for their natural functions, except when no other provision can be made for the good of the whole body. [13]

Artifical insemination, the basis of most of these eugenics plans, was condemned in 1949 and again in 1951 by Pope Pius xii. Let me read a few paragraphs from an excellent book by William E. May, a professor of moral theology at Catholic University, entitled *Human Existence, Medicine and Ethics*:

> Pius, in condemning artificial insemination whether by husbands or donors, had offered two principal considerations. His first objection was that insemination outside the natural act of intercourse would be "to convert the domestic hearth, sanctuary of the family, into nothing more than a biological laboratory." He argued that artificial inseminatation transforms the generating of new human life from an act of procreation into an act of reproduction and that, for this alone, it is dehumanizing and depersonalizing. It was evidently his judgment that artificial insemination drives a wedge between the unitive and procreative meanings of human sexual intercourse, sundering a union that is likely to be inherent and inseperable by human agency. Obviously, artificial insemination by a donor drives these two meanings of human sexual intercourse much further apart than artificial insemination by the husband, but the difference between the two forms is only one of degree or distance. [14]

It is not generally realized that the current abortion movement in the United States and the infamous Nazi race purification program both grew out of the eugenics movement. Let me read a a few paragraphs from a very illuminating article by Michael Schwartz, of the Catholic League of Religious and Civil Rights, entitled *The Nazi-Abortion Link*, which appeared in *The National*

Catholic Register:

The real powers in shaping American policy with regard to population control and abortion are groups such as Planned Parenthood, Zero Population Growth, and the Population Institute. These organizations grew out of the eugenics movement, which had its heyday in the 1920's, and they are still controlled by the social and academic elite groups that played such a prominent role in trying to keep the American race pure half a century ago.

The eugenics movement, which was international but had its strongest base in the United States, is really the *common parent* of both the racial policy of the Nazis and the population control/abortion movement in contemporary America.

American eugenicists were successful in getting a restrictive imigration law passed in 1924 that eliminated most imigration into this country from Eastern and Southern Europe...Eugenicists also succeeded in getting compulsory sterilization laws passed in a majority of the states during those years.

The Supreme Court upheld the constitutionality of those laws in the infamous *Buck vs. Bell* decision of 1927, in which, speaking through Oliver Wendell Holmes, it declared, "Three generations of imbeciles are enough," and ordered the sterilization of Carrie Buck, an allegedly feeble-minded Virginia woman. The law for the Prevention of Progeny with Hereditary Diseases, the basis of Hitler's race purification program, was directly patterned on the model sterilization law proposed by the leaders of the American eugenics movement...

One of the most ardent promoters of eugenics in the 1920's was Margaret Sanger, the founder of Planned Parenthood. In a 1926 address at Vassar College, Mrs. Sanger noted that through the recently passed immigration law the United States had taken action to prevent the deterioration of the population from without. But, she complained, "we make no attempt to cut down the rapid multiplication of the unfit and undesirable at home."

Her solution was "offering a bonus or yearly pension to all obviously unfit parents to allow themselves to be sterilized by a harmless and scientific method...There is only one reply to a request for a higher birth rate among the intelligent, and that is to ask the government to take the burdens of the insane and feeble-minded from off your backs. Sterilization for these is the remedy..."

Dr. Hines was another leading figure in the early Planned Parenthood movement. In his 1936 *Medical History of Contraception* (which Planned Parenthood reprinted in 1965 with a glowing introduction from its president Alan Guttmacher), Hines asked the leading question. "Are Catholic stocks in the United States, taken as a whole, genetically inferior to such non-Catholic libertarian stocks as Unitarians and Universalists, Ethical Culturalists, Freethinkers? Inferior to non-Catholic stocks in general? No one really knows. One is entitled to his hunches, however, and my guess is that the answer will some day be made in the affirmative."...

After the Second World War, when openly elitist statements like these became less palatable to the public, the leaders of the eugenics movement simply shifted their strategy to the "problem" of population growth in general. After all, most of the population growth was occurring among the lower racial groups, the *Untermenschen*, the disenfranchised, such as non-whites, poor whites, and Catholics. [15]

In case there is any doubt about the similarity between Nazi elitism and that of some of the proponents of genetic engineering, let me conclude with a statement by James Watson, the co-discoverer of the double helix of DNA, and now one of the leaders in recombinant DNA research. This is taken from another excellent book entitled *Human Destiny* by John Hammes, a Catholic layman, who is a professor of psychology at the University of Georgia:

In January 1973, the U.S. Supreme Court legalized abortion, and in May of that year James Watson, co-discoverer of the double helix and a Nobel prize winner, extended the court's logic by proposing that it would be even better if a child were "not declared alive" until three days after birth...His reason was that some birth defects were not discoverable until after birth, so the three-day extension would permit legal killing of a defective child. Watson suggested that the doctor should "allow the child to die if the parents so choose" - leaving unsettled the criteria for how defective a child must be in order to merit such a judgment. The phrase "not declared alive" implies that we can determine by mere declaration whether the newborn is to be recognized as alive. Watson was obvioulsy referring to the legal definition of what constituted human life; and since the Supreme Court had decided the future fetus had no legal right to life, Watson was astute enough to observe a logical extension of that loss of privilege. [16]

Rev. De Verne Swezey

We have heard the secular humanists claim that man is now able to take his future evolution into his own hands. I would like to begin my presentation tonight by reading a few comments by Dr. Henry Morris on this claim:

Another common theme among evolutionists is that, since evolution has now "come to consciousness in man," and generated moral and ethical values, as well as an intellectual capacity for understanding the evolutionary process, we are now able to plan and direct all future evolution. One of America's leading evolutionary geneticists, H.J. Muller, said:

"Through the unprecedented faculty of long-range fore-sight, jointly serviced and exercised by us, we can, in securing and advancing our position, increasingly avoid the missteps of blind nature, circumvent its cruelties, reform our own natures, and enhance our own values." [17]

...This belief that man can control future evolution is simply another evidence that evolution is itself a religion. Even assuming that geneticists and biochemists ever acquire enough understanding of genetic mechanisms to do such things, a tremendous number of value judgments will have to be made by someone when they are carried out. Every decision, as to the desirable traits of a future individual or the future course of evolution in general, will evolve a vast system of ethical-values philosophy, and this is obviously religious in essence. [18]

Dr. Schonfield read us a summary of the recombinant DNA controversy from Nicholas Wade's *The Ultimate Experiment: Man-Made Evolution*. Wade is a reporter for *Science*, the weekly bulletin for the Association for the Advancement of Science; in other words, he is a spokesman for the agnostic and atheistic Establishment. So let me read a few excerpts from a book by Richard Hutton, *Bio-Revolution: DNA and the Ethics of Man-Made Life*, which represents more the minority opinion among scientists on recombinant DNA, which is, however, the majority opinion of the public. One of the most vocal scientists involved in the recent recombinant DNA controversy was Robert Sinsheimer of Cal Tech, who tried unsuccessfully to introduce the question of ethics into the debate:

Sinsheimer's arguments...indirectly deride the characteristic scientific arrogance - the monolithic belief that everything boils down to solutions couched in physical and chemical reactions [e.g. the double system of containment]...This arrogance has practically overwhelmed the recombinant debate at times...and most of it comes from the group that is pressing for relative freedom for the research. Its attitude is not something that we can accept with grudging amusement; it is not the kind of egocentrism that permits us to walk away shaking our heads because we think that it cannot effect us. To the contrary, the arrogance displayed by scientists on this issue is particularly galling, precisely because it subverts discussion of an issue which strikes at the very heart of the nature of public debate and responsibility. The scientist is saying, in effect, "Trust me. You cannot be expected to under-

stand the true complexity of the problem." And of his opponents: "They are blinded by jealousy. They have their own
axes to grind. They refuse to see things which, as good
scientists, they should recognize." Sinsheimer's response
raises the question of who is saddled by the most self-interest.
For, when push comes to shove, the only entity whose self-
interest really matters is the one most affected, the public;
who, as Roger Dworkin noted at Asilomar, has the right,
through its legislative representatives, to make its own
mistakes. [19]

In 1979 when the furor over recombinant DNA research had died
down, the NIH quietly relaxed its guidelines. P3 and P4 facilities
are no longer required for what had once been considered
dangerous experiments. Paul Berg had originally said at Asilomar,
that "P2 plus K12 is working in your garage."

...If an accident occurs, the shouts of self-righteous glee
(tinged, perhaps with a touch of sympathy for the victims)
will no doubt rise from the ranks of those who worked so
hard to oppose unrestricted research. If nothing untoward
happens, the researchers will go merrily on their way,
concocting newer and more obscure organisms. And the basic
research will continue to make inroads on the secrets of
nature, leading us to the brink of a technology so fundamentally different from the ones we now know as to portend a
dramatic revolution in the way we conduct our lives.

What strikes the hardest about such a prediction is how
little it seems to have been able to discuss the "other" issues
involved in the research, the issues which have been labeled
irrelevant by the scientific establishment. We have, in a way,
been cleverly deluded into looking at the object of our investigation as though through a pair of binoculars turned
backward. A potentially great problem has been made small;
circumstances which strike at the very heart of the way we
live have been discussed simplistically by decision-makers,
who have managed to define issues as though the only things
at stake were technical in nature, as though ethics and morals

were not involved...

It is quite obvious why scientists wanted to steer clear of the dangers of ethical arguments. Ethics are no longer the companions of scientific thought. Scientists are working to learn more and more about less and less. [Isn't that a wonderful line!] Many of them have learned to fear the uncertainties and ambiguities that go hand and hand with the greater issues that beset us, for those issues are always open to interpretation and never get solved. For those scientists responding to questions about scientific accidents, the efficacy of the containment and the relative dangers of a certain line of research is simple. The figures of one side are compared to those of the other. Numbers replace reality as surely as plastic infantry units stand in for flesh-and-blood soldiers in the Pentagon's War Room. [20]

In 1977 Professor Charles Thomas of the Harvard Medical School was discovered conducting recombinant DNA experiments with SV40, a virus that causes cancer in monkeys, in a P2 laboratory. This was the type of experiment proposed by Paul Berg in 1971 that had originally touched off the whole controversy. Prof. Thomas was at the Asilomar Conference in 1975, and in 1976 had actually helped draft the NIH guidelines which specifically forbade the type of experiment he was conducting. The complaint against Thomas was made by an anonymous technician in his own laboratory. Harvard claimed that it was unaware of the type of experiment being conducted by Thomas, and eventually the NIH, which was funding his research, withdrew their grant. Thomas left Harvard in a huff, saying that the university was dominated by the radical left, evidently the minority group of scientists there who oppose unrestricted research. He was immediately snapped up by the Scripps Clinic and Research Foundation at La Jolla, California. Since the NIH guidelines only apply to scientists receiving federal grants, which usually means the scientists at the universities (they do not apply to private industry), Thomas is now apparently free to conduct any kind of experiment he wants, in any kind of laboratory he wants. This is a combination that had been frequently warned against during the recombinant DNA debate - an unscrupulous, irresponsible scientist, plus unregulated, profit-hungry private industry.

In July of 1978, Dr. Martin Cline performed the first experiment in human genetic engineering. He was refused permission to perform the experiment at the hosptital at UCLA, where his work was being funded by the NIH. The experiment was performed on two young women ages 16 and 21 in hospitals in Italy and Israel. The two women because of defective genes were unable to produce hemoglobin in their blood cells. Cline had first perfomed the experiment on mice. Blood cells producing hemoglobin in the mice had been killed or rendered inoperative by radiation, and new genes were inserted. The experiments on the mice were unsuccessful; no new hemoglobin was produced; but Cline went ahead anyway and repeated the experiment on the human subjects. The two young women showed no change in their condition, and many scientists working in the same field protested the ethics of this experiment.

Because of abuses such as these on the part of Thomas, Cline, and others, many scientists think that research in this and other areas should be brought under some kind of public control. Richard Hutton discusses one of the most frequently suggested solutions to this problem, the so-called "Science Court":

> The Science Court was first suggested in the late 1960's by Dr. Arthur Kantrowitz, a physicist who had helped solve the problem of ballistic missile and spacecraft re-entry years before...The Science Court would act as a bridge between the scientific community and uninformed policy-makers in government by providing an institutional setting in which adversary proceedings could be held. With perhaps five to seven judges drawn from the ranks of scientists and laymen alike, the court could offer a respected influential mechanism to anyone wishing to question the controversial aspects of any line of research and development...It would have been a perfect place for the debate over recombination to have been held after the conferees at Asilomar had shown themselves incapable of dealing with the greater issues implied by the

326 THE SIX DAYS OF CREATION

research.

Because its role would not include issuing verdicts but would be limited to producing advisory reports upon the current state of technical knowledge, it could act as a clearing house for factual disputes that seem to color most scientific debates; it could record the points upon which both sides agree and render judgments on those that are in dispute. Ultimately, as its reports are published, it would act as an informational tool for the public and legislator alike, superseding the myriad methods of trial and error that seem to be the state of the art in scientific debate and providing a unified unbiased viewpoint. [21]

I should hope that the "advisory reports" issued by the Science Court could then could become the basis of possible criminal proceedings for some sort of malpractice in incidents involving the Thomases and the Clines in the scientific community. Hutton concludes with the problem of genetic engineering or eugenics:

The fallibility of scientists surfaces daily. But it becomes most obvious in some examples of ideological science - like the eugenics movement - that have periodically afflicted us throughout history. The pursuit of eugenics, the science of genetically improving the quality of the human race, actually began in the nineteenth century. While it surfaced as a legitimate branch of the rapidly developing discipline of biology, eugenics soon became a catchword, a useful way of explaining some of the more bizarre social policies that needed scientific validation. In its strictest sense, the original concept of eugenics is admirable; after all, who would not agree that we would be better off if such genetic deficiencies as hemophilia and Down's syndrome were removed from the human gene pool? But, in the world of the late nineteeth and early twentieth centuries, "genetic deficiencies" were interpreted mainly to include characteristics inherent to whole classes of people, classes that shared the single, unifying feature of being repugnant to those in power...

"Between 1911 and 1930, thirty-three states passed laws

requiring sterilization for a variety of behavioral traits deemed to be genetically determined. These included, depending on the state, such characteristics as criminality, alcoholism, tendency to commit rape, sodomy or bestiality, and feeblemindedness. Many of these laws are still on the books and have resulted, since that time, in at least 60,000 sterilizations. For instance, it has been reported that the Eugenics Board of the State of North Carolina sterilized 1620 persons between 1960 and 1968, mostly young black women. By far the greatest category of sterilization under these laws was for feeblemindedness. Feeblemindedness can supposedly be defined by the administration of an IQ test. To get some idea of the validity of IQ tests in this regard, we need only look back at the results of Goddard, who was asked in 1912 by the United States Public Health Service to use the tests to determine the frequency of feeblemindedness among new classes of immigrants into the country. Goddard's results demonstrated that the following frequencies of feebleminded- ness pertained: among Hungarians 83 percent, Russians 87 percent, Jews 83 percent, and Italians 79 percent." [22]

It is...the danger of this kind of prejudice and the possibilities of distorted scientific vision that make it necessary for scientists to bow to some kind of societal control. [23]

Dean Smalley

The second of our meetings on the sixth day of creation dealt with the future evolution of man. Our two subtopics were recombinant DNA research and genetic engineering.

Dr. Schonfield gave what might be called the majority report on the scientific community regarding recombinant DNA research and genetic engineering. He emphasized that after several years of intense activity in these areas, not one serious accident had been reported. He urged that the research be given full government and public support.

Rev. Swezey, on the other hand, gave what might be called a minority report on the research and decried the absence of ethical considerations in the pursuit of scientific goals. He urged that scientific research be brought under some form of public control, and suggested that a "Science Court" could more effectively deal with problems such as recombinant DNA research than the Asilomar Conference. He also suggested that the criminal courts should deal in some way with irresponsible and reckless scientists.

Fr. Staatz proposed what he considered a "middle course" between the absolute "yes" to genetic engineering of Dr. Schonfield, and the absolute "no" of Rev. Swezey. He suggested that genetic engineering be accepted in principle, but that each advance in the field be examined on its own merits.

Mrs. Stepan concentrated on the teachings of the Magisterium of the Church regarding the moral problems raised by recombinant DNA research and by scientific research in general, as well as genetic engineering or eugenics. She claimed that both the current abortion movement and the infamous Nazi race purification movement grew out of the eugenics movement.

REFERENCES

1   Nicholas Wade, *The Ultimate Experiment: Man Made Evolution*,
    Walker and Co., New York, 1977, pp.2,3.
2   Wade, *Op. cit.*, pp.132,133.
3   *Idem*, pp.151,152.
4   *Idem*, pp.154,155.
5   Carl Sagan, *The Dragons of Eden*,
    Random House, New York, 1967, p.138.
6   Owen Garrigan, *Man's Intervention in Nature*,
    Hawthorne Books, New York, 1967, p.138.
7   Garrigan, *Op. cit.*, p.136.
8   *Idem*, pp.160,161.

9   *Idem*, pp.178,179.
10 Robert Speaight, *Teilhard de Chardin*,
    Collins, London, 1967, pp.233,234.
11 Bishop Thomas Riley, *Will DNA Research Evoke Moral Concern?*
    The Pilot, Jan 7, 1977, Boston, pp.6,7.
12 Pope John Paul II, *Adress to the Italian Society of Internal Medicine*,
    The Pilot, Nov 14, 1980, Boston, pp.6,7.
13 Pope Pius XI, *Casti Connubii*,
    Terrence McLaughlin, C.S.N., *The Church and the Reconstruction of the Modern
    World*, Doubleday and Co., Image Books, Garden City, N.Y., 1957, pp.140,141.
14 William E. May, *Human Existence, Medicine and Ethics*,
    Franciscan Herald Press, Chicago, 1977, p.47.
15 Michael Schwartz, *The Nazi-Abortion Link*,
    The National Catholic Register, Oct 8, 1978.
    Los Angeles, Cal., pp.1,10.
16 John Hammes, *Human Destiny*,
    Our Sunday Visitor, Inc., Huntington, Ind., 1978, pp.154,155.
17 Henry Morris, *Scientific Creationism*,
    Creation-Life Publishers, San Diego, Cal., 1974, pp.199,200.
    Footnote, p.199, *Science*, Mar 21, 1958.
18 Morris, *Op. cit.*, p.200.
19 Richard Hutton, *Bio-Revolution: DNA and the Ethics of Man-Made Life*,
    New American Library, New York, 1978, p.173.
20 Hutton, *Op. cit.*, pp.174,175.
21 *Idem*, pp.216,217.
22 *Idem*, footnote, p.198,
    Jonathan Beckwith, *Social and Political Uses of Genetics in the United
    States: Past and Present*, New York Academy of Sciences, New York, 1976.
23 *Idem*, pp.197-199.

THE ELEVENTH MEETING
The Existence of the Soul

Dean Smalley

Tonight marks our third meeting on the sixth day of creation which deals with the origin of man. Tonight is also the final meeting in our lengthy dialogue. Since our very first meeting was devoted to the existence of God, we thought it appropriate that this last meeting deal with the existence of the soul. Let me begin as usual by reading the Scriptural account of the sixth day:

> And God said, "Let the earth bring forth living creatures according to their kinds: cattle and creeping things and beasts of the earth according to their kinds." And it was so. And God made the beasts of the earth according to their kinds and the cattle according to their kinds, and everything that creeps upon the ground according to its kind. And God saw that it was good. Then God said, "Let us make man in our image, after our likeness; and let them have dominion over the fish of the sea, and over the birds of the air, and over the cattle, and over all the earth, and over every creeping thing that creeps upon the earth." So God created man in his own image, in the image of God he created him; male and female he created them. And God blessed them, and God said to them, "Be fruitful and multiply, and fill the earth and subdue it; and have dominion over every living thing that moves upon the earth." And God said, "Behold, I have given you every plant yielding seed which is upon the face of all the earth, and every tree with seed in its fruit; you shall have them for food. And to every beast of the earth, and to every bird of the air and to everything that creeps on the earth, everything that has the breath of life. I have given every green plant for food." And it

331

was so. And God saw everything that he had made, and behold, it was very good. And there was evening and there was morning a sixth day (Gen 1:24-31).

Dr. Arthur Schonfield

We began our discussion of the first day of creation with Carl Sagan's *Broca's Brain*, which dealt primarily with the problem of the existence of God. On this our final meeting I would like to read from his *The Dragons of Eden*, which considers mainly the problem of the existence of the soul. The subtitle for this fascinating book is *Speculations on the Evolution of Human Intelligence*. Let me begin by noting Sagan's basic premise regarding human intelligence:

> My fundamental premise about the brain is that its workings - what we sometimes call "mind" - are a consequence of its anatomy and physiology, and nothing more. "Mind" may be a consequence of the action of the components of the brain severally or collectively. Some processes may be a function of the brain as a whole. A few students of the subject seem to have concluded that, because they have been unable to isolate and localize all higher brain functions, no further generation of neuro-anatomists will be able to achieve this objective. But the absence of evidence is not evidence of absence. The entire recent history of biology shows that we are, to a reasonable degree, the results of the interactions of an extremely complex array of molecules; and the aspect of biology that was once considered its holy-of-holies, the nature of the genetic material, has been fundamentally understood in terms of the chemistry of its constituent nucleic acids, DNA and RNA, and their operational agents, the proteins...Both because of the clear trend in the recent history of biology and because there is not a shred of evidence to support it, I will not in these pages entertain any hypothesis on what used to be called the mind-body dualism, the idea that inhabiting the matter of the body is something made of quite different stuff, called mind. [1]

Sagan then speculates on the origin of language, and suggests that both tool making and language arose around the same time. This would mean that *Homo habilis*, the first tool maker, would have had some kind of rudimentary language. Sagan believes that this hypothesis is supported by endocasts of the fossil skulls of *Homo habilis*, who had a brain capacity of around 500 c.c., about the same as a modern chimpanzee. Sagan asks, if *Homo habilis* could speak after a fashion, why can't the chimpanzee? Sagan's chapter on the intelligence of animals is provocatively entitled *The Abstractions of Beasts*, and in it he discusses the remarkable experiments that are presently being conducted in teaching chimpanzees to communicate in sign language.

Until a few years ago, the most extensive attempt to communicate with chimpanzees went something like this: a new-born chimp was taken into a household with a new-born baby, and both would be raised together...At the end of three years, the young chimp had, of course, far outstripped the young human in manual dexterity, running, leaping, climbing, and other motor skills. But while the child was happily babbling away, the chimp could say only, and with enormous difficulty, "Mamma," "Papa," and "cup." From this it was widely concluded that in language, reasoning, and other higher mental functions, chimpanzees were only minimally competent: "Beasts abstract not" [John Locke].

But in thinking over these experiments, two psychologists, Beatrice and Robert Gardner, at the university of Nevada realized that the pharynx and larynx of the chimp are not suited for human speech...It might be, the Gardners reasoned, that the chimpanzees have substantial language abilities which could not be expressed because of the limitations of their anatomy. Was there any symbolic language, they asked, that could employ the strengths rather than the weaknesses of the chimpanzee anatomy?

The Gardners hit upon a brilliant idea. Teach a chimpanzee American sign language, known by its acronym Ameslan, and sometimes as "American deaf and dumb language"...It is ideally suited to the immense manual dexterity of the chimpanzee. It also might have all the crucial design features of verbal language.

There is now a vast library of described and filmed conversations, employing Ameslan and other gestural languages, with Washoe, Lucy, Lana, and other chimpanzees studied by the Gardners and others. Not only are there chimpanzees with working vocabularies of 100 to 200 words; they are also able to distinguish among non-trivially different grammatical patterns and syntaxes. What is more, they have been remarkably inventive in the construction of new words and phrases.

On seeing for the first time a duck land quacking in a pond, Washoe gestured "water bird," which is the same phrase used in English and other languages, but which Washoe invented for the occasion. Having never seen a spherical fruit other than an apple, but knowing the signs for the principal colors, Lana, upon spying a technician eating an orange, signed "orange apple." After tasting a watermelon, Lucy described it as "candy drink" or "drink fruit," which is essentially the same word as the English "water melon." But after she burned her mouth on her first radish, Lucy forever after described them as "cry hurt food." A small doll placed unexpectedly in Washoe's cup elicited the response "baby in my drink."...Eventually Lucy was able to distinguish clearly the meanings of the phrases "Roger tickle Lucy" and "Lucy tickle Roger," both of which activities she enjoyed with gusto. [2]

Since many scientists define man as a language-using animal, once we teach the chimpanzees language, does this mean, Sagan asks, that they will have "human rights?"

If chimpanzees have consciousness, if they are capable of abstractions, do they not have what until now has been described as "human rights?" How smart does a chimpanzee have to be before killing him constitutes murder? What further properties must he show before religious missionaries must consider him worthy of attempts of conversion?

I recently was escorted through a large primate research

laboratory by its director. We approached a long corridor lined to the vanishing point as in a perspective drawing with caged chimpanzees. They were one, two, or three to a cage, and I am sure the accomodations were exemplary as far as such institutions (or for that matter traditional zoos) go. As we approached the nearest cage, its inmates bared their teeth and with incredible accuracy let fly great sweeping arcs of spittle, fairly drenching the lightweight suit of the facility's director. They then uttered a staccato of short shrieks, which echoed down the corridor to be repeated and amplified by other caged chimps, who had certainly not seen us, until the corridor fairly shook with the screeching and banging and rattling of bars...

I was powerfully reminded of those American motion pictures of the 1930's and 40's set in some vast dehumanized state penitentiary, in which the prisoners banged their eating utensils against the bars at the appearance of the tyrannical warden. These chimps are healthy and well-fed. If they are "only" animals, if they are beasts which abstract not, then my comparison is a piece of sentimental foolishness. But chimpanzees *can* abstract. Like other mammals, they are capable of strong emotions. They have certainly committed no crimes. I do not claim to have the answer, but I think it is certainly worthwhile to raise the question: Why, exactly, all over the civilized world, in virtually every major city, are apes in prison?

For all we know, occasional viable crosses between humans and chimpanzees are possible. The natural experiment must have been tried very infrequently, at least recently. If such offspring are ever produced, what will their legal status be? [3]

Sagan then goes from animal intelligence to machine intelligence, and discusses the amazing feats of electronic computers. He gives in some detail an example of a psychotherapy program developed by Joseph Weizenbaum of MIT. In the excerpt I will read, a human psychiatrist "speaks" to the computer via a typewriter on an interactive console in lower case letters, and the computer psychiatrist "replies" in upper case:

doctor, i have terrible news.
YOU SAY YOU HAVE TERRIBLE NEWS
yes, there is a computer at m i t that'll ruin us
WHY DO YOU SAY THAT
i have seen it working
YOU SAY YOU HAVE SEEN IT WORKING
it's frightening - you must see it
YOU THINK I MUST SEE IT
you sound depressed to me
IN YOUR FANTASY PERHAPS WE SOUND DEPRESSED
TO EACH OTHER
yes - perhaps
I UNDERSTAND
i do too
YOU SAY YOU DO TOO...
i can't understand how anyone could be fooled by a mere
machine
CAN'T YOU REALLY
no, after all, there is nothing creative about a computer
YOU ARE BEING NEGATIVE
i am convinced that i am correct
ARE YOU WORRIED TO HAVE BEEN CONVINCED YOU
ARE CORRECT
no, not in the least, not at all, not even a little
YOU ARE BEING NEGATIVE
you said you agreed with me, didn't you
IS THAT WHAT YOU HEARD ME SAY
why don't you try to dissuade me - computers diddle with
numbers, that's all
YOU WISH ME TO TRY TO DISSUADE YOU
you can't
YOU THINK I CAN'T
for example, could a computer in a conversation like this raise
a new topic
YOU SEEM TO HAVE AVOIDED SPEAKING OF YOUR
PARENTS ALTOGETHER...

. The computer psychiatrist lacks sophistication, training

sensitivity, and human intuition; it is mechanical (of course!), inflexible, and relatively unresponsive to emotional nuances and non-verbal cues. And yet it has produced a conversation more intelligent than many. It's response on "a new topic" is stunning. But that response is very likely only a fluke. The program is undoubtedly designed to pay attention to words such as "mother," "father," "parent," and so on; after the computer's clock has ticked away so many minutes, if these words have not been introduced, the program is designed to come up with "You seem to have avoided..." Emerging just at the right moment it did, the remark gives an eerie impression of insight. [4]

These ideas on machine intelligence may seem a little strange at first, but you must admit that, given Sagan's basic assumption, they are very logical. That assumption was, if you remember - "My fundamental premise about the brain is that its workings - what we sometimes call 'mind' - are a consequence of its anatomy and physiology, and nothing more."

The situation is very much like the commentary that has echoed over the centuries after a famous animal story told both by Plutarch and by Pliny: A dog, following the scent of its master, was observed to come to a triple fork in the road. It ran down the leftmost prong, sniffing; then stopped and returned to follow the middle prong for a short distance, again sniffing and then turning back. Finally with no sniffing at all, it raced joyously down the right-hand prong of the forked road.

Montaigne, commenting on this story, argued that it showed clear canine syllogistic reasoning: My master has gone down one of these roads. It is not the left-hand road; it is not the middle road; therefore it must be the right-hand road. There is no need for me to corroborate this conclusion by smell - the conclusion follows by straightforward logic.

The possibility that reasoning at all like this might exist in the animals, although perhaps less clearly articulated, was troubling to many, and long before Montaigne; St. Thomas

Aquinas attempted unsuccessfully to deal with the story. He cited it as a cautionary example of how the appearance of intelligence can exist where no intelligence is in fact present. Aquinas did not, however, offer a satisfactory alternative explanation of the dog's behavior...

We are at a similar point in the consideration of machine intelligence. Machines are just passing over an important threshold: the threshold at which, to some extent at least, they give an unbiased human being, the impression of intelligence. Because of a kind of human chauvinism or anthropocentrism, many humans are reluctant to admit this possibility. But I think it is inevitable. To me it is not in the least demeaning that consciousness and intelligence are the result of "mere" matter sufficiently complexly arranged; on the contrary, it is an exalting tribute to the subtlety of matter and the laws of Nature. [5]

Fr. Robert A. Staatz

Older biblical commentators thought that the phrase "let us make man in our own image, after our likeness," marked the special creation by God of the human soul. Modern biblical scholarship, however, has considerably modified this interpretation. Let me begin again with the Vincentian Bruce Vawter, and his *A Path Through Genesis*:

But in what does this image and likeness consist? This is a ...difficult question. Perhaps the author himself was not quite sure, or at least would have been unable to put it in words...In Christian language we say that man has a spiritual soul with the powers of intellect and free will, and in these he is like God. These conclusions, however, have come to us after much religious thinking and have been aided by Greek philosophy, of which the Hebrew author was ignorant. It is very likely that he saw man's similarity to God at least partially fulfilled in his having been created to rule over the earth; just as God is sovereign over all, man was intended to share in this dominion by God's will. But there is no reason to think that he completely comprehended the mystery of man any more than we do. At any rate, he knew that man was somehow like God, that he had in him a spark of the divine, and knowing this he has a considerable advantage over not a few modern people to whom man is just a few pounds of chemicals, another biped whose mating habits can be judged by the same standards as, say, those of wasps. [6]

We see then that the notion of "soul" was derived more from Greek philosophy than from Scripture. Let me now discuss this notion from the point of view of philosophy and science. Here again is Fr. Owen Garrigan in his *Man's Intervention in Nature*:

> ...All speculations about the origin of man and related problems go back to an age from which written tradition is unknown and oral tradition quite improbable in any reliable sense. We do not know for certain if a philosophically "human" being arose a million years ago in a transition of hominids [the *Australopithecines*] to *Homo erectus* (who seems to have been a tool user with elements of true language). Or perhaps the critical transition was from *Homo erectus* to *Homo sapiens* [Neanderthal Man] (definitely modern man) within the last hundred thousand years. In either case, early man has left evidence of only a low cultural level and relatively few intellectual achievements.
>
> In the context of an evolving universe, the origin of the soul raises several fundamental questions. Man is distinctly human by reason of his soul. The soul is that by which man lives. The soul is the immaterial principle of life, the breath of God, spirit. It is not visible. Hence, its origin is not observable. What answers, then, can we give to the question: "Did the human soul evolve?" and "Will it evolve in the future?" The evolutionary panorama comes into focus only by telescoping time so that past and future are brought closer to the present. Since the roots of mankind are buried in an evolving universe, these two questions are important not only to man's ancestors and progeny, removed by centuries and millenia from the present. They are of profound and urgent concern to the man

of today. If we do not know what we were and what me may become, we do not fully know what we are. [7]

Garrigan goes on to discuss the possibility of the evolution of the soul. I should mention that "matter" and "form" are terms used in Aristotelian philosophy. Man is composed of matter - a body, and form - a soul.

> ...The human soul is the root cause of one's being an individual human person. An individual becomes independent of his parents and becomes a person "made in the image and likeness of God." To be a person is an all-or-nothing phenomenon. Just as a woman cannot be partially pregnant, so one cannot be only partially a person. Of course, personality may mature only gradually over a period of time. Infant's personalities do not emerge fully formed all at once. It is possible even for one who is an adult chronologically to close himself off from others and thereby delay or prevent the full realization of his personal power. To be a person is to be constantly challenged to the fulfilling of an ongoing task, a constant emergence into fullness of being. But there is no middle ground. And in this sense the soul could not evolve. (This line of reasoning would hold for the process of the production of the race as well as of each individual, for phylogeny [evolution of the race] as well as for ontogeny [development of the embryo].
> But there is a sense in which a principle of life (a philosophical "form" or soul) might evolve. What is observed in the world about us is that living beings evolve. The existence of the two principles of life, matter and form, is only inferred from observing the beings. The inference from the evolution of beings to the evolution of matter is accepted without much question. There must be some level on which correlative inference to the evolution of forms is equally acceptable. [8]

Fr. Garrigan is a great admirer of Teilhard de Chardin, who, if you remember his "law of complexity-consciousness," has no inhibitions about the past and future evolution of the soul.

Taking his cue from the intellect and will of man, Pierre Teilhard de Chardin found some attenuated spontaneity in a subatomic event, some diminished consciousness in a molecule, the glimmer of personality in the playfulness of a cat. The disintegration rate of a radioactive substance may be statistically constant, but each individual event is unpredictable and spontaneous. A protein molecule can "recognize" its substrate and cofactors. The more complex the matter aggregate, the greater the degree of consciousness. In this line of thought the possibility is not excluded that *in some way* each of these subhuman diminished participations in consciousness and freedom contributed as providential antecedents to the production of human consciousness and freedom.

Insofar as these speculations about the origin of the human soul avoid the pitfall of an objectionable panpsychism [a Greek word meaning "everything alive"], they are attractive in their simplicity. They satisfy the concept of the unity of man's nature and they make man less anomalous in the evolutionary plan of God. For mankind is of a piece with the universe. The human soul is not independent of, or joined only accidently to, the body. The analysis from which the soul's existence is inferred is irreversible. That is, we can take a real person and argue to the philosophical principles of his being. But this is not to say that we can reverse the process and construct a real being from these same principles. The distinction between body and soul, abstractly arrived at, does not impair the reality that each man is one, a complete and individual human person. The soul is not a prisoner of the body. Nor does God take ready-made souls from a stockpile and insert them into appropriate chunks of matter. Souls are not distributed along some computerized, automated, or mechanical assembly line. [9]

Garrigan concludes his discussion of the soul with an excellent summary of the theolgy of Teilhard de Chardin:

Christian tradition does not rest satisfied with what the soul is not. It affirms without hesitation that God is responsible for the totality of man's being, body and soul. To be human is to be whole. Without both material and spiritual dimensions man in not completely himself. Integral human beings with their material dimensions intact, have a spiritual relationship to God and an eternal destiny...

Man is, moreover, at the pinacle of creation, a microcosm who sums up in himself the whole created universe, whose mission is to dominate the universe and offer his dominion back to the Creator. "Hominization" is part of the grand scheme whereby all creation is given in man a mind and a heart to praise its Creator...

The risen Christ working now through those who share his life, remakes and restores all things in himself. And the proper object of the Incarnate Redeemer's love is the whole man, the human creature who is both animal and rational. The positive reality of man's creation and re-creation in Christ, from which man emerges as a single integrated whole, transcends any attempt to reduce the body-soul relationship to a tidy dichotomy between matter and spirit. [10]

In conclusion let me say that the scientific fact of the evolution of man's body seems to demand some form of evolution for his soul. This makes it necessary for the Church to reformulate its notion of just what a soul is, and is not.

Mrs. Maria Stepan

Dr. Schonfield began his presentation tonight with a statement from Carl Sagan, "my fundamental premise about the brain is that its workings - what we sometimes call 'mind' are a consequence of its anatomy and physiology and nothing more." This is not the opinion of one of the world's leading brain researchers, Sir John Eccles, who is himself an evolutionist. Eccles recently attended a congress held in Dallas, Texas on the theme *The Reality of God and the Dignity of Man*. Let me quote from a report on this congress by Joseph W. Koterski which appeared in *The Wanderer*:

Most prominent among the scientists attending the conference was Sir John Eccles, a Nobel laureate in brain physiology and the author of many books on the subject. It was Eccles' life-long research on the function of the brain which won him world-wide recognition in the 1960's.

Using the term "mind" and "soul" interchangeably, Eccles argued that "The mind has an authentic existence free of the brain." While integrally linked to the brain, the mind is not part of the brain. For Eccles, the phenomenon of self-consciousness on the part of such a mind is the "miracle" which dethrones monistic materialism, the view that material forces provide a sufficient explanation for all reality. "Self-consciousness," he said, "is completely unexplainable by those who do not believe in God." [11]

Despite the title of his chapter on animal intelligence, *The Abstractions of Beasts*, the examples Carl Sagan gives such as "Roger tickle Lucy," are not examples of abstractions. All abstractions involve universal ideas, such as "man." The examples given by Sagan all involve singular ideas such as "Roger." Let me read from a standard text in philosophical psychology concerning the notion of abstraction. Here is Msgr. Paul Glenn in his *Psychology: A Class Manual in the Philosophy of Organic and Rational Life*:

> Man's mind or intellect holds such ideas as *being, unity, goodness, truth, ideals, virtue, honor, ambition, purpose, beauty, steadfastness, patriotism*, etc. Can any organ lay hold of such things? Can you smell ideas? Can you imagine what ambition would look like, and draw a picture of it? These are individual limitations or settings (*abstract* comes from the Latin *ab* "from" and *traho*, "I draw"), and hence they are beyond the grasp of any bodily part. They are things which require a supra-organic power to apprehend them, a *spiritual* power. But this power is resident in a spiritual substance; this substance is the soul. [12]

It is of course from arguments such as these that we prove from reason the existence of the soul. Let me read Msgr. Glenn developing one of these philosophical arguments for the existence of the soul:

By what sentient faculty can you do a sum in mathematics? By what organ can you discover that two and two make four? You can see two bricks; you can hear two sounds; you can smell two odors; you can touch and feel two bodily objects; you can taste two flavors; you can imagine two dragons. But you cannot by any sense or sense-organ lay hold of *two* - that is of *two* by itself; not two this or that, but simply *two*. But the mind of man can understand what two means. A man, confronted with the exacting problem of adding two and two, does not pause and say, "Two *what*?" When little boys and girls first go to school the teacher trains them to make pure mathematical concepts (or *ideas*) by connecting the quantities with definite and sensible materials. The teacher says, "If John had two apples and Mary gave him two more apples, how many apples had John?" But in a very short time the minds of the smallest children are ready to dispense with the apples and with other material substances, and are able to deal with *quantity in the abstract*. And so the children add two and two, and three and five, and nine and seven, not being puzzled by the task of handling quantities *without any sensible thing that is quantified*. What organ could begin to do such a thing? The brain? You might as well say the eye or the ear. For no organ deals with objects in the abstract; no organ can deal with objects in the universal. The brain is the organ of the interior senses,...of imagination, for example, and sense-memory. Now, imagination and sense-memory can deal with their object when it is no longer outwardly and physically present; but to do this they must project the object within themselves in an image that is *individual, concrete, circumstanced*. This is an example of the highest type of organic operation, and it is still a matter of concreteness and circumstance. But thinking and reasoning are not limited by concreteness, individuality, and circumstance. Hence thinking and reasoning are operations of a character superior to any organic operation. They are supra-organic; they are of spiritual character. Hence they come from a spiritual first principle. This is the soul. [13]

Also the amusing story about the dog coming to the three forks in the road is not, as Sagan claimed, an example of "canine syllogistic reasoning." In a syllogism the major premise is always universal: "All men are mortal." "My master has gone down one of these roads," is not a universal major premise. Sagan claims that St. Thomas Aquinas does not offer a satisfactory explanation of this story, so let's see exactly what St. Thomas had to say:

Whether Choice Is to Be Found in Irrational Animals...

Obj. 3 Further, according to... [Aristotle] "It is from prudence that a man makes a good choice of means." But prudence can be found in irrational animals: hence it is said..."those animals which like bees, cannot hear sounds, are prudent by instinct." We see this plainly, in the wonderful cases of sagacity manifested in the works of various animals, such as bees, spiders, and dogs. For a hound in following a stag, on coming to a crossroad tries by scent whether the stag has passed the first or the second road: and if he find that the stag has not passed there, being thus assured, takes to the third road without trying the scent; as though he were reasoning by way of exclusion, arguing that the stag must have passed by this way, since he did not pass by the others, and there is no other road. Therefore it seems that irrational animals are able to choose...

Reply Obj. 3 As stated in...[Aristotle], "movement is in the act of the movable, caused by a mover." Wherefore the power of the mover appears in the movement of that which it moves. Accordingly, in all things moved by reason, the order of reason which moves them is evident, although the things themselves are without reason: for an arrow through the motion of the archer goes straight towards the target, as though it were endowed with reason to direct its course. The same may be seen in the movements of clocks and all engines put together by the art of men. Now, as artificial things are in comparison to human art, so are all natural things in comparison to Divine art. And accordingly, order is to be seen in things moved by nature, just as in things moved by reason...and thus it is that, in the works of irrational animals, we notice certain marks of sagacity, insofar as they have a natural inclination to set about their actions in a most orderly manner through being ordained by the Supreme art. For which reason, too, certain animals are called prudent or sagacious; but not because they reason or exercise any choice about things. This is clear from the fact that all that share in one nature invariably act in the same way. [14]

St. Thomas would say that the appearance of prudence and sagacity in Washoe and the dog are not prudence and sagacity themselves. They are rather the result of the natural instincts given by God to these irrational animals, and not an indication of incipient rationality. The only reason that Carl Sagan finds this answer inadequate is because he is unable to accept the existence of God.

Let me proceed to St. Thomas on the soul of man. We saw that St. Thomas teaches that Adam's *body* was produced immediately by God, so *a fortiori* he would teach that the rational soul is produced immediately by God:

Whether the Rational Soul Is Produced by God Immediately?

...Some have held that angels acting by the power of God produce rational souls. But this is quite impossible, and is against faith. For it has been proved that the rational soul cannot be produced except by creation. Now, God alone can create or the first agent alone can act without presupposing the existence of anything; while the second cause always presupposes something derived from the first cause...: and every agent that presupposes something to its act, acts by making a change therein. Therefore, everything else acts by producing a change, whereas God alone acts by creation. Since therefore, the rational soul cannot be produced by a change in matter, it cannot be produced save immediately by God. [15]

This, of course, refutes Fr. Staatz's claim that the soul has somehow evolved in the past, and will continue to evolve in the future. St. Thomas is saying that no creature, which is what evolution is, has anything to do with the origin of the soul.

Let me conclude by turning from the Tradition to the Magisterium of the Church. The existence of the soul is a defined dogma of the faith and this was reiterated as recently as 1968 by Pope Paul VI in his *Creed of the People of God*. Let me first read the section of the creed on the soul, and then a brief commentary on this passage by Msgr. Eugene Kevane from his *Creed and Catechetics*. In the official footnotes attached to the Creed, Pope Paul refers to the 1950 encyclical *Humani Generis* of Pope Pius XII, which we have seen before. If you remember, Fr. Vawter claimed that the notion of the soul was more Greek than biblical; this claim Msgr. Kevane rejects:

"We believe in only one God, Father, Son and Holy Spirit, Creator of things visible such as this world in which our brief life passes, of things invisible such as the pure spirits which are also called angels, and Creator in each man of his spiritual and immortal soul." [And here is Msgr. Kevane:]

This affirmation of the Creed implies a definite concept of man, as composed of body and soul, that needs special emphasis today when there is no lack of Catholic theologians who put it in doubt as something "Greek" instead of "biblical"...Such a doubt has grave consequences for our doctrine on eschatology or the last things, for without this definite concept of man's composition of body and soul...the doctrine on the state of souls between death and resurrection becomes impossible. Pope Benedict XII in his Constitution *Benedictus Deus* teaches explicitly that souls after death come either into heaven or into the pains of hell before the resurrection of the body and the General Judgment. Furthermore, the Second Vatican Council teaches the spirituality and immortality of the soul when it treats of the dignity of the human person...

The reference given by Pope Paul to the encyclical *Humani Generis* of Pope Pius xii reads as follows: "The Catholic faith commands us to hold that our souls are created immediately by God."...A spiritual and immortal soul cannot be the mere product of the generative action of the human parents. Hence Paul vi, noting certain doctrinal tendencies of our times insists that God creates the human soul in each human being. [16]

Rev. De Verne Swezey

I would like to begin my presentation tonight by commenting on Carl Sagan's claim that sign language using chimpanzees are currently in the process of crossing the threshold of self-consciousness and intelligence. If you remember Sagan said: "A small doll placed unexpectedly in Washoe's cup elicited the response 'Baby in my drink.'" This sentence is the favorite example of the humanists to illustrate the incipient rationality of these animals. Let us see just what happened in this particular instance.

Dr. Herbert Terrace of Columbia University has conducted the most extensive study to date of chimpanzees using sign language. This is from his *Nim* (another sign language using chimp) which appeared in 1979:

> The potential for confusion in inadequate reporting is made plain by another exchange that appears in both films. Washoe is with her teacher Susan Nichols, who has a cup and a doll. Ms. Nichols points to a cup and signs *that*. Washoe signs *baby*. Ms. Nichols brings the cup and doll closer to Washoe, allowing her to touch them, then slowly pulls them away, signing *that* and pointing to the cup. Washoe signs *in* and looks away, Ms Nichols brings the cup and doll closer to Washoe again who looks at the two objects once more and signs *baby*. Then, as Ms. Nichols brings the cup still closer, Washoe signs *in*. *That*, signs Ms. Nichols and points to the cup. *My drink*, signs Washoe. Now the question is, is this utterance by Washoe - *baby in baby in my drink* - either

spontaneous or a significant creative use of words? It is actually a "run-on" sequence with very little relationship among its parts. Only the last two signs were uttered without prompting on the part of the teacher. The sequence of the prompts, moreover (pointing to the doll and then pointing to the cup), follows the order called for to construct an English prepositional phrase. In short, careful analysis makes the chimpanzee's linguistic achievement less remarkable than it might at first seem. [17]

Even within the ranks of the humanist establishment itself (I am not speaking of the counter-culture) there are many, including Jacob Bronowski, who reject the interpretation placed on the accomplishments of these chimpanzees by Carl Sagan and others. Some scientists call them "tricks" similar to those you could teach a dog, or mere mimetic behavior as in a parrot's "Polly wanna cracker." Some also compare these accomplishments to "Clever Hans," the famous Viennese "talking horse." Hans' trainer would ask, "how much is four plus four?" and Hans would stamp eight times on the floor. But on closer observation it was discovered that Hans was merely watching his trainer, who would unknowingly indicate by body language when Hans had reached the correct sum. Dr. Terrace, by running the films of sign language using chimps and their trainers in slow-motion, finds that something similar is happening here. The trainers are unwittingly cueing the chimps to give the proper sign.

There is no reason to believe that these films, limited as they are, show Washoe at much less than her best. One could wish for more comprehensive records (as far as I know, these are the only films of apes signing publicly available), but nothing in them suggests anything other than a consistent tendency for the teacher to initiate the signing and for the ape to interrupt and mirror the teacher. *Teaching Sign Language*, the longer of the two films, contains 155 of Washoe's utterances. One hundred and twenty were single-sign utterances, and occurred mainly in vocabulary testing sessions. Every one of Washoe's multisign sequences (24 two-sign, 6 three-sign, and 5 four-sign sequences) was preceded by a similar utterance from her teacher. The *Nova* film also included short segments about Nim's brother Ally and the gorilla Koko. It shows that all of Koko's and most of Ally's utterances (in each case, simple signs) were prompted. [18]

Dr. Terrace is forced to conclude, reluctantly, that what appeared at first glance to be spontaneity and originality on the part of the signs used by the chimps, had actually been prompted beforehand by the teachers:

> I must conclude - though reluctantly - that until it is possible to defeat *all* plausible explanations short of the intellectual capacity to arrange words according to a grammatical rule, it would be premature to conclude that a chimpanzee's combinations show the same structure evident in the sentences of a child. The fact that Nim's utterances were less spontaneous and less original than those of a child and that his utterances did not become longer, both as he learned new signs and as he acquired more experience in using sign language, suggests that much of the structure and meaning of his combinations was determined, or at least suggested, by the utterances of his teachers. [19]

In other words Dr. Terrace is practically admitting that this is another case of what some humanists call "The Clever Hans Syndrome." Let me go on now from Carl Sagan's "intelligent" animals to his "intelligent" machines. I turn again to the counter-culture critic Theodore Roszak and his *Where the Wasteland Ends.* He is commenting on the humanist claim that what we call "soul" is simply the result of the physiology of the brain.

> ..."I myself, like many scientists," announces Nobel laureate Francis Crick, "believe that the soul is imaginary and that what we call our minds is simply a way of talking about the functions of our brains." And he goes on: "Once one has become adjusted to the idea that we are here because we have evolved from simple chemical compounds by a process of

natural selection, it is remarkable how many of the problems of the modern world take on a completely new light." Indeed they do. It is the funereal gleam by which we travel the wasteland, the light of dying stars. [20]

Theodore Roszak also comments on Carl Sagan's final exhortation during our preceding meeting, that we must pursue "knowledge for its own sake" if we are to survive:

...A popular mythology of "mad doctors" haunts the history of nineteenth-and-twentieth-century science: Dr. Franken-stein, Dr. Moreau, Dr. Cyclops, Dr. Cagliari, Dr. Strange-love...cold-blooded manipulators and makers of monsters. Easy enough to write off this literary tradition as fictitious exaggeration. But to do so would be a sad mistake; the myth of the mad doctor refuses to be dispelled. It survives because it embodies a profound, popular realization of the moral ambiguity of science; a legitimate fear that the scientist does not exist primarily to serve the human good, but to pursue a fleshless ideal called "knowledge for its own sake," in the presence of which even one's fellow humans are reduced to mere experimental material. And, of course, these mad doctors are not simply literary inventions. They have emerged from the science fiction and bad dreams of our society to move among us. Have we not known in our times Nazi physicians who could treat imprisoned men and women as laboratory specimens in their ghoulish search for knowledge..."for its own sake?"
...But we need not look abroad to Nazi or Communist societies to find science beset by well-rationalized reduction-ism. There are more than enough research zealots in the contemporary West pursuing "knowledge for its own sake" with a maniacal energy that sets personal curiosity and careerist advantage above every humanistic consideration. Their work undeniably produces what their profession values as "results"; but at what a cost in simple humanity. The question grows more troubling with each passing year: how much of what yesterday's science fiction regarded as unspeak-

ably dreadful has become today's award-winning research? [21]

Roszak appends a list of just six of the many current top priority research projects, among which is the pursuit of what Carl Sagan calls "machine intelligence":

Artificial Intelligence and Mechanistic Counterfeiting:

The more objectified the study of behavior grows, the more remote it becomes (at least for many scientists) as a form of experience known from within. Until it finally becomes quite sensible to speak of machines that "see" or "remember," "think" or "create" - as well as people, or even better. Thus Professor I.J. Good predicts the UIM, the ultra intelligent machine. "When we have the very intelligent machine we can educate it in the theory of machine intelligence. It will then design a much better machine, even if it needs to be creative to do so. This process can be repeated until we have an ultra-intelligent machine and we shall have an intelligence explosion that will nullify Lukasiewicz's ignorance explosion. [By this he means that knowledge is expanding so fast that the fraction of it that anyone can know is tending rapidly to zero.] The UIM will enable us to solve any practically soluble problem and we shall perhaps achieve world peace, the elixir of life, the piecemeal conversion of people into UIPs (ultra-intelligent people), or the conversion of the world's population into a *single* UIP."

...Within recent years, I have come across glowing reports of computer machines that have "consciences," that "teach" and "learn," that "compose music," and that "feel" and "hurt," even machines that do or will soon do architecture. Nicholas Negroponte and Leon Grosier head the Architecture Project at MIT, which hopes to produce machines that will desgin better buildings than people can...Certainly their computers could not produce a more impersonal, machine-tooled architecture than our cities are now being cursed with.

The prospectus for artificial intelligence machines is limitlessly optimistic. It includes their use as a superintelligent governing apparatus to run national economy and to plan military strategy...Richard Landers looks forward to the day when our closest friends will be "conversation machines"...so much better than real people. "When the day comes that conversation machines are developed, I strongly believe that many will prefer them to humans as telephone partners - particularly the machines that are 'tunable' to one's personality." [22]

Dean Smalley

Since the first meeting in our long dialogue dealt with the existence of God, we thought it appropriate that this final meeting be on the existence of the soul.

Dr. Schonfield presented the humanist claim that what we call "soul" or "mind" is simply the result of the physiology of the brain. He stated that *Homo habilis* was probably the first to cross the threshold of self-consciousness and intelligence and that both chimpanzees using sign language and electronic computers are currently in the process of crossing that threshold.

Fr. Staatz asserted that the notion of "soul" was derived more from Greek philosophy than from Scripture. He claimed that the scientific fact of the evolution of man, seems to demand some kind of evolution of the soul, and therefore requires a new appraisal of just what the soul is and is not. He claimed that the old scholastic distinction between "matter" and "spirit," degraded the unity of man and his oneness with the universe.

Mrs. Stepan began her presentation with Sir John Eccles, the Nobel laureate, a leading brain researcher, himself an evolutionist, who maintains, contrary to Carl Sagan, that the study of the brain points clearly to the existence of the soul. Mrs. Stepan also gave us a brief glimpse of one of the classical arguments from reason for the existence of the rational soul. She claimed that both the Tradition and the Magisterium of the Church rejects Fr. Staatz's notion of the evolution of the soul, and insists on its immediate creation by God out of nothing.

Rev. Swezey drew attention to the split within the ranks of the humanist establishment concerning the claims made for sign language using chimpanzees. He suggested that this phenomenon was probably another case of the "Clever Hans Syndrome." He also offered Theodore Roszak's highly critical comments on the pursuit of "knowledge for its own sake," and on "machine intelligence."

So we come to the end of *The Six Days of Creation*, and I will conclude by attempting a brief summary of our entire dialogue. But I think I should remind you once again of my own liberal Protestant position which I was surprised to discover is almost identical to that of Fr. Staatz, but I will try to make it as objective as I can. You will remember that our dialogue was intended to explore the "ultimate questions" concerning the existence of God, the origin of religion, the origin of the universe, the origin of life, the origin of man, the existence of the soul, to name just a few - quite a large order.

Dr. Schonfield gave the secular humanist answers to these questions. We come, he said, from a primordial explosion of matter and energy, the Big Bang, and are going ultimately to a Big Crunch, and this cycle will continue for all eternity. We are matter, nothing more, which has evolved by sheer chance into such a complexity as to become self-conscious and intelligent. He implied throughout, that in science alone, do we find the answers to all the "ultimate questions."

Fr. Staatz rejected both the concordist and fundamentalist interpretations of the first chapters of Genesis, saying that they were based on a false notion of the literary form of these chapters, which are not history but myth. With the single exception of the Oscillating Universe, he found no serious conflict between the "new theology" and any of the current scientific theories regrarding the origin and evolution of both the universe and man. Fr. Staatz's position, then, was that the answers to all the "ultimate questions" were to be found in both science and religion, but that these answers were never final or complete, but always part of an ongoing process.

Mrs. Stepan maintained that many of the current scientific theories regarding the origin of the universe, of life, etc., could easily be harmonized with the Scriptural account of those origins, and therefore a legitimate scientific theory should lead an unbelieving scientist of good will to God. However, some scientific theories she rejected out of hand, such as polygenism, many Adams and Eves, because she claimed they were incompatible with defined dogmas of the Church, such as original sin. The answers to the "ultimate questions," she stated, have been revealed by God in Scripture and Tradition, as interpreted by the Magisterium of the Church.

Rev. Swezey rejected most of the current scientific theories on the origin and evolution of the universe and man, and claimed that in the Bible alone, God had revealed the answers to all the "ultimate questions."

This concludes our dialogue on the six days of creation, and what better way to end, than by reading the Scriptural account of the seventh day, the day of rest:

> Thus the heavens and earth were finished, and all the host of them. And on the seventh day God finished his work which he had done. So God blessed the seventh day and hallowed it, because on it God rested from all the work which he had done in creation (Gen 2:1-3).

REFERENCES

1   Carl Sagan, *The Dragons of Eden*,
    Random House, New York, 1977, p.7.
2   Sagan, *Op. cit.*, pp.108-111.
3   *Idem*, pp.120,121.
4   *Idem*, pp.206-208.
5   *Idem*, pp.209,210.
6   Bruce Vawter, c.m., *A Path Through Genesis*,
    Sheed and Ward, New York, 1955, pp.44,45.
7   Owen Garrigan, *Man's Intervention in Nature*,
    Hawthorne Books, New York, 1967, p.94.

8 Garrigan, *Op. cit.*, pp.96,97.

9 *Idem*, p.97.

10 *Idem*, pp.97,98.

11 Joseph W. Koterski, *Distinguished Scholars Examine Modern Thought and the Turn to Theism*, *The Wanderer*, April 7, 1983, St. Paul, Minn., p.9.

12 Msgr. Paul Glenn, *Psychology: A Class Manual in the Philosophy of Organic and Rational Life*, B. Herder, St. Louis, 1948, pp.189,190.

13 Glenn, *Op. cit.*, pp.187-189.

14 St. Thomas Aquinas, *Summa Theologica*, (*I-II, Q13, a2*),
Benziger Brothers, Boston, 1947, pp.643,644.

16 Msgr. Eugene Kevane, *Creed and Catechetics*,
Christian Classics, Westminster, Md., 1978, pp.13,103,104.

17 Herbert Terrace, *Nim*,
Alfred A. Knopf, New York, 1979, p.220.

18 Terrace, *Op. cit.*, pp.220,221.

19 *Idem*, p.221.

20 Theodore Roszak, *Where the Wasteland Ends*,
Doubleday and Co., Garden City, N.Y., 1972, p.173.

21 Roszak, *Op. cit.*, pp.229-231.

22 *Idem*, pp.247,248.

WORKS CITED

Abell, George, *Exploration of the Universe*,
  Holt, Rinehart and Winston, New York, 1964.
Alexander, George, *How Life on Eath Began, Reader's Digest*,
  November, 1982, Pleasantville, New York.
Aquinas, St. Thomas, *Summa Contra Gentiles*,
Rickaby, Joseph, s.j., *Of God and His Creatures*,
  B. Herder, St. Louis, 1905.
Aquinas, St. Thomas, *Summa Theologica*,
  Benziger Brothers, New York, 1947.
Asimov, Isaac, *The Universe*,
  Walker and Co., Avon Books, New York, 1966.
Belloc, Hilaire, *A Companion to Mr. Wells's "Outline of History,"*
  Sheed and Ward, London, 1926.
Bennett, Owen, o.f.m., conv., *Cosmos: A Trap or a Home?*
  Homiletic and Pastoral Review,
  New York, December, 1983.
Broderick, James, s.j., *Robert Bellarmine*,
  Newman Press, Westminster, Md., 1961.
Bronowski, Jacob, *The Ascent of Man*,
  Little, Brown and Co., Boston, 1973.
Brown, Raymond, s.s., *Biblical Reflections on Crises Facing the
  Church*, Paulist Press, New York, 1975.
Browne, Malcolm, W., *Scientists Expect New Clues to the Origin
  of the Universe, World Science, 1979 Year Book,
  Illustrated World Encyclopedia*, New York, 1979.
Calder, Nigel, *Violent Universe*,
  Viking Press, New York, 1969.
Calder, Nigel, *Einstein's Universe*
  Viking Press, New York, 1979.

Campos, de Redig, D., *Cappella Sistina,*
Instituto Geographico Agostini, S.p.A., Novara, 1959.
Catran, Jack, *Gee-Whiz Scientists Searching for Life,*
Los Angeles Times, March 13, 1983.
Clement, Hal, *Jupiter: Eden with a Red Spot,*
Included in: Ben Bova, *Closeup: New Worlds,*
St. Martin's Press, New York, 1971.
Faricy, Robert, s.j., *Teilhard de Chardin's Theology of the*
Christian in the World, Sheed and Ward, New York, 1967.
Ferris, Timothy, *The Red Limit,*
Wilson, Morrow and Co., New York, 1977.
Flood, Fr. P.J., *Evolution and Sacred Scripture,*
Claves Regni, June, 1932,
Quoted in: Messenger, Fr. E.E., *Theology and Evolution,*
Sands and Co., London, 1949.
Garrigan, Fr. Owen, *Man's Intervention in Nature,*
Hawthorne Books, New York, 1967.
Glenn, Msgr. Paul, *A Class Manual in the Philosophy of*
Organic and Rational Life, B. Herder, New York, 1947.
Hammes, John, *Human Destiny,*
Our Sunday Visitor Inc., Huntington, Ind., 1978.
Hebblethwaite, Peter, s.j., *The Council Fathers and Atheism,*
Paulist Press, Deus Books, New York, 1967.
Hunt, Ignatius, o.s.b., *Understanding the Bible,*
Sheed and Ward, New York, 1962.
Hutton, Richard, *Bio-Revolution:* DNA *and the Ethics of*
Man-Made Life, New American Library, New York, 1978.
Jaki, Stanley, o.s.b., *The Road of Science and the Ways to God,*
University of Chicago Press, Chicago, 1978.
Jaki, Stanley, o.s.b., *Cosmos and Creator,*
Scottish Academic Press, Edinburgh, 1980,
In USA: Regnery Editions, New York, 1980.
The Jesuit Fathers of St. Mary's College, *The Church Teaches,*
B. Herder Book Co., St. Louis, 1955.
John Paul II, Pope, *Address to the Italian Society of Internal*
Medicine, The Pilot, Boston, Nov 14, 1980.
John Paul II, Pope, General Audience, Sept 12, 1979,
L'Osservatore Romano, Vatican City, Sept 17, 1979.

John Paul II, Pope, General Audience, Sept 19, 1979,
L'Osservatore Romano, Vatican City, Sept 24, 1979.

John Paul II, Pope, *Address to the Pontifical Academy of Science*, L'Osservatore Romano, Vatican City, Nov 26, 1979.

Johnson, J.W.G., *Evolution: The Hoax That's Destroying Christendom*, (Tape), Keep the Faith Inc., Montvale, N.J., 1983.

Kevane, Msgr. Eugene, *Creed and Catechetics*,
Christian Classics, Westminster, Md., 1978.

Koestler, Arthur, *The Sleepwalkers*,
MacMillan Co., New York, 1959.

Koestler, Arthur, *The Ghost in the Machine*,
MacMillan Co., New York, 1968.

Korin, Henry, C.S.SP., *An Introduction to the Philosophy of Animate Nature*, Herder Book Co., St. Louis, 1955.

Lustig, Lawrence, *Science and Superstition: An Age of Unreason, 1976 Brittanica Book of the Year*,
Encyclopedia Brittanica, London, 1976.

Manteau-Bonamy, F.H.M., O.P., *Immaculate Conception and the Holy Spirit*, Prow Books, Franciscan Marytown Press,
Libertyville, Ill., 1977.

May, William, E., *Human Existence, Medicine and Ethics*,
Franciscan Herald Press, Chicago, 1977.

McGrath, Msgr. William, *The Lady of the Rosary*,
Included in: Delaney, John, J., *A Woman Clothed with the Sun*,
Doubleday and Co., Image Books, Garden City, N.Y., 1961.

McHugh, L.C., S.J., *Are There Others Out Yonder?*
Included in: *Rational Life in Outer Space*,
America Press, New York, 1966.

McKee, Fr. John, *The Enemy Within the Gate*,
Lumen Christi Press, Houston, Tex., 1974.

Millar, Ronald, *The Piltdown Men*,
Ballantine Books, New York, 1972.

Monod, Jacques, *Chance and Necessity*,
Translated from the French by Austryn Wainhouse,
Vintage Books, Random House, New York, 1972.

Morris, Henry, *Scientific Creationism*,
Creation-Life Publishers, San Diego, Cal., 1974.

O'Connell, Fr. Patrick, *Science of Today and the Problems*

Of Genesis, Christian Book Club of America,
Hawthorne, Cal., 1968.

O'Connell, Fr. Patrick, *Original Sin in the Light of Present-Day Science*, Lumen Christi Press, Houston, Tex., 1973.

O'Toole, Fr. George, *The Case Against Evolution*,
MacMillan Co., New York, 1925.

Overbye, Dennis, *The Universe According to Guth*,
Discover, June 1983, Time Inc., New York.

Paul vi, Pope, *Ecclesiam Suam*,
Paulist Press, Glenn Rock, N.J., 1964.

Pius ii, Pope, *Cum Sicut Accepimus*,
Denziger, *Enchiridion Symbolorum*,
Herder, Rome, 1973.

Pius x, Pope, *Pascendi Gregis*,
National Catholic Welfare Conference, Washington, D.C., 1963.

Pius xi, Pope, *Casti Connubii*,
Included in: McLauglin, Terrence, c.s.n., *The Church and the Reconstruction of Society*, Doubleday and Co., Image Books, Garden City, N.Y., 1957.

Pius xii, Pope, *Address to the Pontifical Academy of Science*,
L'Osservatore Romano, Vatican City, Dec 1, 1941.

Pius xii, Pope, *Humani Generis*,
Weston College Press, Weston, Mass., 1951.

Pius xii, Pope, *The Proofs of the Existence of God in the Light of Modern Natural Science*, *L'Osservatore Romano*,
Vatican City, Nov 23, 1957.

Pope, Hugh, o.p., *The Catholic Student's "Aids" to the Bible*,
Benziger Brothers, N.Y., 1913.

Riley, Bishop Thomas, *Will DNA Research Evoke Moral Concern?*, *The Pilot*, Boston, Jan 7, 1977.

Rifkin, Jeremy, *Entropy: A New World View*,
Viking Press, New York, 1980.

Roman Martyrology, The,
Newman Bookshop, Westminster, Md., 1947.

Rome and the Study of Scripture,
Abbey Press, St. Meinrad, Ind., 1964.

Roszak, Theodore, Review of:
Monod, Jacques, *Chance and Necessity*,

Book World, New York, Oct 24, 1971.

Roszak, Theodore, *Where the Wasteland Ends*,
   Doubleday and Co., Anchor Books, Garden City, N.Y., 1972.

Ruffini, Cardinal Ernesto, *The Theory of Evolution Judged by Reason and Faith*, Translated from the Italian by Fr. Francis O'Hanlon, Joseph F. Wagner, New York, 1959.

Sagan, Carl, *Broca's Brain*,
   Random House, New York, 1979.

Sagan, Carl, *The Dragons of Eden*,
   Random House, New York, 1967.

Schumacher, Msgr. Leo, *The Truth about Teilhard*,
   Twin Circle Publishing Co., New York, 1968.

Schwartz, Michael, *The Nazi-Abortion Link*,
   The National Catholic Register, Los Angeles, Oct 8, 1978.

Simpson, George Gaylord, *This View of Life*,
   Harcourt, Brace and World, New York, 1964.

Speaight, Robert, *Teilhard de Chardin*,
   Collins, London, 1967.

Steinmueller, Msgr. John, *A Companion to Scripture Studies*,
   Joseph F. Wagner, New York, 1969.

Steinmueller, Msgr. John, *The Sword of the Spirit*,
   Stella Maris Books, Fort Worth, Tex., 1977.

Terrace, Herbert, *Nim*,
   Alfred A. Knopf, New York, 1979.

Tuzo, J., *Land Masses in Motion*,
The Book of Popular Science, Vol. 2,
   Grolier, Inc., New York, 1972.

Vawter, Bruce, C.M., *Genesis*, Included in:
Fuller, Johnson and Kearns, *A New Catholic Commentary on Holy Scripture*, Thomas Nelson and Sons, London, 1969.

Vawter, Bruce, C.M., *A Path Through Genesis*,
   Sheed and Ward, New York, 1956.

Wade, Nicholas, *The Ultimate Experiment: Man-Made Evolution*,
   Walker and Co., New York, 1977.

Editorial, *The Wanderer*,
   St. Paul, Minn., Dec 27, 1979.

Wilson, Clifford, *Ebla Tablets: Secrets of a Forgotten City*,
   Creation-Life Publishers, Master Books, San Diego, Cal., 1979.

INDEX

Abell, George, *Exploration of The Universe:*
"Tired light" hypothesis, pp.114,115.

Abiogenesis:
Term coined by T.H. Huxley, p.130.

Age of the Earth:
Based on decay rate of radioactive uranium, pp.100,101.
J.A. Eddy on age of sun, pp.109,110.
Criticism of uranium decay method by Dr. Morris, pp.116,117.
Young age from decay of earth's magnetic field, pp.117,118.

Age of the Universe:
Based on "red shift," pp.101-103.
Fr. Hunt on, p.107.
Pope Pius XII on, p.108.
Fr. Hugh Pope on Ussher chronology, pp.112,113.

Roman Martyrology on, p.113.
Mrs. Stepan on, pp.113,114.
Defense of Ussher chronology by Dr. Morris, pp.118-120.

Alexander, George, *How Life on Earth Began:*
Concordance between science and Bible, pp.142,143.

Anthropic Principle:
Points to existence of God, pp.47-49.

Aquinas, St. Thomas, *Summa Contra Gentiles:*
God and triangle, according to Sagan, p.8.
Things impossible to God, according to St. Thomas, p.19.
Oscillating Universe, p.86.
Creation cannot be demonstrated by science or philosophy, p.111.

362

Plants not living, according
to Dr. Morris, pp.152,153.
Curse on earth after Fall,
according to Dr. Morris,
p.152.
Mrs. Stepan's criticism of
fundamentalist position on
plants, pp.176,177.
St. Thomas against a
strictly literal interpretation
of Curse, pp.177,178.

Galileo Galilei:
Introduction to by Dr.
Bronowski, pp.162,163.
Bruno and St. Robert
Bellarmine, according to
Bronowski, p.162.
Secret Vatican Archives,
pp.163,164.
Absolute injunction of
1616, according to
Bronowski, p.165.
Threatened with torture,
p.166.
Results of condemnation
(Samson analogy),
according to Bronowski,
pp.166-168.
Vatican II and Galileo,
according to Fr. Nead,
pp.168,169.
Fr. Broderick on,
pp.171-173.
Pope John Paul II on,
p.175.
Mrs. Stepan's attempt to
"demythologize" the Case,

pp.178-185.
Geocentric system of
Ptolemy, pp.178,179.
Heliocentric system of
Copernicus, pp.179,180.
Tychonic system, (phases of
Venus), pp.180-182.
Kepler (ellipses), p.181.
Galileo and phases of
Venus, p.182.
Galileo's theory of the tides,
p.183.
Newton, p.184.
Alleged absolute injunction,
according to Mrs. Stepan,
p.185.
Huxley on Case, according
to Mrs. Stepan, pp.185,186.
Sherwood Taylor and
Galileo Case, p.186.
"Mythography" of Case,
according to Koestler,
p.187.
Koestler on Bruno, p.188.
Koestler on St. Robert
Bellarmine, pp.187,188.
Trial, according to Koestler,
pp.189,190.
Threat of torture, according
to Koestler, pp.189,190.
Condemnation of Galileo,
pp.190,191.
Decline of science in
Catholic countries (Samson
analogy of Bronowski),
pp.191,192.
Tragic split between religion
and science, pp.192-194.

PSALM 148

Laudate Dominum de caelis

Praise ye the Lord from the heavens:
  praise him in the high places.
Praise ye him, all his angels:
  praise ye him, all his hosts.
Praise ye him, O sun and moon:
  praise him, all ye stars and light.
Praise him, ye heavens of heavens:
  and let all the waters that are above the earth praise the name of
  the Lord.
For he spoke and they were made:
  he commanded, and they were created.
He hath established them for ever, and for ages of ages:
  he hath made a decree, and it shall not pass away.
Praise the Lord from the earth, ye dragons and all ye deeps:
  Fire, hail, snow, ice, stormy winds, which fulfill his word:
Mountains and all hills, fruitful trees and all cedars:
  Beasts and all cattle: serpents and feathered fowls:
Kings of the earth and all people:
  princes and all judges of the earth:
Young men and maidens:
  let the old with the younger
Praise the name of the Lord:
  for his name alone is exalted.
The praise of him is above the heaven and earth:
  and he hath exalted the horn of his people.
A hymn to all his saints:
  to the children of Israel, a people approaching him, Alleluia.

(Douay-Rheims)

Also by Thomas Mary Sennott

The Woman of Genesis

"*The Woman of Genesis* by Brother Thomas Mary is a delightful defense of the traditional wording of...Genesis 3:15:...'*She*
shall crush thy head, and thou shalt lie in wait for her heel.'...*The
Woman of Genesis* is addressed to ordinary readers to strengthen
their faith in Mary's role in our salvation. It succeeds admirably."

Fr. John A. Hardon, s.j.,   *The Wanderer, Reflections*

The Woman of Genesis   Paper $4.50

The Ravengate Press
Box 103
Cambridge, MA, 02238